FUN WITH THE FAMILY™

in IOWA

HUNDREDS OF IDEAS
FOR DAY TRIPS WITH THE KIDS

BETSY RUBINER

D0650978

The Globe Pequot Press

GUILFORD, CONNECTICUT

The prices and rates listed in this guidebook were confirmed at press time. We recommend, however, that you call establishments to obtain current information before traveling.

Text design by Nancy Freeborn
Maps created by XNR Productions, Inc. © The Globe Pequot Press

ISBN 0-7627-2286-X

Manufactured in the United States of America
First Edition/First Printing

For my parents, whose wanderlust I inherited.

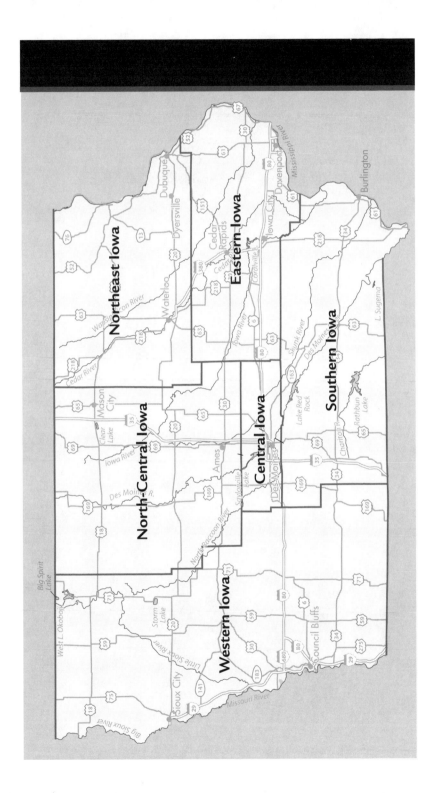

Contents

Acknowledgments vi

Introduction vii

Northeast Iowa 1

Eastern Iowa 35

Southern Iowa 71

Central Iowa 109

North-Central Iowa 137

Western Iowa 169

Appendix: Events and Celebrations 205

General Index 211

Activities Index 218

About the Author 222

Acknowledgments

This book would not have been possible without my husband, Dirck Steimel, and our children, Noah and Lily, who gamely helped me explore Iowa and field-test attractions, restaurants, and lodgings. Thanks also to my stepdaughter, Emma, who enthusiastically joined us on several adventures. I am also indebted to friends and neighbors, as well as children and parents I met on the road, for their invaluable travel tips. The fourth and fifth graders at Des Moines's Downtown School offered terrific suggestions. And a big thank you to the Iowa Department of Tourism and the countless local chamber of commerce staff, museum guides, park rangers, attractions operators, and restaurant and hotel workers who cheerfully answered the nitpickiest of questions.

Introduction

Hollywood helped lure me to Iowa.

In 1989, I left a Kansas City movie theater thinking, *I never knew Iowa was so beautiful. I should go there some time.* I'd just seen the film *Field of Dreams*, a baseball fairy tale set on a heavenly eastern Iowa farm.

A year later, as fate would have it, my husband Dirck and I were offered reporting jobs at the *Des Moines Register*. We left Kansas City and moved to Des Moines where, years later, we're raising two native Iowans, our son Noah, 11, and daughter Lily, 10. Even before this book project, we were busy exploring Iowa—hiking, biking, canoeing, horseback riding, apple picking, you name it. We've enjoyed small county fairs and big city museums, rodeos and arts festivals, Native American powwows and Dutch tulip celebrations, Americana cafes and Thai restaurants, Des Moines riverfront concerts, and University of Iowa Hawkeye football games. In Iowa we have some of the best of both worlds, urban and rural. We love the big-city culture, sophistication, and diversity in Des Moines. We also love having farms, tiny towns, and state parks nearby.

During our travels we've learned that Iowa *is* beautiful, with forests and prairies, pancake-flat cropland and rolling hills, lakes and rivers. But like any place, it's not *all* beautiful. This guide, I hope, will help point you in the right directions.

I've carved the state into six regions. We start in **Northeast Iowa**, bordered by Minnesota and Wisconsin, then move down the Mississippi River through **Eastern Iowa** and on to **Southern Iowa**, where we travel westward. Next we go to **Central Iowa** and then up to **North-Central Iowa**. Finally, we'll visit **Western Iowa**, starting in the north.

Children's Books about Iowa and Famous Iowans

- *Artist in Overalls: The Life of Grant Wood* by John Duggleby
- *I is for Iowa* by Mary Ann Gensicke
- *Iowa Fun Facts and Games* by Mary Ann Gensicke
- *Iowa is for Iowa People* by Mary Ann Gensicke
- *My First Book about Iowa* by Carole Marsh
- *Kate Shelley and the Midnight Express* by Margaret K. Wetterer
- *Kate Shelley: Bound for Legend* by Robert D. San Souci
- *Tomas and the Library Lady* by Pat Mora

Each section is organized geographically, often moving in a loop. This way, you don't have to backtrack, and you can plan your itinerary by flipping ahead or back a few pages. To help find what you're looking for, there are two indexes (one general, one by activity type) and a calendar of events and celebrations. I've also included in each chapter a list of our family favorites and reference maps, based on an Iowa Department of Transportation map distributed free of charge. To get one, call (515) 242–4705 or (800) 345–IOWA, or visit www.traveliowa.com. A free Iowa travel guide, calendar of events, and special maps (large-print and bicycle maps) are also available.

I've included primarily child-friendly attractions, restaurants, and lodgings, but some are grown-up places that are fine for well-behaved children (and well-behaved parents). I've tried to give you a heads up about the latter so you can decide what's best for your family. Also, you'll notice that several attractions are in flux. That's because an almost $2 billion effort to develop cultural and community projects is under way in Iowa—spurred by $225 million in state grants. So you're visiting Iowa during a very exciting time. Happy trails.

Lodging, Restaurant, and Attraction Fees

In the "Where to Eat" and "Where to Stay" sections, dollar signs indicate general price ranges or averages. For meals, the prices are generally for individual adult entrees. (Children's meals are usually less.) These may vary according to the meal served (lunch vs. dinner for example.)

For lodging, the rates are generally for a double room for a family of three or more, often with a complimentary breakfast (especially at bed-and-breakfasts). Rates for lodging may be higher during peak vacation seasons and holidays.

Rates for attractions are per person; these ratings appear at the end of the italicized information in the heading for each attraction.

Rates for Lodging

$	up to $50
$$	$51 to $75
$$$	$76 to $100
$$$$	more than $100

Rates for Restaurants

$	entrees less than $10
$$	entrees $10 to $15
$$$	entrees $16 to $20
$$$$	entrees more than $20

Rates for Attractions

$	up to $5
$$	$6 to $10
$$$	$11 to $20
$$$$	more than $21

For Quick Reference

For Quick Reference I've tried whenever possible to find places to eat and stay that have a local flair, but I've also, by necessity, included some chain motels (most of which serve a free continental breakfast). To find other large chain motels not listed but fairly common throughout Iowa, here are some numbers:

- AmeriInn, (800) 634-3444
- AmeriHost, (800) 434-5800
- Best Western, (800) 937-8376
- Clarion, (877) 424-6423
- Comfort Inn and Suites, (800) 228-5150
- Courtyard by Marriott, (888) 236-2427
- Country Inn and Suites, (800) 456-4000
- Days Inn, (800) 329-7466
- EconoLodge, (800) 553-2666
- Fairfield Inn, (800) 228-2800
- Hampton Inn and Suites, (800) 426-7866
- Heartland Inn, (800) 334-3277
- Holiday Inn/Holiday Inn Express, (800) 465-4329
- Quality Inn, (800) 228-5151
- Ramada, (800) 272-6232
- Sheraton, (800) 325-3535
- Super 8, (800) 800-8000
- For state park cabin rental, see www.state.ia.us/dnr/organiza/ppd/cabins.htm#fees.
- For state park camping fees and information, visit www.state.ia.us/dnr/organiza/ppd/camping.htm.
- For locations of Iowa Welcome Centers (tourism offices scattered throughout the state), log on to www.traveliowa.com/contacts/welcome.htm.

Attractions Key

The following is a key to the icons found throughout the text.

 Swimming

 Animal Viewing

 Boating / Boat Tour

 Food

 Historic Site

 Lodging

 Hiking / Walking

 Camping

 Fishing

 Museums

 Biking

 Performing Arts

 Amusement Park

 Sports / Athletic

 Horseback Riding

 Picnicking

 Skiing / Winter Sports

 Playground

 Park

 Shopping

 Plants / Gardens / Nature Trails

Northeast Iowa

Plan to spend a lot of time outdoors—hiking, biking, canoeing, fishing, horseback riding, and skiing—when you visit northeast Iowa. Known for its natural beauty and fall foliage, this region of rolling farmland, winding rivers, and wooded bluffs above the Mississippi is home to several popular state parks, as well as Effigy Mounds, Iowa's only National Monument. Bordered by Wisconsin and Minnesota, this area also includes the film site of the 1989 movie *Field of Dreams* with its baseball field carved out of a heavenly cornfield. And don't forget to ride a paddle wheeler on the Mississippi.

Indoors, you'll also find interesting, sometimes unusual attractions in the northeast's largest cities, Dubuque and Waterloo, and in small, charming river towns like Guttenberg. You can visit Laura Ingalls Wilder's home in Burr Oak and a museum about Norwegian immigrants in Decorah. See a collection of hand-carved wooden clocks in Spillville, an old ice house in Cedar Falls, and an outdoor tram elevator in Dubuque.

Begin your trip in the region's southeast corner, exploring Dubuque and neighboring towns before traveling north along (or near) the Mississippi on "The Great River Road." After you reach McGregor and Marquette, you'll drive inland to the Decorah area on State Highways 76 and 9, then west on State Highway 24 and south on US 63 into Waterloo and Cedar Falls.

For More Information

Eastern Iowa Tourism Association. P. O. Box 189, Dyersville 52040; (800) *891–3482 or (563) 875–7269, www.easterniowatourism.org.*

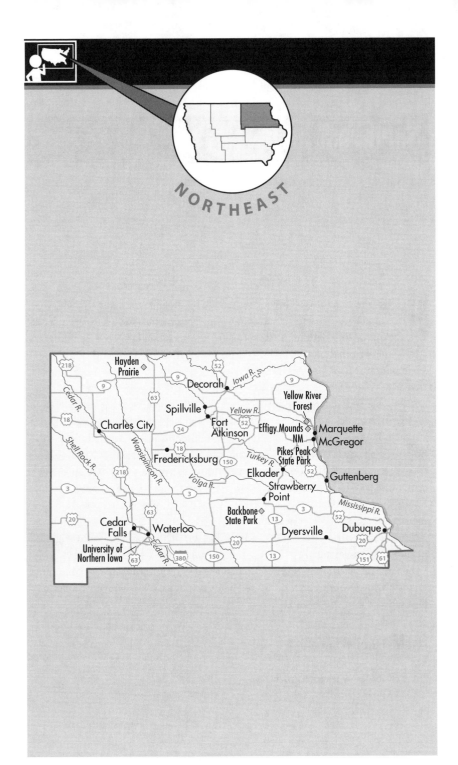

Hayden Prairie

218

52

9

Iowa R.

Decorah

9

63

Spillville

Yellow R.

Yellow River Forest

Cedar R.

18

Charles City

24

Fort Atkinson

52

Effigy Mounds NM

Marquette

McGregor

Shell Rock R.

Wapsipinicon R.

18

Fredericksburg

150

Turkey R.

Pikes Peak State Park

52

218

3

Volga R.

Elkader

Strawberry Point

Guttenberg

20

Cedar Falls

63

Waterloo

Backbone State Park

13

3

52

Mississippi R.

Dyersville

Dubuque

University of Northern Iowa

63

380

150

20

13

20

151

61

Cedar R.

Betsy's Top Ten
Picks for Fun in Northeast Iowa

1. Fenelon Place Elevator, Dubuque

2. Crystal Lake Cave, Dubuque

3. Spook Cave, McGregor

4. Effigy Mounds, Harpers Ferry

5. Pikes Peak State Park, McGregor

6. Canoeing on the Upper Iowa

7. Riding the *Spirit of Dubuque* paddle wheeler on the Mississippi

8. Backbone State Park, Strawberry Point

9. Laura Ingalls Wilder Park, Burr Oak

10. Driving the Great River Road

Dubuque

Iowa's oldest city, Dubuque, is a scenic river town with leafy residential neighborhoods atop limestone bluffs. Downtown has the feel of an old East Coast factory town, with a well-preserved historic district of brick row houses and elegant Victorian mansions converted into inns. But when you catch a glimpse of the barges slowly plying the Mississippi, you know you're still in the Midwest. Each year, Dubuque holds two arts festivals with fun children's activities: Dubuquefest, the third weekend in May, and Riverfest, the second weekend in September.

FENELON PLACE/FOURTH STREET ELEVATOR (all ages)

512 Fenelon Place, Dubuque 52001; (563) 582–9496. Runs continuously between 8:00 A.M. and 10:00 P.M. daily from April through November. $.

My kids love this unusual outdoor elevator, and yours will too. It was built in 1882 by a banker looking for a quick way to get from his house up on the bluff (Fenelon Place) to work downtown (Fourth Street). And he saved enough time to catch a quick nap after lunch at home. Some Dubuque residents still use the elevator to get to work. Billed as the world's shortest, steepest scenic railway, the elevator lifts you 189 feet while traveling only 296 feet. One-way or round-trip, it's a quick ride with terrific views of the Mississippi River and neighboring Wisconsin and Illinois.

Travel in Old-fashioned Style

Brush up on your Dubuque history during a narrated tour via horse-drawn carriage or trolley. **Rustic Hills Carriage Tours,** on Fourth Street near the elevator, offers half-hour tours daily. For reservations call (563) 580–0558; for information, (563) 556–6341. **Trolleys of Dubuque,** 98 East Fourth Street, offers one-hour tours. For reservations and information, call (800) 408–0077 or (563) 556–2750.

MISSISSIPPI RIVER MUSEUM (ages 5 and up)

98 East Third Street, Dubuque 52001; (800) 226–3369 or (563) 557–9545. Open 10:00 A.M. to 5:30 P.M. daily from May through October; 10:00 A.M. to 5:00 P.M. daily from November through April; closed holidays. $$, ages 3 and under **Free.**

This museum, housed in a 1902 brick freight house in the Port of Dubuque's Ice Harbor, is supposed to quadruple in size when a $55 million expansion is completed by spring 2003. Additions will include a River Discovery Center and Aquarium with huge tanks filled with Mississippi River aquatic life, a one-and-a-half-acre wetland, "touch pools" with exotic animals to touch, a working boatyard, and replicas of barges, keelboats, and steamboats. Covering 900 years of river history, the museum has an orientation film narrated by Garrison Keillor.

Culture for Kids

- **Five Flags Theater.** Fourth and Main Streets, Dubuque; (888) 412–9758 or (563) 589–4254. Modeled after the Moulin Rouge in Paris, this 1910 theater presents music, ballet, and theatrical productions often suitable for children.

- **Grand Opera House.** 135 Eighth Street, Dubuque; (563) 588–1305. Children's shows are among the offerings staged by a community theater in this elegant 1890 opera house.

Coming Attractions The Mississippi River Museum expansion is part of a $188 million redevelopment of Dubuque's riverfront scheduled to be completed by 2004. It will include a new riverfront hotel and indoor water park, a conference/education center, and a river walk atop the flood wall.

SPIRIT OF DUBUQUE SIGHTSEEING CRUISES (all ages)

Third Street, Ice Harbor, Dubuque 52001; (800) 747–8093 or (563) 583–8093, www.spiritofdubuque.com, mail@spiritofdubuque.com. Open daily from May through October. Call for cruise schedule. $$.

Tour the Mississippi on this authentic paddle wheel riverboat. During the summer, there are two ninety-minute narrated sightseeing cruises each weekday afternoon and four cruises on Saturday. The boat has an open-air sightseeing deck and an enclosed area. Reservations are recommended.

MINES OF SPAIN RECREATION AREA/E. B. LYONS INTERPRETIVE AND NATURE CENTER (all ages)

8999 Bellevue Heights, Dubuque 52003; (563) 556–0620. The park is open from 4:00 A.M. to 10:30 P.M. year-round. The center is open from 9:00 A.M. to 4:00 P.M. Monday through Friday and noon to 4:30 P.M. Saturday and Sunday from April through October; limited hours during other months. **Free.**

Just south of Dubuque off US 52 South, this 1,380-acre recreation area of woods, wetlands, and prairie along the Mississippi River is a National Historic Landmark with trails for hiking and cross-country skiing. The nature center offers environmental programs for all ages, plus nature displays, a bird and butterfly garden, a picnic area, and an old farm site. Some trails are steep and challenging. For a great view, drive up to the Julien Dubuque monument, honoring the city's founder.

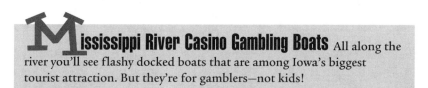

Mississippi River Casino Gambling Boats All along the river you'll see flashy docked boats that are among Iowa's biggest tourist attraction. But they're for gamblers—not kids!

CRYSTAL LAKE CAVE (all ages)

7699 Crystal Lake Cave Drive, Dubuque 52003; (563) 556–6451. Open 9:00 A.M. to 6:00 P.M. daily from Memorial Day through Labor Day, reduced hours in May, September, and October. $$ for adults, $ for ages 5 through 11, ages 4 and under Free.

Three miles south of Dubuque on US 52, this is the largest living cave in Iowa open to visitors. More than 40 feet underground, it has almost a mile of well-lit passageways, an underground lake and intricate formations (some resembling well-done bacon, others hollow soda straws). Look too for rare cave crystals called anthodites. The guided tour lasts forty-five minutes. Remember to bring a jacket—the cave temperature is 52 degrees.

The Great River Road

A 3,000-mile stretch of roads borders the Mississippi River on both sides from Canada to the Gulf of Mexico. The 237-mile segment that runs through Iowa is one of the state's prettiest drives.

CZIPAR'S APPLE ORCHARD (all ages)

8562 Route 52 South, Dubuque 52003; (563) 582–7476. Open 8:30 A.M. to 6:00 P.M. daily, generally from Labor Day weekend through Thanksgiving. Free.

During a fall drive on the Great River Road, stop here for apples. About 4 miles south of Dubuque in a scenic spot overlooking the Mississippi, this third-generation orchard has about eighteen apple varieties, including some more exotic ones like Greening (my favorite), Honeycrisp, Jon-a-Red, and the Arkansas Black Apple (also known as Black Twig).

Luxembourg in Iowa

On the Great River Road south of Dubuque is the tiny historic village of St. Donatus (population about 150). Settled by Luxembourg immigrants, it has a charming old-world feel with its restored nineteenth-century limestone buildings, including barns, a blacksmith shop, and the 1848 Gehlen House, which is now a bed-and-breakfast with a gift shop. It's at 101 North Main Street. For information call (800) 280-1177 or (563) 773-8200 or visit www.bellevueia.com/gehlenhouse/index.cfm.

SUNDOWN MOUNTAIN SKI RESORT (ages 4 and up)

17017 Asbury Road, Dubuque 52002; (888) 786–3696 or (563) 556–6676, www.sundownmtn.com. Open 9:00 A.M. to 9:00 P.M. Sunday through Thursday, until 10:00 P.M. Friday and Saturday, from late November through mid-March. $$$$ for adults, $$–$$$$ for ages 6 through 11, ages 5 and under Free.

Sundown is one of the state's best skiing and snowboarding spots, with the highest vertical drop in Iowa and southern Minnesota (475 feet), plus a gentle slope for beginners and SKIwee lessons for ages four through twelve. There are twenty-one trails carved into a century-old cedar forest, five chairlifts, a seven-acre terrain park, ski rental, and two restaurants. The Kids' Ski Club offers reduced rates for fourth through sixth graders who ski a lot.

STORYBOOK HILL CHILDREN'S ZOO (all ages, especially younger children)

12345 North Cascade Road, Dubuque 52003; (563) 588–2551. Open 11:00 A.M. to 7:00 P.M. daily from Memorial Day weekend through Labor Day. Free.

This small petting zoo with farm animals, a playground, and picnic facilities is in FDR Park on Dubuque's north end.

Picnic Possibilities Visit Eagle Point Park, a 146-acre public park that overlooks the Mississippi's lock and dam #11. It has a lily pond, gardens, a playground, nature trails, and a horseshoe pitching area. Go west on Shiras Avenue to Rhomberg Avenue.

Where to Eat

Betty Jane's Candies. *3049 Asbury Road, Dubuque; (563) 582–4668.* Opened in 1938, this shop serves ice cream and fancy handmade chocolates, including its famous Gremlins (chocolate-covered caramel and pecans). $

Breitbach's Country Dining. *563 Balltown Road, Balltown; (563) 552–2220.* Iowa's oldest restaurant (open since 1852) and run by the same family for six generations, Breitbach's serves a hearty meat, soup, and vegetables buffet that includes fried chicken, barbecued ribs, mashed potatoes, and pie (try the red raspberry) in a rustic 1846 former stagecoach house. A scenic 15-mile drive up the Mississippi from Dubuque, Balltown has about sixty residents. $

Dempsey's Steakhouse. *395 West Ninth Street, Dubuque; (563) 582–7057.* This casual steak and pasta restaurant downtown has a children's menu. $$

Elizabeth's Tollbridge. *2800 Rhomberg Avenue, Dubuque; (563) 556–5566.* Overlooking Mississippi lock and dam #11, this white-tablecloth restaurant that serves Mediterranean and California-inspired cuisine is best known for fresh fish and river views. $$$

Shot Tower Inn. *390 Locust Street, Dubuque; (563) 556–1061.* Next to the downtown civic center, the Shot Tower Inn restaurant has pizza, ribs, sandwiches, and Mexican entrees. $

Yen Ching. *926 Main Street, Dubuque; (563) 556–2574.* This popular Chinese restaurant serves Hunan and Mandarin favorites. $

Where to Stay

Country Inn and Suites. *1315 Associates Drive, Dubuque; (800) 456–4000 or (563) 583–2500.* This seventy-room hotel on the west side, off the Northwest Arterial, has an indoor pool. $$–$$$$

Days Inn. *111 Dodge Street, Dubuque; (800) 772–3297 or (563) 583–3297.* With 154 rooms near downtown, the Days Inn has one of Dubuque's few outdoor hotel pools. $$–$$$

Four Mounds Inn Bed & Breakfast. *4900 Peru Road, Dubuque; (563) 556–1908, www.fourmounds.com.* A gorgeous 1908 Craftsman-style Mission mansion high above the Mississippi north of downtown, this inn is part of a former gentleman's farm on sixty secluded acres with hiking trails, five guest rooms, and a family-perfect cabin that sleeps up to six. $$$–$$$$

Heartland Inn–West. *4025 McDonald Drive, Dubuque; (800) 334–3277 ext. 12 or (563) 582–3752.* West of downtown near US 20, the Heartland has eighty-four rooms and an indoor pool. $$–$$$

Grand Harbor Resort and Waterpark. *350 Bell Street, Dubuque; (800) 690–4006, www.grandharborresort.com.* Opened in 2002, the resort has 194 rooms, a 25,000-square-foot indoor waterpark, a restaurant, and a cafe.

For More Information

Dubuque Convention and Visitors Bureau. *300 Main Street, Suite 200,* *Dubuque 52004; (800) 798–8844 or (563) 556–4372, www.traveldubuque.com.*

Dyersville

About 25 miles west of Dubuque on US 20, Dyersville was the *Field of Dreams* film location and is home to three farm toy companies (plus several farm toy stores).

Corn Mazes Ever try to find your way out of a maze made from maize? A popular form of "agritainment," corn mazes dot Iowa during the late summer and fall when the corn shoots up to 12 feet high. They're often found on farms or at other tourist attractions. Designs and difficulty vary, but the basic idea is to follow the path that winds through the pattern and ends in the middle or the rear. Parental supervision is a wise idea, especially with young children and complex mazes.

A popular northeast Iowa maze is the **Country Heritage Community Maize Maze** on County Road B64 a mile east of Elgin (877–4NE–IOWA). It's open from noon to dusk, Wednesday through Sunday, from July through October. The maze is across from the Gilbertson Nature Center, 22580 A Avenue. For more information on Iowa mazes, log on to www.campsilos.org/mod3/students/mazes.shtml.

LEFT AND CENTER FIELD OF DREAMS (all ages)

29001 Lansing Road, Dyersville 52040; (800) 443–8981 or (563) 875–6012, www.leftandcenterfod.com. Open 9:00 A.M. to 6:00 P.M. daily from April through November, until 8:00 P.M. from Memorial Day through Labor Day. **Free**. *The corn maze is open 9:00 A.M. to 5:00 P.M. daily from August through October. $, ages 5 and under* **Free**.

This is your chance to try out the baseball diamond from the movie *Field of Dreams*. You can even borrow a baseball, bat, and glove here, plus there's a snack shop and seasonal corn maze. From June through September, on the last Sunday of the month, there's also a **Free** two-hour show at noon ("*The Greatest Show on Dirt*") featuring "ghost players" in old uniforms who sometimes invite children to play ball with them. In the 1989 movie, after a seemingly sane Iowa farmer hears a voice urging him to build a baseball diamond in his cornfield, the ghosts of Shoeless Joe Jackson and other players show up to play. Today, that ball diamond has two owners, each with a chunk of the diamond and a souvenir shop. This attraction includes left and center field, plus a third-base souvenir shop.

FIELD OF DREAMS MOVIE SITE (all ages)

28963 Lansing Road, Dyersville 52040; (563) 875–8404 or (888) 875–8404, www.fieldofdreamsmoviesite.com/distance.html, shoelessjoe@fieldofdreams moviesite.com. Open 9:00 A.M. to 6:00 P.M. daily from April through November. **Free**.

This is the other chunk of the *Field of Dreams* ball diamond (the infield and the pretty farmhouse from the movie).

 NATIONAL FARM TOY MUSEUM (ages 3 and up)
1110 16th Avenue Court SE, Dyersville 52040; (563) 875–2727, www.nftm online.com. Open 8:00 A.M. to 7:00 P.M. daily. $, ages 5 and under Free.

Thousands of toy trucks and tractors are on display at this two-floor museum, and children can play with some in a play area. They can also learn about farming and farm equipment. An exhibit that shows how corn and grain harvesting have changed from ancient times features replicas of old machines. Other attractions include a ten-minute movie and a life-size tractor display.

Where to Eat

Country Junction Restaurant. *913 Fifteenth Avenue SE, Dyersville; (563) 875–7055.* At the junction of US 20 and State Highway 136, this local favorite serves home-style cooking for breakfast, lunch, and dinner. $-$$

Dyersville Family Restaurant. *226 First Avenue East, Dyersville; (563) 875– 2181.* This downtown restaurant serves sandwiches, steaks, and soup, and has a children's menu. $

Picnic Possibilities Visit Commercial Club Park, on State Highway 136, a small city park with picnic tables, a playground, and a public pool.

Where to Stay

Comfort Inn. *527 Sixteenth Avenue SE, Dyersville; (563) 875–7700.* Near the movie site, the Comfort Inn has fifty rooms and an indoor pool. $$

Super 8. *925 Fifteenth Avenue SE, Dyersville; (800) 800–8000 or (319) 875–8885.* Close to the National Farm Toy Museum, this is a forty-five-room chain hotel near the junction of State Highway 136 and US 20. $

For More Information

Dyersville Area Chamber of Commerce, *1100 Sixteenth Avenue Court SE, Dyersville 52040; (866) DYERSVILLE or*

(563) 875–2311, www.dyersville.org, dyersvillechamber@dyersville.org.

Strawberry Point

A 15-foot-high fiberglass strawberry ("the world's largest") looms above the city hall in the small town of Strawberry Point, about 39 miles northwest of Dyersville on State Highways 13 and 3. Early settlers in Strawberry Point (founded in 1853) discovered wild strawberries when they arrived.

BACKBONE STATE PARK (all ages)

1347 129th Street, Dundee 52038; (563) 924–2527, backbone@dnr.state. ia.us. Open 4:00 A.M. to 10:30 P.M. daily. **Free.**

Dedicated in 1920, Backbone is Iowa's first state park and one of its best-known nature preserves, offering hiking, camping, and picnic spots with great views. You can also boat and fish in Backbone Lake. Unfortunately, swimming has been an issue recently, with the beach occasionally closed due to high bacteria levels, so check before you go. Located in the tiny town of Dundee, 4 miles south of Strawberry Point, this 1,780-acre park got its name from a narrow, steep ridge of bedrock said to look like the devil's backbone. The ridge is also one of northeast Iowa's highest points. Backbone has 21 miles of multiuse and hiking trails through old cedar forests and up rocky bluffs, plus 7 miles of designated bike trails. There are sixteen cabins for rent, sleeping four to nine, and some have heating and air-conditioning. Half are available year-round, the other half from April through October. Summer rentals are by the week only, with a two-night minimum stay the rest of the year. The cabins are very popular, so make sure to reserve far in advance. Reservations are accepted as of January. Call (563) 933–4225. Backbone also has two campgrounds with 127 campsites.

Where to Eat

Joe's Pizza. *624 Commercial Street, Strawberry Point; (563) 933–2376.* This pizzeria and ice-cream shop is on the south edge of town on State Highways 3 and 13. $

Strawberry Point Drug. *104 West Mission Street, Strawberry Point; (563) 933–4762.* The marble-topped early-1900s soda fountain at this local drug store serves ice-cream sodas, sundaes, and malts. (Another place to find ice cream is at the Conoco Service Station downtown, known for large soft-serve portions.) $

Happy Trails

The following are some of the many Northeast Iowa trails for biking, hiking, jogging, walking, and in-line skating.

- **Cedar River Greenbelt and Harry Cook Nature Trails,** a 9-mile crushed limestone trail in Mitchell County.

- **Wapsi–Great Western Trail,** a 10½-mile crushed limestone trail in Howard and Mitchell Counties near Riceville.

- **Prairie Farmer Recreational Trail,** an 18-mile crushed limestone trail in Winneshiek County, from Calmar to Cresco.

- **Heritage Trail,** a 26-mile crushed limestone trail between Dubuque and Dyersville.

- **Shell Rock River Trail,** an almost 5-mile trail in Butler County near Waverly.

- **Cedar Valley Trail System,** a 63-mile asphalt and concrete trail system in the Cedar Falls/Waterloo area. Try starting at George Wyth State Park off of US 218 in Cedar Falls.

Where to Stay

Franklin Hotel. *102 Elkader Street, Strawberry Point; (563) 933–4788.* This 1902 brick hotel has a lobby with nineteenth-century chandeliers and oak woodwork, a restaurant, and seven guest rooms. $

For More Information

Strawberry Point Chamber of Commerce. *P.O. Box 444, Strawberry Point 52076; (563) 933–2260, www.strawberrypt.com.*

Elkader

A pleasant town on the Turkey River, Elkader is about 14 miles north of Strawberry Point on State Highway 13.

OSBORNE NATURE CENTER (all ages)

29862 Osborne Road, Elkader 52046; (563) 245–1516. Open 8:00 A.M. to 4:00 P.M. Monday through Saturday and noon to 4:00 P.M. Sunday from April through December, closed Sunday the rest of the year. **Free.**

Picnic and camp near where the buffalo roam at this popular 300-acre nature center on State Highway 13 about 5 miles south of Elkader. This is one of Iowa's largest wildlife farms, with more than fifty species of birds and animals (most alive, some stuffed). See white-tailed deer, wild turkey, wolves, a cougar, and other animals native to Iowa at what feels like an old-fashioned zoo. Some quarters are cramped pens lacking native habitat, but an expansion is under way and the three buffalo (and two elk) have a roomier, albeit fenced-in, space. There's also a simple pioneer village, primitive camping, and picnic areas, plus three nature and hiking trails, each with a specific theme (trees, wildlife, and heritage). In the winter, you can cross-country ski, sled, and ice-skate on the center's pond. During the annual Heritage Days on the second full weekend in October, there are demonstrations by blacksmiths and shingle makers, and you can sample pioneer food, including buffalo stew and homemade root beer. The highlight is the Iowa Championship Buffalo Chip Throwing Contest. (FYI, buffalo chips are made from dried manure.)

Canoeing on the Turkey and Volga Rivers A large stream flowing through four northeast Iowa counties, the Turkey River runs through a wide, scenic valley. The Volga River is a tributary of the Turkey. Many paddlers start at Elkader, where you can rent canoes from **Turkey River Canoe Rental** (563-245-1559). For information about the best places to canoe, visit the Clayton County Web site, www.claytoncounty-iowa.com.

Where to Eat

Johnson's Restaurant and Cafe. *916 High Street NE, Elkader; (563) 245–2371.* This casual restaurant, known for its daily buffet, also serves sandwiches. $$

Keystone Restaurant. *107 South Main Street, Elkader; (563) 245–1992.* Overlooking an old Stone Arch bridge over the Turkey River with indoor and out-door seating, the Keystone serves sandwiches, hamburgers, and fish. $

Marcia's Sweet Shoppe. *133 South Main Street, Elkader; (563) 245–2886.* This old-fashioned ice-cream parlor also serves hand-dipped and homemade candies. $

St. Olaf Tavern. *106 South Main Street, St. Olaf; (563) 783–7723.* About 8 miles northeast of Elkader, St. Olaf's serves enormous pork tenderloins, plus burgers and sandwiches. $

The Shanti. *17455 Gunder Road, Elgin; (563) 864–9289.* If you like your burgers big—one pound big—try the infamous "gunderburger" in the tiny town of Gunder, about 8 miles northwest of Elkader. (The mailing address is Elgin because Gunder's population is thirty-two.) $

Where to Stay

Elkader Inn. *24886 Highway 13, Elkader; (563) 245–2020.* Located north of town on a busy highway, this hotel has fifteen rooms. $$

For More Information

Clayton County Development Group. *132 South Main Street, P.O. Box 778, Elkader 52043; (800) 488–7572 or* *(563) 245–2201, www.claytoncounty-iowa.com, info@claytoncounty-iowa.com.*

Guttenberg

Perched on the Mississippi 20 miles east of Elkader, Guttenberg (pronounced *GUT-ten-berg,* not *GOOT-ten-berg*) has old German buildings and a lovely mile-long river walk. Settled by German immigrants in 1832, Guttenberg was named after the fifth-century inventor of movable type, Johannes Gutenberg (with one "t") of Gutenberg Bible fame.

 THE AQUARIUM (all ages)
331 South River Park Drive, Guttenberg 52052; (563) 252–1156. Open 8:00 A.M. to 8:00 P.M. daily from May through October. **Free.**
  This 1930s aquarium and fish hatchery is full of freshwater fish from the Mississippi and cold-water trout from local streams, plus turtles and a display of buttons made from Guttenberg shells. In the spring you may also see northern pike being hatched.

LOCKMASTER'S HOUSE HERITAGE MUSEUM (ages 7 and up)
Located on the grounds of lock and dam #10, Guttenberg 52052; (563) 252–1531. Open noon to 4:00 P.M. Tuesday through Sunday from Memorial Day through mid-October. **Free.**

This is the last lockmaster's house on the Mississippi, with early twentieth-century furnishings, including some old cooking utensils children will enjoy. There are also interesting old photos of Guttenberg and the lock and dam system. Barges carrying millions of tons of cargo pass through lock and dam #10, which was built in the 1930s.

Where to Eat

Bill's Boat Landing. *101 South Front Street, Clayton; (563) 964–2112.* Boats pull right up to this restaurant in the small fishing village of Clayton, just north of Guttenberg. Dining room windows overlook the Mississippi, and there's an outdoor patio where people (sometimes in wet bathing suits) eat burgers, steaks, and seafood, plus hot dogs and chicken nuggets from the children's menu. $–$$

The Clayton Litehouse. *100 Front Street, Clayton; (563) 964–2103.* Also in Clayton on the Mississippi, this restaurant serves steak, seafood, and a lighter menu. It's closed from November through January. $$

Guttenberg Bakery and Cafe. *422 South River Park Drive, Guttenberg; (563) 252–2225.* This small bakery with fresh bread and sweets, located across from a riverfront park, also serves sandwiches. $

The Picket Fence Cafe. *531 South River Park Drive, Guttenberg; (563) 252–3820.* Because the owners of this tiny cafe and gourmet food store, which serves sandwiches and salads, are also farmers, they use their own butchered meat. $

Picnic Possibilities Try **Ingleside Park in Guttenberg**, a small, grassy park along the Mississippi by the Lockmaster's House where you'll find picnic tables, a shelter house, a playground, and a good view of barges as they pass through lock and dam #10.

Where to Stay

Claytonian Inn. *100 South Front Street, Clayton; (563) 964–2776.* A short drive north of Guttenberg, this bed-and-breakfast is part hotel and part motel, with individually themed rooms. $$

Guttenberg River Inn and Cafe. *308 South River Park Drive, Guttenberg; (877) 521–4790 or (563) 252–3706.* This three-story limestone building across from the Mississippi has two spacious suites, each well suited for a family, with a private bath, shared kitchen, and common area. A full breakfast is served, and there's an upscale cafe on the ground floor with a children's menu, vegetarian entrees, steak, and fresh seafood. $$$–$$$$

For More Information

Guttenberg Civic and Commerce Club. *323 South River Park Drive, Guttenberg 52052; (877) 252–2323 or (563)* 252–2323, *www.guttenberg-iowa.org/, gutnberg@alpinenet.com.*

McGregor/Marquette

Follow the Great River Road (County Road X56 to State Highway 340) along the Mississippi about 17 miles to the neighboring river towns of McGregor and Marquette, which are lined with antiques and specialty shops in nineteenth-century storefronts. Across the Mississippi, you'll also find places to eat and stay in Prairie du Chien, Wisconsin's second oldest city.

Amazing Iowa Facts "The Greatest Show on Earth" traces its roots to McGregor, home of John Ringling, founder of the Ringling Brothers Circus. Local legend has it that John and his four brothers caught the circus bug when a circus troupe traveling on a Mississippi steamboat stopped in McGregor in 1870. The Ringling brothers staged their first impromptu circus for neighbors under a tent strung up with clothesline, starring neighborhood dogs and a billy goat. By the 1920s John Ringling was a multimillionaire circus owner, but a decade later, during the depression, he lost the circus.

PIKES PEAK STATE PARK (all ages)
15316 Great River Road, McGregor 52157; (563) 873–2341, www.state.ia.us/ dnr/organiza/ppd/pikepeak.htm, Pikes_Peak@dnr.state.ia.us. Open 4:00 A.M. to 10:30 P.M. daily. Free.

Located 2 miles southeast of McGregor, Pikes Peak is one of my family's favorite places to hike and picnic. With the highest bluff on the Mississippi (500 feet), the park has stunning views. To the south you'll see the Mississippi meet the Wisconsin River. To the north, suspension bridges connect Iowa and Wisconsin. The park is named after Zebulon Pike, who explored the Mississippi Valley in 1805. (A few years later in Colorado, he went to what is also now known as Pikes Peak.) The main picnic area includes a rustic stone shelter, overlook, and playground. The campground has seventy-seven campsites and modern bathrooms and showers. There are also 13 miles of mostly rugged dirt trails through the woods. The most popular is an easy half-mile round-trip loop through a wooded valley to a little waterfall called Bridal Veil Falls.

RIVER JUNCTION TRADE COMPANY (ages 3 and up)

312 Main Street, McGregor 52157; (563) 873–2387. Open 9:00 A.M. to 5:00 P.M. Monday through Saturday year-round; closed Sunday. **Free.**

Young wanna-be cowboys and adventurers will be fascinated by this old general store that sells "complete outfits for the frontiersman." Packed with nineteenth-century western gear and memorabilia, including holsters, gun belts, chaps, saddles, and swords, the shop supplies the costumes used in Hollywood westerns and Civil War reenactments. The friendly shopkeepers are very patient with families that wander in and ask lots of questions.

PAPER MOON (all ages)

156 A Street, McGregor 52157; (563) 873–3357. Open 10:00 A.M. to 5:00 P.M. daily from April through December, Wednesday through Saturday from January through March. **Free.**

Don't miss this wonderful, whimsically decorated three-story book and gift store filled with carefully selected and beautifully displayed stuff (books, toys, clothing, jewelry, food, you name it) for kids *and* parents.

SPOOK CAVE AND CAMPGROUND (ages 5 and up)

13299 Spook Cave Road, McGregor 52157; (563) 873–2144, spookcave@ alpinecom.net. Cave tours available 9:00 A.M. to 5:30 P.M. daily from Memorial Day weekend through late August, weekends in September and October. $$ for adults, $ for ages 4 through 12, ages 3 and under **Free.**

If you like adventure, go here. If you're claustrophobic, don't. The only way to see this cave, hidden under a 90-foot-high bluff on the Bloody Run Creek, is by boat on an underground river. You enter through an awfully small hole in the bluff and glide through a very narrow tunnel with low ceilings, so be prepared to do a lot of ducking. The thirty-five-minute boat tour is led by a guide who explains how the cave was discovered in 1853. (For years, early settlers were intrigued by strange noises they heard coming from a hole at the bottom of the bluff.) The cave is fully lighted, but it's about 47 degrees, so remember a sweater. Surrounding the cave is a pretty ninety-three-acre campground, open from May through October. It's on a two-acre lake with a sandy beach and swim area, hiking trails, a stocked trout stream, playgrounds, showers and flush toilets, and a game room. Also available is one cabin fit for two adults and two children with a kitchen (but no bathroom.)

Pinky the Elephant You know you're in Marquette when you spot the local mascot, a giant pink elephant sporting a jaunty top hat. Pinky started out at the Pink Elephant Supper Club, but was relocated to the Marquette Riverboat Casino. Rumor has it that Pinky once went waterskiing on the Mississippi to mark the visit of then President Jimmy Carter.

EFFIGY MOUNDS NATIONAL MONUMENT (all ages)
151 Highway 76, Harpers Ferry 52146; (563) 873–3491, www.nps.gov/efmo. The park is open sunrise to sunset daily. The visitor center is open 8:00 A.M. to 4:30 P.M. daily, with extended hours from late spring through fall; closed on major winter holidays. April through October, $, ages 16 and under Free.

Located 3 miles north of Marquette, this 1,481-acre park has prehistoric Native American burial and ceremonial mounds dating back to 500 B.C. To see them, you hike along wooded trails on high bluffs with amazing Mississippi River views. With hardy kids, try the 7-mile round-trip northern trail, which takes about three hours. With young children, go as far as the Fire Point marker, which is about 2 miles round-trip and includes a variety of mounds plus a bluff view. With very young children, especially in strollers, try the new quarter-mile boardwalk behind the visitor center; it leads to the Yellow River through ponds and wetlands with wildflowers and good bird-watching. (You won't see any mounds, but there are three in front of the visitor center.) Inside the visitor center, there's a display of Native American artifacts and stuffed bald eagles, turkeys, and bear cubs. Check the Web site for ranger-led hikes and programs during the summer. You can't picnic at Effigy Mounds because it's a sacred burial ground, but there are picnic areas south of the visitor center on State Highway 76.

PAINT CREEK RIDING STABLES AND CAMPGROUND (all ages)
1048 Sandhill Road, Waukon 52172; (563) 535–7253. Season runs from May through October; the rest of year, weather permitting. Open 9:00 A.M. to 6:00 P.M. daily. Trail rides, $$$; hayrides, $$$$. Reservations are required.

x

x

About 15 miles north of Effigy Mounds off State Highway 76, this working horse ranch offers supervised trail rides and hayrides, most on the weekend, and has a campground that's open year-round. To go on a guided trail ride, children must be nine years old and accompanied by an adult. Families can stay overnight in a furnished farmhouse that sleeps up to eight people. There is also primitive camping (with a portable toilet and shower in the farmhouse basement) via tent, pop-up camper, or RV. The campground has a one-acre pond with paddleboats, a playground, a horseshoe court, and a shelter house.

A Rubiner Family Adventure One of our many family visits to Effigy Mounds turned out to be during Hawk Watch Weekend, an annual event held the first full weekend in September. Our kids, then six and seven, were fascinated by the live raptors, owls, and hawks, some of which were recovering from injuries. We saw bird banding and, best of all, we watched a peregrine falcon be released back into the wild. The sight of that falcon soaring off to freedom high above the Mississippi will remain etched in our memory for years to come. Not coincidentally, my son Noah did a school project on falcons the next year.

YELLOW RIVER STATE FOREST (all ages)

729 State Forest Road, Harpers Ferry 52146; (563) 586–2254, www.state. ia.us/dnr/organiza/forest/yr.htm. Open dawn to 10:30 P.M. daily. **Free.**

One of the best places in Iowa to hike, camp, and trout fish, the 8,503-acre Yellow River Forest in gorgeous Allamakee County includes one of the Midwest's most remote and wild stream valleys. Home to sixty-five bird species, including turkeys, bald eagles, and turkey vultures, it's also popular for cross-country skiing. The headquarters and recreation facilities are located on County Highway B25, about 3 miles west of Harpers Ferry. A best bet is the forest's Paint Creek Unit, which includes the Big Paint Creek, Little Paint Creek, and equestrian campgrounds, plus hiking trails, picnic areas, scenic overlooks, 6 miles of trout stream stocked from April through October, and a marsh for catching bass and panfish.

Where to Eat

McGregor's Marina Beer and Bratz Garden. *Riverfront and Main Streets, McGregor; (563) 873–9613.* Run by the owners of the marina next door (with pontoon rentals), this casual open-air cafe on the Mississippi serves brats, fish and chicken baskets, and ice cream, and does carry-out. $

White Springs Night Club. *30157 Klien Brewery Road, McGregor; (319) 873–9642.* A sentimental favorite, this funky old roadhouse 2 miles west of downtown on Business US 18 has good, greasy, no-frills food, including great onion rings, salty and smoky barbecued ribs, homemade fries, and yummy fried chicken. $

Where to Stay

Grumpster's Log Cabin Getaway. *535 Ash Street, McGregor; (563) 873–3767, grumpstr@alpinecom.net.* Each of the two modern log cabins at this wonderful hideaway in the woods sleeps up to six and includes kitchenette, bath, loft, fireplace, sitting porch with rockers, and a gas grill. $$$$

Little Switzerland Inn and Aunt Sadie's Log Cabin. *126 Main Street, McGregor; (563) 873–2057, www.alpine com.net/lsibandb/switzerland.html.* In a pretty three-story building downtown, built in 1862 as home of Iowa's oldest weekly newspaper, this inn has five rooms with private baths, including two suites with extra loft sleeping— perfect for a family of four. There's also an authentic 1848 log cabin that has rustic birch bark walls and a stone fireplace and sleeps six. A full gourmet breakfast included. $$$–$$$$

The Natural Gait Cabins and Lodge. *1878 Old Mission Drive, Harpers Ferry; (800) 291–2143 or (563) 535–7231, www.naturalgait.com.* About 15 miles north of McGregor on the Yellow River, this bucolic place nestled in a river valley has three furnished log cabins, each sleeping six to eight, and a lodge with six bedrooms (shared bath). Horse-drawn carriage and sleigh rides, pond fishing, and primitive camping are also available. $$$$

For More Information

McGregor–Marquette Chamber of Commerce. *146 Main Street, McGregor 52157; (800) 896–0910.*

Decorah

A scenic 41-mile drive northwest along State Highways 76 and 9 leads you to Decorah, a well-preserved town on the Upper Iowa River that's proud of its Norwegian heritage and is a draw for outdoor enthusiasts. A good time to visit is during Decorah's annual Nordic Fest in late July.

Canoeing the Upper Iowa River

One of Iowa's most popular rivers for canoeing and tubing, the Upper Iowa parallels the Iowa–Minnesota border through three northeast Iowa counties. Many people put in near Decorah, where the river winds past 200-foot-high bluffs. Try the 15-mile stretch from Kendallville to Bluffton, starring the famous "chimney rock" formation, or from Bluffton to Decorah. For canoes, kayaks, and inner tube rental, call **Hruska Canoe Livery** in Kendallville (563–547–4566), **Randy's Bluffton Store and Campground** in Bluffton (563–735–5738), or **Chimney Rock Cabins, Campground, and Canoe Rental** in Cresco (877–787–CAMP, www.chimneyrocks.com). For more information about the river, see the Web site www.clayton county-iowa.com.

DECORAH TROUT HATCHERY (all ages)

2325 Siewers Spring Road, Decorah 52101; (563) 382–8324. Open during daylight hours daily. **Free**.

A fun place to see fish of all sizes in tanks, this hatchery stocks seventeen trout streams in and around Decorah. To get here, take Trout Run Road off of State Highway 9.

A Rubiner Family Adventure

One sunny fall day we were strolling along Decorah's lovely main drag, Water Street, when we spotted a storefront sign: QUALITY CHICKS. We giggled our way into the **Decorah Hatchery,** a cozy chicken hatchery that's been around since the 1930s. We'd missed hatching season, when the place is filled with peeping chicks and huge, egg-filled wooden incubators. But my daughter Lily left with a yellow T-shirt reading "Another Quality Chick." The next Halloween, Lily was the only "Quality Chick" in the neighborhood, proudly wearing the T-shirt and a headdress sprouting bright yellow chicken feathers. By the way, hatching season at the Decorah Hatchery is from April through July, and there are chicks there through August. All quality chicks, and other visitors, are welcome.

VESTERHEIM NORWEGIAN-AMERICAN MUSEUM (ages 5 and up)

523 West Water Street, Decorah 52101; (563) 382–9681, www.vesterheim.org. Open 9:00 A.M. to 5:00 P.M. daily from May through October, 10:00 A.M. to 4:00 P.M. daily from November through April. $, ages 6 and under **Free**.

Learn about Norwegian-American culture at this beautifully restored nineteenth-century brick complex, the nation's oldest, largest museum devoted to an immigrant group. Guided tours of the museum's historic buildings include two furnished homes (one from America, the other from Norway), a schoolhouse, and a prairie church. Exhibits feature costumes, folk arts, and *Tradewind,* the smallest sailboat to cross the Atlantic. Now displayed in a three-story-high gallery with its sails fully rigged, the boat sailed to the United States in 1933.

A Rubiner Family Adventure

Our canoe wobbled in the Upper Iowa River as my son Noah, then nine, crawled into the bow for the first time, trading places with my husband, who moved to the middle. Watching from the stern, I braced myself. But Noah soon proved he could paddle, and my daughter Lily, then eight, did too. Occasionally their paddles dinged the canoe. Once we got caught in a current and hit the grassy riverbank with a soft thud, ducking to miss tree limbs. Still, we kept moving and we kept afloat. Yet again, we'd drifted into new territory.

To keep the trip fresh during our occasional stays in Decorah, we don't just canoe. The first fall, we also stayed at a bed-and-breakfast, visited Laura Ingalls Wilder's home, and hiked near the Mississippi. Another fall, we bunked in a riverside cabin, toured a hatchery, and discovered a hidden waterfall. Even if we didn't add new adventures, the trip would still change. On our first float, when Noah was seven and Lily six, we easily fit into one canoe. Dirck and I paddled while the kids snacked, splashed, and sometimes squabbled. Three years later, the kids not only helped paddle, they helped weigh down the canoe. Scraping the rocky riverbed, the overloaded canoe got stuck several times. Dirck and I had to step into the cold water and push us off (much to the kids' amusement). Next trip, we'll rent two canoes. And maybe Noah and Lily will try a stint in the stern.

We never know what's around the bend.

SEED SAVERS EXCHANGE/HERITAGE FARM (all ages)

3076 North Winn Road, Decorah 52101; (563) 382–5990, www.seedsavers.org. Open 9:00 A.M. to 5:00 P.M. daily from Memorial Day until October. **Free.**

Behind this picture-postcard perfect 170-acre farm with a big red barn and vast gardens is a mission: to save endangered varieties of vegetables, fruits, herbs, and flowers. The organizers of this nonprofit farm collect and plant heirloom seeds, reviving traditional varieties grown by Native Americans and immigrants. (These efforts won the farm's founder a MacArthur Foundation "genius award.") You can visit the gift shop in the barn and tour the lovely preservation gardens, featuring thousands of heirloom varieties. Especially pretty is the old orchard, filled with 700 nineteenth-century apple varieties—the nation's largest apple display. From Decorah, drive 5.5 miles north on US 52, then right on North Winn Road (W-34) to the farm.

WILLOWGLEN NURSERY (all ages)

3512 Lost Mile Road, Decorah 52101; (563) 735–5570. Open 10:00 A.M. to 6:00 P.M. daily except Monday from May through September. **Free.**

Trying to find this out-of-the-way Eden filled with beautiful flowers, you might get lost on lonely gravel roads. That's half the fun. When you arrive, children will especially enjoy the water gardens (complete with tadpoles, fish, and frogs) and can help choose flowers to plant at home.

LAURA INGALLS WILDER PARK AND MUSEUM (all ages)

3603 236th Avenue, Burr Oak 52101; (563) 735–5916. Open 9:00 A.M. to 5:00 P.M. daily from May through October, other times by appointment. $.

The author of the famous "Little House" children's series lived in lots of places as a child, but this place—in Burr Oak, a small town about 16 miles north of Decorah—is the only one that remains on its original site, and inside are some of her belongings. The building is a former hotel, which the Ingalls family moved to in 1876. Laura's father managed the hotel while nine-year-old Laura, her mother, and her sisters helped with the chores. A year later they moved back to Minnesota. In 1973 Burr Oak residents raised money to reopen the old hotel as a museum.

Where to Eat

Cafe Deluxe. *421 West Water Street, Decorah; (563) 382–5589.* There is a hip, alternative feel to this downtown cafe that's popular for Sunday brunch but also serves casual lunch and dinner fare. $

Mabe's Pizza. *110 East Water Street, Decorah; (563) 382–4297.* Pizza, burg-ers, broasted chicken, pasta, salad, and sandwiches are served at Mabe's, which is popular with students from Decorah's Luther College. $

Stone Hearth Inn. *811 Commerce Drive, Decorah; (563) 382–4614.* A children's menu and hefty Midwestern por-tions of prime rib and pork loin are available in the Stone Hearth's rustic-decor dining room with a stone fireplace. $$

Victorian Rose. *104 East Water Street, Decorah; (563) 382–4164.* Our children were warmly welcomed in this fancy dining room in the recently restored Hotel Winneshiek, where the chef uses local organic produce and poultry to reinvent classic dishes. $$–$$$

Whippy Dip. *130 College Drive, Decorah; (563) 382–4591.* A busy summer family hangout, this locally owned soft-serve ice-cream stand also serves hot dogs and has picnic tables (beware of bees). $

Picnic Possibilities Try **Phelps Park,** on Upper Broadway Street in a historic residential district, which has a network of trails. Or visit **Dunning's Springs,** a lovely waterfall that's in the middle of Decorah but hard to find. To get there, take College Drive north to Ice Cave Road. Turn right and go a quarter mile; a sign on the left marks a dirt road that dovetails a stream through the woods.

Where to Stay

Hotel Winneshiek. *104 East Water Street, Decorah; (563) 382–4164, www.hotelwinn.com, info@hotelwinn.com.* Built in 1904, this historic downtown hotel was reopened in 2000 after a fifteen-month restoration. It has an elegant octagonal lobby, an interesting restaurant, and twenty-six rooms, including five suites. $$$–$$$$

Pulpit Rock Campground. *505 Pulpit Rock Road, Decorah; (563) 382–9941.* We've canoed on the Upper Iowa right up to this campground, which has tent and RV sites, plus modern shower and bathroom facilities. Open from April through October, it's almost a mile north of the intersection of State Highway 9 and US 52. From US 52, take the Will Baker Park exit. $

For More Information

Winneshiek County Tourism. *300 West Water Street , Decorah 52101; (800) 463–4692, www.decorah-iowa.com.*

Spillville

About 10 miles south of Decorah on State Highway 325 (off US 52), Spillville was settled by Czech immigrants. Czech composer Antonin Dvořák lived here briefly in 1893, completing his famous *New World Symphony.*

BILY CLOCKS MUSEUM/ANTONIN DVOŘÁK EXHIBIT (ages 4 and up)

323 Main Street, Spillville 52168; (563) 562–3569, www.spillville.ia.us/about.html. Open 10:00 A.M. to 4:00 P.M. weekends (and on call daily) in March and November, 10:00 A.M. to 4:00 P.M. daily in April, 8:30 A.M. to 5:00 P.M. daily from May through October. $.

This unassuming brick building where Antonin Dvořák lived during his brief stay in Spillville now houses a remarkable collection of large wooden clocks hand-carved by brothers Joseph and Frank Bily (*BEE-lee*). Bohemian Czech farmers, the brothers spent their winters carving wood, and during thirty-five years produced forty clocks, many with movable figures, music boxes, and chimes. (One clock marks Charles Lindbergh's transatlantic flight; another features the twelve apostles, who appear on the hour.) Upstairs, there's an exhibit on Dvořák.

Maple Syrup Alert Golden brown maple syrup is made the old-fashioned way at **Green's Sugar Bush** (563-567-8472), a fifth-generation syrup producer located about 15 miles south of Decorah at 111th Avenue in Castalia. An annual Maple Fest celebration, which includes a pancake/sausage breakfast and horse-drawn wagon rides, takes place usually on the last Sunday in March and the first Sunday in April. The syrup-making process begins by boring holes into hard maple trees. The sap drips into pails that are then pulled in tanks through the woods by horses. Fun Fact: It takes about forty gallons of evaporated sap to make a gallon of syrup.

FORT ATKINSON STATE PRESERVE (all ages)

Three blocks north of State Highway 24, Fort Atkinson 52142; (563) 425–4161. Open daily during daylight hours. **Free.**

Much of this 1840s fort is gone, but it's fun to walk inside the high walls past the remaining blockhouse and stockade. Located 5 miles southwest of Spillville on State Highway 24, the fort was an army post built to contain the Winnebago Indians after they were forcibly moved to Iowa from Wisconsin. After eight years, the Winnebago Indians were moved out of Iowa, and the army left. During the last full weekend in September, the Fort Atkinson Rendezvous, a free event, re-creates 1840s frontier life with cannon drills, buckskinners, tomahawk throwing contests, and venison stew.

Where to Eat

The Train Station Restaurant. *202 North Maryville Street, Calmar; (563) 562–3082.* About 4 miles southeast of Spillville in Calmar, this family restaurant next to the railroad tracks is known for its broasted chicken and "flash burger" (a hamburger steak topped with cheese and hash browns, toast on the side). $

Where to Stay

Taylor-Made B&B. *330 South Main Street, Spillville; (563) 562–3958.* The eleven Taylor children helped their parents fix up this Victorian home with a wooden porch in 1993. Today there are five rooms (each with a private bath) and two cabins (each with kitchen, porch, and bathroom). A full breakfast is served in a bay window dining area. $$-$$$

Fredericksburg

Fredericksburg is located on US 18, about 29 miles south of Spillville.

HAWKEYE BUFFALO RANCH (ages 3 and up)

3034 Pembroke Avenue, Fredericksburg 50630; (563) 237–5318, www. hawkeyebuffalo.com. Guided tours by reservation year-round. $–$$, ages 6 and under **Free.**

During a one-hour guided tour (via pickup or tractor-pulled wagon) of this working ranch about an hour north of Waterloo, you can hand feed buffalo, sample buffalo meat, throw a tomahawk, see llamas and burros, and search for green Aracuna chicken eggs. You'll also learn about the historical and spiritual connection between Native Americans and buffalo, and witness a Lakota Sioux "smudge" feather ceremony, during which a feather is used to waft smoke from burning sage over guests gathered in a circle. Located on 500 acres of rolling hills and timberland, the ranch has been owned since 1854 by the McFarland family. Inside the 1860 American ranch house are two guest rooms. Breakfast features buffalo bacon; buffalo steak dinners are available upon request. The gift shop sells painted buffalo skulls and tanned hides. Nearby, eighty-acre Split Rock Park has a man-made lake and beach for swimming and fishing, plus a campground with modern facilities. Reservations are recommended.

Waterloo

Take US 18 west and then US 63 south from Fredericksburg about 49 miles to Waterloo.

WATERLOO CENTER FOR THE ARTS (all ages)

225 Commercial Street, Waterloo 50703; (319) 291–4490, www.wplwloo.lib. ia.us/arts/. Open 10:00 A.M. to 5:00 P.M. Monday through Friday and 1:00 to 4:00 P.M. Saturday and Sunday. The Junior Art Gallery is open 1:00 to 4:00 P.M. Saturday and Sunday. **Free.**

This attractive modern museum in downtown Waterloo has a junior art gallery for children, with traveling exhibits on different cultures. The center also has the nation's largest public collection of Haitian art, plus Midwest and American Decorative Art.

BLACKHAWK CHILDREN'S THEATRE (ages 4 and up)

225 Commercial Street, Waterloo, 50703; Box office (319) 291–4494, www. cedarnet.org/wcpbhct/. Season runs September through April. Tickets cost $$ for adults, $ for children.

This award-winning children's community theater stages about five children's productions a year in the Hope C. Martin Theatre, part of the Waterloo Center for the Arts and an offshoot of the Waterloo Community Playhouse.

GROUT MUSEUM OF HISTORY AND SCIENCE (ages 4 and up)

503 South Street, Waterloo 50703; (319) 234–6357, www.groutmuseum district.org/index.html. Open 10:00 A.M. to 4:30 P.M. Tuesday through Saturday and 1:00 to 4:30 P.M. Sunday. $.

A fifty-seat planetarium with a seventeen-foot dome and a "touch and see" discovery zone for young children are highlights at this museum devoted to the history of Waterloo and Northeast Iowa. The museum also has five full-scale dioramas of a blacksmith shop, carpenter shop, log cabin, toolshed, and general store. The top floor features displays about Iowa's geology, first inhabitants, and wildlife. Check the museum's calendar for family activity nights and seasonal celebrations.

Amazing Iowa Facts Thomas and Alleta Sullivan of Waterloo lost the most sons during World War II of any American parents. Their five sons were killed in 1942 when their Navy ship was torpedoed by a Japanese submarine. (After this, family members were not allowed to serve in the same troop.) The Oscar-winning 1998 movie *Saving Private Ryan* was loosely inspired by the Sullivan brothers. The Sullivan Brothers Veterans Museum, an addition to the Grout Museum, is scheduled to be completed in 2004.

BLUEDORN SCIENCE IMAGINARIUM (all ages)

322 Washington Street, Waterloo 50703; (319) 233–8707. Open 1:00 to 4:30 P.M. Sunday and Tuesday through Friday and 10:00 A.M. to 4:30 P.M. Saturday from September through May; 10:00 A.M. to 4:30 P.M. Tuesday through Saturday and 1:00 to 4:30 P.M. Sunday from June through August. $, ages 2 and under Free.

Opened as part of the Grout Museum in 1993, this hands-on science museum is a fun way to learn about physics, light, sound, and momentum. You can race bubbles, ride a wild gyroscope, create your own laser show with a laser spirograph, fire an air cannon, and visit a learning laboratory just for kids. Live science demonstrations are held at 3:00 P.M. daily from September through May, with additional demonstrations held at 11:00 A.M. and 1:30 P.M. during the summer.

WATERLOO BLACK HAWKS HOCKEY (ages 5 and up)

Young Arena, 125 Commercial Street, Waterloo 50704; (319) 291–4300, for tickets call (319) 232-1261. $$.

In Waterloo for more than forty years, this junior A hockey team's players—ages twenty and under—are being groomed for college and professional teams. Their sixty-one-game schedule starts in mid-September and ends in late March.

WATERLOO BUCKS BASEBALL (ages 5 and up)

850 Park Road, Waterloo 50702; (319) 232–5633, www.waterloobucks.com. Season runs from early June through August. $–$$, ages 5 and under Free. *A family pass is available.*

A semipro summer collegiate team, the Waterloo Bucks play in historic Riverfront Stadium, built in 1946 with wood-backed bleachers under a covered grandstand. The Bucks, promising young players being groomed for college and the major leagues, play a sixty-four-game season.

CEDAR VALLEY ARBORETUM AND BOTANIC GARDENS (all ages)

1927 East Orange Road, Waterloo 50704; (319) 226–4966, gardens@cedar net.org. Open 10:00 A.M. to 2:00 P.M. Tuesday, noon to 7:00 P.M. Thursday, 8:00 A.M. to 4:00 P.M. Saturday, and noon to 4:00 P.M. Sunday from May through September. $, up to age 17 **Free.**

Kids can dig for fossils and "dinosaur bones," wander through a prairie butterfly garden maze, and watch fish, frogs, and turtles in a water channel at this seventy-four-acre arboretum's interactive children's garden. The garden also has a stage where children's stories that feature gardens (like *Peter Rabbit* and *Alice in Wonderland*) are performed. Located at the Hawkeye Community College, the arboretum has 450 trees and a dozen gardens.

LOST ISLAND WATER PARK (all ages)

2225 East Shaulis Road, Waterloo 50701; (319) 234–3210, www.thelostisland. com. Open 10:00 A.M. to 6:30 P.M. daily from late May through late August. Golf and go-carts available, weather permitting, 2:00 to 10:00 P.M. Monday through Saturday and 2:00 to 6:00 P.M. Sunday (also available Friday through Sunday in early May). $$, ages 2 and under **Free.** *Golf, per game, and go-carts, per ride, $.*

This elaborate water park is designed to look like a tropical Polynesian village, with palm trees, thatched huts, tree houses, tiki gods, even mock volcanoes. Visitors can ride in tubes along a 3-foot-deep lazy river. For older children (at least 48 inches tall) there's a large wave pool with 3-foot-high waves every five minutes and several slides (including a hot-pink speed slide). For younger children there's Starfish Cove, an ankle-deep area with water sprays, umbrellas, and a small tiki hut with a slide. Children too small for the water slides can try the slides in the park's tree house. The Castaway Cafe sells pizza, fries, cotton candy, and fruit smoothies. There's also a picnic area, an 18-hole adventure golf course, and go-cart tracks. The park is located in southern Waterloo, off US 20 near the Crossroads Mall.

Where to Eat

A.J.'s Eatery. *1415 East San Marnan Drive, Waterloo; (319) 232–7660.* Near the water park and arboretum in a shopping area, this neighborhood eatery has a children's menu and serves beef, fish, chicken, pasta, and burgers. $

Brown Bottle Restaurant. *West Fifth and Commercial Streets, Waterloo; (319) 232–3014.* This upscale Italian dinner spot in an old brick building downtown has a children's menu and serves good prime rib. $$

Doughy Joey's. *Fourth and Jefferson Streets, Waterloo; (319) 274–0996.* Located downtown by the museums and art center, Joey's serves pizza, sandwiches, and soup. Children use crayons to draw on the paper tablecloths and papered walls. $

The Hawkeye State Iowa got its nickname from Sac Indian Chief Black Hawk, who was forced to move to Iowa when the United States took his tribal land near Rock Island, Illinois. In 1832 Black Hawk led his people in a brief, unsuccessful effort to regain their land during the Black Hawk War. More than 1,000 people died, and Chief Black Hawk was imprisoned. Freed a year later, he wrote a well-regarded autobiography, earned the respect of President Andrew Jackson, and spent his last years in Iowa before dying in 1838. Today, Waterloo is the seat of Black Hawk County. Chief Black Hawk is buried in southern Iowa's Davis County.

Where to Stay

Best Western Starlight Village. *214 Washington Street, Waterloo; (319) 235–0321.* Centrally located, this eleven-story white stucco tower hotel has 215 rooms, an indoor pool, and a restaurant. $$

Fairfield Inn by Marriott. *2011 LaPorte Road, Waterloo; (319) 234–5452.* Located off US 20 near a shopping center south of downtown, this chain hotel has fifty-seven rooms and indoor pool. $$–$$$

Ramada Inn–Convention Center. *205 West Fourth Street, Waterloo; (319) 233–7560.* A ten-floor high-rise downtown next to the convention center, the Ramada has 236 rooms, an indoor pool, a restaurant, and a glass-enclosed atrium lobby. $$$

For More Information

Waterloo Convention and Visitors Bureau. *215 East Fourth Street, Waterloo 50703; (319) 233–8350 or (800) 728–8431, www.waterloocvb.org.*

Cedar Falls

From Waterloo, it's a short jog via US 218 to Cedar Falls, home of the University of Northern Iowa (originally called the Iowa State Normal School when it opened in 1876 to train public school teachers).

HARTMAN RESERVE NATURE CENTER (all ages)
657 Reserve Drive, Cedar Falls 50613; (319) 277–2187. Open daily sunrise to sunset. Interpretive center open 8:00 A.M. to 4:30 P.M. Monday through Friday year-round, also open 1:00 to 5:00 P.M. Sunday from Labor Day through Memorial Day. **Free.**

This 287-acre wooded area connected to recreational trails has an interpretive center with displays and children's programs. The center has three habitats: forest, wetland, and prairie. The wetland has river otters and ospreys.

ICE HOUSE MUSEUM (all ages)
First and Clay Streets, Cedar Falls 50613; (319) 266–5140. Open 2:00 to 4:30 P.M. Wednesday, Saturday, and Sunday from May through October. **Free.**

Before there were refrigerators, there was ice. This old icehouse once held up to 8,000 tons of natural ice. Listed on the National Register of Historic Places, it's now a museum where you can learn how ice was harvested from the Cedar River during the late nineteenth-century. This icehouse, which was built in 1921 after a wooden one burned down, stored ice until 1934.

ulture for Kids

- **The Waterloo/Cedar Falls Symphony Orchestra** performs a family concert and free Lollipop concerts for children ages four through ten at the Gallagher-Bluedorn Performing Arts Center on the UNI campus. Call (319) 273-3373.

- **The Cedar Falls Municipal Band** holds summer outdoor concerts at the Overman Park band shell.

UNIVERSITY OF NORTHERN IOWA MUSEUM (ages 3 and up)
3219 Hudson Road, Cedar Falls 50613; (319) 273–2188, www.uni.edu/ museum. Open 9:00 A.M. to 4:30 P.M. Monday through Friday, 1:00 to 4:00 P.M. Saturday and Sunday; closed holidays. **Free***.*

African antelope skeletons, mastodon bones, and Peruvian textiles are among the 100,000 objects in this natural history museum with special exhibits and programs often well suited for children. The museum also oversees the Marshall Center School, a restored 1893 one-room schoolhouse open to visitors by reservation.

University of Northern Iowa Panthers When you watch UNI's football and men's basketball, you're visiting Iowa's only domed stadium, the UNI-Dome. Also popular is women's basketball and volleyball, which are played in the West Gym. For tickets call (319) 273-3663 or check out www.unipanthers.com/ticket/.

Where to Eat

The Broom Factory. *110 North Main Street, Cedar Falls; (319) 268–0877.* Enjoy steak, pasta, prime rib, and Cajun food in a former nineteenth-century broom factory overlooking the Cedar River near the Ice House Museum. A children's menu is available. $–$$

Mainly Lou's. *118 Main Street, Cedar Falls; (319) 266–7337.* Located down-town in an old building, Lou's serves homemade pasta, soup, and sandwiches, and does carryout. $

Montage. *222 Main Street, Cedar Falls; (319) 268–7222.* Serving contemporary cuisine with multiethnic influences— Caribbean, Pacific Rim, Southwest, and Latin—this is a grown-up place suitable for adventurous, well-behaved young eaters. $$

Picnic Possibilities Visit 1,762-acre **Black Hawk Park** at 2410 West Lone Tree Road, just north of downtown.

Where to Stay

AmericInn Lodge and Suites. *5818 Nordic Drive, Cedar Falls; (319) 277– 6166.* Two miles south of Cedar Falls on State Highway 58 in an industrial park, this fifty-eight-room chain hotel has an indoor pool. $$

Country Inn and Suites. *2910 South Main Street, Cedar Falls; (319) 268–1800.* About a half mile from UNI's Gallagher-Bluedorn Performing Arts Center off State Highway 58, this hotel has sixty-five rooms and an indoor pool. $$$

Holiday Inn–University Plaza. *5826 University Avenue, Cedar Falls; (319) 277–2230.* Popular with parents visiting UNI students or attending Panthers games, the two-story "holidome hotel" about a mile from the UNI-Dome has indoor and outdoor pools, a restaurant, a game room, and 112 rooms. $$$

Other Things to See and Do in Northeast Iowa

- **Cable Car Square.** Dubuque, (563) 583–5000
- **Dubuque Museum of Art.** Dubuque, (563) 557–1851
- **Dubuque Arboretum and Botanical Gardens.** Dubuque, (563) 556–2100
- **Dyer-Botsford Victorian House and Doll Museum.** Dyersville, (563) 875–2504
- **Volga River State Recreation Area.** Fayette, (319) 425–4161
- **Montauk.** Clermont, (563) 423–7173.
- **Fish Farm Mounds State Preserve.** New Albin, (563) 568–4110
- **Porter House Museum.** Decorah, (563) 382–8465
- **Hayden Prairie.** Chester, (563) 547–3634
- **"World's Smallest Church."** Festina, (800) 463–4692
- **Little Brown Church.** Nashua, (641) 435–2027
- **Old Bradford Pioneer Village.** Nashua, (641) 435–2567
- **Floyd County Historical Society Museum.** Charles City, (641) 228–1099
- **Fossil and Prairie Park.** Rockford, (641) 756–3490
- **Spirit of Greene River Cruise.** Greene, (888) 823–4794 or (641) 823–4791
- **Hub City Railway Museum.** Oelwein, (319) 283–2861
- **Cedar Rock State Park.** Quasqueton, (319) 934–3572
- **Little Red School House.** Cedar Falls, (319) 266–5149

For More Information

Cedar Falls Tourism and Visitors Bureau. *10 Main Street, Cedar Falls 50613; (800) 845–1955 or (319) 268–4266, www.cedarfallstourism.org.*

Eastern Iowa

astern Iowa is a rich stew, both culturally and geographically. It includes two of Iowa's largest metropolitan areas—Cedar Rapids and the Quad Cities—and Iowa's only North American settlement, the Meskwaki Nation. Here you'll find the old-world redbrick villages of the Amana Colonies, one of the state's top tourist attractions, and the cutting edge college town of Iowa City, the state's largest university. Along the way, you'll drive through bucolic farmland and beside the mighty Mississippi.

So expect a filling trip: Explore caves and gorges, watch baseball at a river-front stadium, visit a Czech Village, and enjoy a Native American powwow. You can also learn about two famous (and very different) Iowans who hail from this region, artist Grant Wood and President Herbert Hoover.

To make a broad loop of the area, start in the northwest corner, in Tama County. Travel south on US 63 to Grinnell and Montezuma, then east along (or near) Interstate 80 to Iowa City. Next you'll dip southeast to Muscatine, then follow the Mississippi River north through the Quad Cities, Clinton, and Bellevue. Driving back inland through rolling countryside, you'll end up in Cedar Rapids.

For More Information

Eastern Iowa Tourism Association. P.O. Box 189, Dyersville 52040; (800) *891–3482 or (563) 875–7269, www. easterniowatourism.org.*

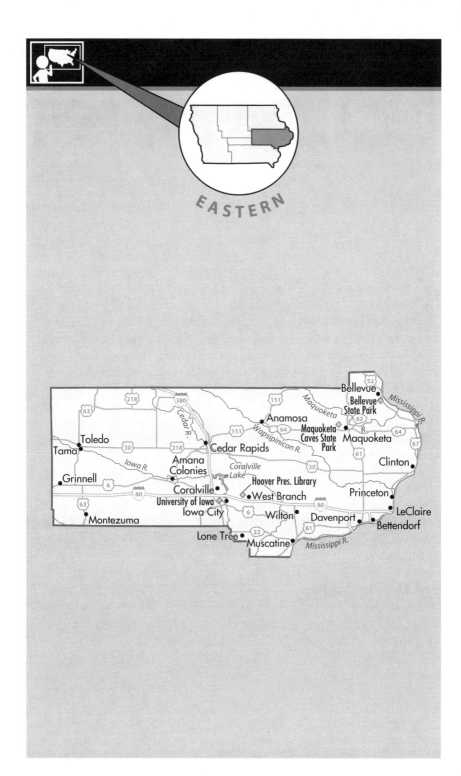

EASTERN

Betsy's Top Ten Picks for Fun in Eastern Iowa

1. Maquoketa Caves, Maquoketa
2. University of Iowa Hawkeyes games, Iowa City
3. Eulenspiegel Puppet Theatre, West Liberty
4. Devonian Fossil Gorge, Iowa City
5. Meskwaki Indian Powwow, Tama
6. Amana Colonies
7. Browsing in Prairie Lights bookstore, Iowa City
8. River Bandits baseball on the Mississippi, Davenport
9. Wilton Candy Kitchen, Wilton
10. Bellevue Butterfly Gardens, Bellevue

Tama/Toledo

Located at the intersection of US 63 and US 30, Toledo and Tama are in rural Tama County, home of Iowa's only Native American settlement. The Meskwaki Indians own almost 3,500 acres along the Iowa River, including the Meskwaki Bingo and Casino in Tama (which is off-limits to children).

 TAMA COUNTY HISTORICAL MUSEUM (ages 6 and up)
200 North Broadway, Toledo 52342; (641) 484–6767. Open 1:00 to 4:30 P.M. Tuesday through Saturday. **Free**, *donation appreciated.*
This former county jail, circa 1870, displays Meskwaki Indian and pioneer artifacts. Nearby, a carefully restored pioneer family log home is open for tours.

Meskwaki Powwow To learn about Meskwaki traditions, drop by the four-day celebration held on the second weekend in August, featuring food (including Indian Fry Bread), traditional dancing, culture, and arts. The first day is Children's Day, with most dances performed by children. The Powwow grounds are on County Highway E49, west of Tama. Admission is charged; children five and under free. Call (641) 484-4678.

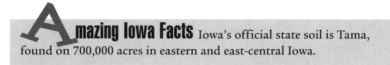

Amazing Iowa Facts Iowa's official state soil is Tama, found on 700,000 acres in eastern and east-central Iowa.

Where to Eat

The Fireside Inn. *US 63 and US 30, Toledo; (641) 484–5244.* Located in a commercial area at the junction of two highways, the Fireside Inn has prime rib, steaks, a salad bar, and a children's menu. $–$$

Rube's Steakhouse. *118 Elm Street, Montour; (641) 492–6222.* About 7 miles west of Tama–Toledo, this well-known grill-your-own-enormous-steak joint has a children's menu. $$$

Picnic Possibilities Try Lincoln Highway Bridge Park, off US 30 on Fifth Street, the site of the only remaining original bridge from the old Lincoln Highway, built in 1915 as America's first transcontinental highway.

Where to Stay

Meskwaki Bingo Casino Hotel. *1504 305th Street, Tama; (800) 728–GAME.* Off US 30 about 5 miles west of Tama–Toledo, the 204-room hotel is part of a casino complex and includes an all-you-can-eat buffet and an indoor pool. Reminder: No one under age 21 can enter the casino. $$–$$$

For More Information

Tama–Toledo Area Chamber of Commerce. *P.O. Box 367, Toledo 52342; (641) 484–6661, www.tama toledo.com.*

Grinnell

About 19 miles south of Tama–Toledo in Poweshiek County on US 6 is Grinnell, home of Grinnell College, a small, progressive liberal arts college. Grinnell was the first college west of the Mississippi to grant bachelor of arts degrees and among the first to admit women and African-Americans to full degree programs.

CARROLL'S PUMPKIN FARM (all ages)

244 400th Avenue, Grinnell 50112; (641) 236–7043. Open 10:00 A.M. *to 7:00* P.M. *Monday through Saturday and 1:00 to 7:00* P.M. *Sunday during October only. $, ages 2 and under* Free.

On a beautiful autumn day, this forty-acre farm with fields of corn and soybeans is the perfect place to pick a Halloween pumpkin. It's also an agricultural theme park of sorts, where you can take a hayride, navigate a cornfield maze, play in a barn full of grain, and pet baby goats. Other highlights include a pumpkin catapult that pitches pumpkins into a pond and a playground in a straw barn. On the weekends there's often live harmonica and accordion music. Caramel apples are sold at a concession stand.

Amazing Iowa Facts "Go West, young man," New York newspaper editor Horace Greeley advised a young abolitionist minister in 1853. The minister, Josiah Bushnell "J. B." Grinnell, went west—and founded the town of Grinnell.

Where to Eat

Kelcy's. *812 Sixth Avenue, Grinnell; (641) 236–3132.* Daily lunch specials (spaghetti, meat loaf, casseroles), steak and prime rib dinners, burgers, sandwiches, and homemade desserts are offered at this casual restaurant north of the town square. $$–$$$

Pagliai's Pizza. *816 Fifth Avenue, Grinnell; (641) 236–5331.* Located north of the downtown square, this family-owned restaurant serves garden-fresh pizza and pasta. $$

Where to Stay

Carriage House B&B. *1133 Broad Street, Grinnell; (641) 236–7520.* The Carriage House, near Grinnell College, is a Victorian house with a cushioned swing on the wraparound porch. It has six rooms, each with private bath (including one with a double bed, twin bed, and available cot), and serves

fresh Irish soda bread and homemade jams for breakfast. $$

Country Inn of Grinnell. *1710 West Street South, Grinnell; (800) 456–4000 or (641) 236–9600.* This forty-eight-room chain hotel, off Interstate 80 about 4 miles from downtown, has an indoor pool and three suites. $$

For More Information

Grinnell Chamber of Commerce.
833 Fourth Avenue, Grinnell 50112; (641)
236–6555, www.grinnellchamber.org,
chamber@grinnellchamber.org.

Montezuma

Montezuma is about 21 miles southeast of Grinnell at the junction of US 63 and State Highway 85, 9 miles south of Interstate 80.

 FUN VALLEY SKI AREA (ages 3 and up)
1066 500th Avenue, Montezuma 50171; (641) 623–3456. Open December through March, 4:00 to 9:00 P.M. Tuesday through Thursday, noon to 9:00 P.M. Friday and Sunday, and 10:00 A.M. to 9:00 P.M. Saturday. Daily skiing or snowboarding lift ticket and rental, $$$; tubing, $$.

Designed for beginner and intermediate skiers, Fun Valley has a 240-foot-high slope, about a quarter mile long, with one triple and two double chairlifts. There's also tubing, a snowboard jumping area, and fast food.

Where to Eat

The Apple Basket. 105 South Fourth Street, Montezuma; (641) 623–3845. A popular restaurant on the town square, the Apple Basket serves huge steaks and fresh seafood. Reservations are recommended on weekends. $$

For More Information

Montezuma Community Boosters.
P.O. Box 111, Montezuma 50171; (641) 623–5640.

Amana Colonies

Travel northeast from Montezuma to the Amana Colonies, located off Interstate 80 at exit 225 along and near US 6. Founded in 1855 as a religious communal society by German immigrants fleeing persecution, the seven pristine redbrick villages known as "The Amanas" began as a utopian living experiment and are now one of Iowa's top tourist spots. Utopia ended in the 1930s, but the well-preserved villages endure, filled with German restaurants, lodgings, shops, museums, and wineries. Home to 1,400 people, the major villages are Amana, Middle Amana, Lower Amana, and Homestead.

MUSEUM OF AMANA HISTORY (ages 5 and up)

4310 220th Trail, Amana 52203; (319) 622–3567, www.amanaheritage.org. Open 10:00 A.M. to 5:00 P.M. Monday through Saturday, and noon to 5:00 P.M. Sunday from April through October; open Saturday year-round. $, ages 7 and under Free.

Each summer this history museum, located in three nineteenth-century buildings, offers the Amana Colonies for Kids program, which includes a huge scavenger hunt, hands-on education workshops, live entertainment, and walking tours for little or no extra cost. The workshops for school-age children and a one-hour children's theater show called *Struwwel Peter* are offered Tuesday through Saturday from late June through mid-August. Reservations aren't needed. The workshops teach crafts like calligraphy, quilting, and lithography. *Struwwel Peter* highlights fables and folktales of Iowa's German settlers. Walking tours led by costumed interpreters are offered Monday through Saturday from July through mid-August. Another option is a historical audio driving tour. A CD about Amana history and CD converters are available for rent at the museum. In mid-September there's a self-guided tour of Amana Colony artisans' studios and workplaces. Call (319) 622–3678.

MINI-AMERICANA BARN MUSEUM (ages 5 and up)

413 P Street, South Amana 52334; (319) 622–3058, www.barnmuseum.com. Open 9:00 A.M. to 5:00 P.M. daily from April through October. $.

Inside this old horse barn are more than 200 miniature replicas of barns and homesteads, including a Southern Louisiana plantation and Abe Lincoln's home, all carved from wood by Iowan Henry Moore. It's billed as the largest collection of miniature replicas in the United States built by one man.

Amazing Iowa Facts The first microwave oven was invented in Amana. The Amana Radarange was unveiled in 1967 by Amana Home Appliances.

AMANA COLONIES NATURE TRAIL (all ages)

Located at the junction of US 151 and US 6, near Homestead. Open year-round except during deer hunting season.

Hike or cross-county ski this 3-mile trail through the woods and along the Iowa River to a scenic bluff overlooking a 250-year-old Indian dam.

Splish Splash If you need to cool offer during a summer visit, try the indoor pool at Amana Elementary School, 3023 220th Trail, Middle Amana. There's a lifeguard and playground. Admission is charged. For hours call (319) 622–3792.

Where to Eat

The Ronnenberg. *4408 220th Trail, Main Amana; (888) 348–4686 or (319) 622–3641.* Formerly a communal kitchen used by original Amana settlers, the Ronnenberg has served German-American food family-style in big pass-around bowls for fifty years. Lighter meals and sandwiches are also available. $-$$

Schatzi's Ice Cream and Sandwich Shop. *4201 F Street, Amana; (319) 622–3183.* Tenderloins, hamburgers, and fries, plus soft-serve ice cream and frozen yogurt are available at this little shop off US 151. $

Zuber's Dugout Restaurant. *2206 V Street, Homestead; (319) 622–3911.* Zuber's serves a hearty German meal (a main course with side dishes like sauerkraut, applesauce, and fried potatoes with gravy) and is decorated with baseball memorabilia. It was opened by a former major-league baseball pitcher, the late Bill Zuber. $-$$

Picnic Possibilities Visit 160-acre **Lily Lake,** on Highway 220 outside Middle Amana, which is covered with yellow lotus lily blooms from late July to mid-August. There's also a 3.1-mile hard-surface trail around the lake for biking and in-line skating.

Where to Stay

Amana Holiday Inn. *Off Interstate 80 at exit 225 in Williamsburg; (319) 668–1175.* This 155-room hotel has an indoor pool, a playground, and a restaurant where children eat for free. $$-$$$$

Die Heimat Country Inn. *4434 V Street, Homestead; (888) 613–5463 or (319) 622–3937.* Originally an 1854 stagecoach stop, this charming B&B has eighteen rooms and serves a full breakfast. $$–$$$

Dust to Dawn Bed and Breakfast. *2616 K Street, Middle Amana; (319) 622–3029.* Located in an 1860s home, this antiques-filled B&B has seven rooms, a deck, and a sunroom, and serves a continental breakfast. $$

For More Information

Amana Colonies Convention and Visitors Bureau. *39 38th Avenue, Suite 100, Amana 52203; (800) 579–2294 or (319) 622–7622, www.amanacolonies.com, info@amanacolonies.com.* There are also two Iowa Welcome Centers, one at exit 225 off Interstate 80 and the other at the visitors bureau.

Iowa City

About 20 miles southeast of the Amanas along Interstate 80 is Iowa City, home of the University of Iowa, the state's largest university, with its powerhouse Hawkeye football and basketball teams. A hip, happening college town of about 60,000 people (45 percent of them students), Iowa City has some of Iowa's best restaurants, markets, bookstores, museums, galleries, and performing arts. Surrounded by lush farmland, Iowa City also has one of the nation's largest teaching hospitals and most famous university creative writing programs. Flannery O'Connor, Kurt Vonnegut Jr., and Philip Roth are all former Iowa Writers' Workshop students or faculty. The neighboring town of Coralville is often lumped in with Iowa City.

 IOWA CHILDREN'S MUSEUM (all ages)
1451 Coral Ridge Avenue, Coralville 52241; (319) 625–6255, www.theicm.org. Open 9:00 A.M. to 6:00 P.M. Tuesday through Thursday, 9:00 A.M. to 8:00 P.M. Friday, 10:00 A.M. to 6:00 P.M. Saturday, and 11:00 A.M. to 6:00 P.M. Sunday. $.
Located in the Coral Ridge Mall off Interstate 80 at exit 240, this 28,000-square-foot museum has hands-on exhibits about community, science, early childhood development, and cultural diversity. Designed to encourage teamwork and stimulate young minds, the exhibits also include a make-your-own pizzeria, a broadcast area where children can do their own newscasts, and a child-size grocery store. There's also a science experiment center, a play hospital and ambulance, and a special toddler/preschooler room.

Culture for Kids

- **University of Iowa's Hancher Auditorium.** *231 Hancher Auditorium, Iowa City 52242; (800) HANCHER or (319) 335–1160, www.uiowa.edu/ hancher, hancher-box-office@uiowa.edu.* This university performing arts center offers top-notch Broadway fare, concerts, and dance events, some specifically for children.

- **Eulenspiegel Puppet Theatre Company.** *319 North Calhoun Street, West Liberty 52776; (319) 627–2487, www.puppetspuppets.com, owlglass@ avalon.net.* Since 1974, this small puppet theater has entertained Iowa children, using handcrafted puppets to perform international folktales. The forty-five-minute performances are held in West Liberty, about 15 miles east of Iowa City, at the New Strand Theater, 111 East Third Street, or at the North Calhoun Street location.

OLD CAPITOL MUSEUM (ages 5 and up)

24 Old Capitol Street, University of Iowa campus, Iowa City 52242; (319) 335– 0548, www.uiowa.edu/~oldcap. Open 10:00 A.M. to 3:00 P.M. Monday through Saturday and noon to 4:00 P.M. Sunday. **Free**.

A 2001 fire destroyed the golden dome of this beautifully restored Greek Revival building that served as Iowa's first state capitol from 1846 to 1857. But the dome, a cherished symbol of the university and the state, is being rebuilt and may reopen by spring 2003 for guided tours. Call to double-check.

UNIVERSITY OF IOWA MUSEUM OF ART (ages 3 and up)

150 North Riverside Drive, Iowa City 52242; (319) 335–1727, www.uiowa. edu/~uima. Open 10:00 A.M. to 5:00 P.M. Tuesday through Saturday, until 9:00 P.M. Friday, and noon to 5:00 P.M. Sunday. **Free**.

Hands-on art activities for children are typically offered on Sundays at this fine-arts museum featuring work by major twentieth-century artists, including Iowa's own Grant Wood (a former University of Iowa art professor). Part of a sprawling arts complex on the Iowa River's west bank, the museum also has one of the nation's best African art collections.

University of Iowa Hawkeyes Every kid should go to at least one Hawkeye football or basketball game. For tickets, call 800–IAHAWKS—and call early.

MUSEUM OF NATURAL HISTORY (all ages)
*MacBride Hall, Clinton and Jefferson Streets on the University of Iowa campus,
Iowa City 52242; (319) 335–0482. Open 9:30 A.M. to 4:30 P.M. Monday
through Saturday and 12:30 to 4:30 P.M. Sunday.* **Free.**
See a 9-foot-tall model of an Ice Age sloth, a 47-foot whale skeleton,
and dioramas depicting a nineteenth-century Meskwaki village in the
museum's Iowa Hall and Mammal Hall, which cover about a billion
years of history. There's also a collection of 1,100 mounted birds and a
fossil display.

A Rubiner Family Adventure It was too good to be true.
But when friends offered us free tickets to the Iowa-Michigan football
game—*on the 50-yard line*—we jumped at the opportunity. Our children,
then ages six and seven, would not only experience a classic fall outing
in Iowa, they'd see the Iowa Hawkeyes play the Michigan Wolverines
from my home state. But instead of a gorgeous, bright, crisp autumn
day, we got an ugly, gray, soggy autumn day. Like many other families,
we tried waiting out the rain by hanging out at the Coralville Mall,
Prairie Lights, and the New Pioneer Co-op. No luck. The weather didn't
improve. So we decided to brave the elements. Bundled up in sweaters,
parkas, and blankets, we joined a surprisingly large crowd of similarly
foolhardy spectators to watch the football players slip and slide across a
muddy field. It was a lot of fun—for about an hour. Then we sloshed off
to find some hard-earned hot chocolate.

 **DEVONIAN FOSSIL GORGE AND CORALVILLE LAKE
(ages 5 and up)**
*2850 Prairie du Chien Road Northeast, Iowa City 52240; (319) 338–3543,
www.coralvillelake.org. Visitor center open 7:30 A.M. to 4:00 P.M. daily; closed
weekends from January to mid-April. The gorge is open dawn to dusk year-round.*
Free.
A paradise for young explorers, this gorge was created by the famous
flood of 1993 (yes, 1993) and is about 3½ miles north of Interstate 80
exit 244 near the Coralville Dam. The flood eroded a 15-foot-deep
channel, exposing the bedrock beneath. On a pretty day, children can be
spotted hopping from one flat shelf of rock to the next, peering into
shallow pools of green mossy water and shouting, "Here's one!" as they
bend over to scan the rocks for fossils, some of them 375 million years

old. Small plaques in the gorge explain what you're seeing, but you'll need a guide brochure. They're in a box at the entry plaza or at the visitor center, which also shows a short video about the 1993 flood. (If the center's front door is locked, go around the corner to the office door.) Try to visit during the spring or fall when the light is best and it's not too hot, or on an early summer morning. Coralville Lake offers swimming and boating, plus trails for hiking, biking, and cross-country skiing.

WILSON'S ORCHARD (all ages)

2924 Orchard Lane Northeast, Iowa City 52240; (319) 354–5651. Open 10:00 A.M. until dusk from August through October. **Free**.

Choose from among 150 varieties of apples at this pick-your-own orchard.

PRAIRIE LIGHTS (all ages)

15 Dubuque Street, Iowa City 52240; (319) 337–2681, www.prairielights.com. Open 9:00 A.M. to 10:00 P.M. daily except Sunday when closed at 6:00 P.M.

Famous writers and students from the Iowa Writers' Workshop hang out at Prairie Lights, a nationally known bookstore located downtown. So do everyday book lovers. With three floors to explore, it is Iowa's largest independent bookstore and hosts free readings by noted writers that are broadcast statewide on Iowa public radio. It's also a welcoming place for families with a good children's book department (in the basement) and a helpful, knowledgeable staff. There's also a pleasant upstairs cafe.

Where to Eat

Bread Garden Cafe. *224 South Clinton Street, Iowa City; (319) 622–3278.* This pleasant bakery across from campus has hearty soups, sandwiches, and luscious desserts. $

The Monkey House. *1604 Sycamore Street, Iowa City; (319) 338–1698.* Located in the Sycamore Mall, this family entertainment center with a karaoke stage, toddler play area, games, and rides also serves kid-friendly food—pizza, grilled cheese, chef salads, chicken wings—at tables with chalkboards for playing games. There's a $5.00 admission for children up to age fifteen. $

Pagliai's Pizza. *302 East Bloomfield Street, Iowa City; (319) 351–5073.* A family-owned Iowa City favorite, Pagliai's serves freshly made pizza in a brick building north of downtown. $

Whitey's Ice Cream. *112 East Washington Street, Iowa City; (319) 354–1200.* Sundaes, "upside-down shakes and malts," and ice cream in exotic flavors (blueberry root beer, anyone?) are served at Whitey's downtown shop, which also has an outlet in the Coral Ridge Mall. $

Picnic Possibilities

Pick up food at the **New Pioneer Co-op** at 22 South Van Buren Street in Iowa City or 1101 Second Street off US 6 West in Coralville. Or shop at the Saturday morning **farmers' market** at the Chauncey Swan Parking Ramp between Washington and College Streets, held from May through October. Then head to Iowa City's pretty **City Park,** along the Iowa River near Dubuque Street, which has a playground and summer amusement park rides. Another option is **College Green Park,** at Washington and Dodge Streets, which has a playground. For more information on Iowa City's thirty-three parks, call the Iowa City Recreation Department at (319) 356–5100.

Where to Stay

AmericInn. *2597 Holiday Road, Coralville; (319) 625–2400.* Located near the Coral Ridge Mall, this seventy-six-room hotel has an indoor pool. $$–$$$.

Highlander Inn. *2525 North Dodge Street, Iowa City; (800) 333–3333 or (319) 354–2000.* This ninety-five-room hotel on the northeast side at the intersection of Interstate 80 and State Highway 1 has an indoor pool and a restaurant. $$–$$$

Iowa House Hotel. *Corner of Madison and Jefferson Streets, Iowa City; (319) 335–3513.* With 103 rooms and suites, the Iowa House is in the Iowa Memorial Union on the U of I campus. $$$–$$$$

Sheraton of Iowa City. *210 South Dubuque Street, Iowa City; (319) 337–4058.* Right on Iowa City's lively downtown pedestrian mall, the Sheraton has 234 rooms and suites, an indoor pool, and a restaurant. $$$$

For More Information

Iowa City/Coralville Convention and Visitors Bureau, *408 First Avenue, Coralville 52241; (800) 283–6592 or (319) 337–6592, www.icccvb.org, cvb@icccvb.org.*

West Branch

West Branch, about 9 miles east of Iowa City, is a small town with a big museum honoring President Herbert Hoover, the only Iowan to hold that office.

HERBERT HOOVER NATIONAL HISTORIC SITE AND PRESIDENTIAL MUSEUM (ages 3 and up, depending on the exhibit)

210 Parkside Drive, West Branch 52358; (319) 643–5301, www.hoover.nara. gov. Open 9:00 A.M. to 5:00 P.M. daily year-round except for major holidays. $, ages 16 and under **free.**

Learn about the thirty-first U.S. President, Herbert Hoover, by visiting this complex that includes a presidential library and museum, Hoover's gravesite, and grounds reconstructing the president's childhood hometown. Children will most enjoy the grounds, featuring Hoover's birthplace cottage, a blacksmith shop, Quaker meetinghouse, one-room schoolhouse, and seventy-six-acre tallgrass prairie. The museum may spark the interest of older children. It offers quiz games and traces Hoover's life. (An Iowa blacksmith's son, Hoover was orphaned at age ten and became president in 1928.) The first weekend in August is Hoover Fest, which includes a children's activities tent and a fireworks show with live music by the Cedar Rapids Symphony.

Where to Eat

Herb 'n Lou's. *105 North Downey Street, West Branch; (319) 643–7373.* Named after President Hoover and his wife (Lou Henry Hoover), this pizza place in the old downtown also serves deli sandwiches, soups, and salads. $

Main Street Sweets. *106 East Main Street, West Branch; (319) 643–2629.* Basic kid food—subs, burgers, huge pork tenderloins, corn dogs, fries, and ice cream—is available at this restaurant with a small indoor eating area and a courtyard with picnic tables. $

For More Information

West Branch Chamber of Commerce. *Box 365, West Branch 52358; (319) 643–2111.*

Lone Tree

Lone Tree is about 16 miles south of West Branch.

BOCK'S BERRY FARM (all ages)

5888 Sand Road SE, Lone Tree 52755; (319) 629–5553. Open 7:30 A.M. *to 7:00* P.M. *Tuesday through Sunday from May through July, 9:00* A.M. *to 6:00* P.M. *Tuesday through Sunday from August through October, 10:00* A.M. *to 5:00* P.M. *Tuesday through Sunday in November and December, and 10:00* A.M. *to 5:00* P.M. *Saturday and Sunday from January through April.* **Free**.

Ten miles south of Iowa City, Bock's offers fruit picking (strawberries, blueberries, raspberries, and pumpkins), a farm animal petting zoo, and a gift shop in an old barn.

Muscatine

Take State Highway 22 east about 20 miles to Muscatine, an old Mississippi River town that today has a large Hispanic population.

PEARL BUTTON MUSEUM (ages 6 and up)

117 West Second Street, Muscatine 52761; (563) 263–1052, www.pearlbutton. org. Open noon to 4:00 P.M. *Tuesday through Saturday or by appointment.* **Free**.

This is the world's only museum detailing how pearl buttons were made from the shells of Mississippi River clams, a major Muscatine industry from the 1850s until the 1930s, when plastic buttons came along. Located in an old brick and sandstone building that's part of a downtown historic district near the river, the museum features an authentic 1900s riverboat used to harvest clams, a pearl factory production line, and a ten-minute video. By the late 1800s, 37 percent of the world's pearl buttons were made in

Amazing Iowa Facts All purple and green ketchup is made in Muscatine at the Heinz Ketchup plant.

Muscatine at some forty companies that employed half the local workforce.

Marvelous Melons Muscatine is famous for musk melons—a large sweet cantaloupe—and watermelon. During the summer you'll find local farmers' markets along State Highway 70 and US 61 south, including Hoopes Melon Shed, 4701 Grandview Avenue, (563) 263–7302.

KARKOSH KORNERS DISPLAY GARDENS AT PEARL CITY PERENNIAL PLANTATION (all ages)

2820 Highway 22, Muscatine 52761; (563) 262–5555. Open 9:00 A.M. *to 6:00* P.M. *Monday through Friday, 9:00* A.M. *to 5:00* P.M. *Saturday, and noon to 5:00* P.M. *Sunday from April through October.* **Free**.

There's a charming children's zoo with llamas, peacocks, and other domestic animals at this plantation with ten acres of display gardens, plus meadows, winding trails, a picnic area, and a historic farm home. Wander along landscaped paths to visit the many gardens, including a water garden with exotic fish.

Amazing Iowa Facts In 1926 Muscatine butcher Frank Angell created a loose-meat sandwich from ground beef and spices that was "made right." The Maid-Rite Sandwich (sort of a dry Sloppy Joe) was born. Today there are more than eighty Maid-Rite franchises in seven states. Maid-Rite also pioneered the drive-up and walk-up windows. In small Iowa towns the local Maid-Rite is often a gathering spot for farmers. Kids like it too.

Where to Eat

Cookie Crumbs. *203 East Second Street, Muscatine; (563) 288–6651.* Soups, sandwiches, salads, and big cookies are served at this small bakery and cafe in the downtown historic area. $

Floodwaters. *101 West Mississippi Drive, Muscatine; (563) 264–1940.* Located in the old Hotel Muscatine, this casual restaurant serves contemporary Ameri-can food, from seafood pasta to steaks and sandwiches. $–$$

Habanero Grill and Cantina. *114 East Second Street, Muscatine; (563) 263–3188.* Located near the pearl button museum, Habanero is a local downtown favorite that serves authentic Mexican cuisine. $

Picnic Possibilities Try **Riverside Park** on Mississippi Drive downtown, which has a playground and great river view, or **Mark Twain Lookout** (east of Riverside Park on State Highways 22 and 92 near the bridge to Illinois).

Where to Stay

Comfort Inn. *115 Cleveland Street, Muscatine; (563) 263–1500.* The forty-nine-room Comfort Inn, near US 61 and State Highway 38 has several suites, some with mini kitchens, and an indoor pool. $$$

Holiday Inn Holidome. *2915 US 61 North, Muscatine; (563) 264–5550.* Located northeast of town, this 112-room hotel has a large indoor recreation area with a pool, restaurant (where kids eat free), waterfall, and small pond. $$–$$$$

Strawberry Farm B&B. *3402 Tipton Road, Muscatine; (563) 262–8688.* Situated on an 1840s strawberry farm on the outskirts of town, this lovely Victorian redbrick farmhouse has three rooms and two baths, and serves breakfast. $$–$$$

Varner's Caboose. *3911 Highway 22, Montpelier; (563) 381–3652.* This 1958 Rock Island Line caboose in a tiny town near Muscatine sleeps four people, with breakfast included. $$

For More Information

Muscatine Convention and Visitors Bureau. *319 East Second Street, Suite 102, Muscatine 52761; (800) 257–3275* *or (563) 263–8895, www.muscatine.com, visitorinfo@muscatine.com.*

Wilton

Wilton is about 10 miles north of Muscatine, off State Highway 38.

WILTON CANDY KITCHEN (all ages)

310 Cedar Street, Wilton 52778; (563) 732–2278. Generally open 8:00 A.M. *to 5:00* P.M. *daily.*

Except for the Styrofoam dish that's used to serve the ice-cream sundaes, you'll feel like you're in the movie *Back to the Future* when you visit the Wilton Candy Kitchen, which claims to be the nation's oldest ongoing ice-cream parlor, soda fountain, and confectionery. Opened in 1867, it sure feels old, with a marble soda fountain, walnut and leather-upholstered booths and oval white marble tables, a sloping stamped tin ceiling, and leaded glass light fixtures. Owned since 1910 by the same Greek-American family, it's on the National Register of Historic Places and located in a small, pokey downtown. There's also a little museum with interesting local memorabilia. Try a malt.

Where to Eat

White Way Restaurant/Cafe. *718 Fifth Street, Durant; (563) 785–6202.* Located in a small town 5 miles northeast of Wilton, this thirty-five-year-old diner has earned national attention for its homemade American entrees, including pork chops and catfish, served with a twenty-item salad bar. It also has a children's menu. $

Davenport/The Quad Cities

From Wilton, take I–80 east about 19 miles to the Quad Cities, which include Davenport and Bettendorf in Iowa, plus Rock Island, Moline, and East Moline in Illinois. (Yup, that's five cities.) In Iowa, small towns considered part of the Quad Cities include LeClaire, Long Grove, and Princeton.

Vintage Tractors in Moline Visit a re-created 1950s farm tractor store, complete with old-fashioned equipment and costumed interpreters, at the **John Deere Collectors Center** on the riverfront in Moline, Illinois. It's across from the John Deere Pavilion, 1400 River Drive, which has exhibits showing how farm equipment has evolved from the horse-drawn plow to high-tech combines. Call (309) 765–1000.

CHANNEL CAT WATER TAXI (all ages)

On Mound Street in the historic village of East Davenport; (309) 788–3360. The taxi leaves on the hour from 11:00 A.M. to 8:00 P.M. Monday through Friday and on the half hour starting at 9:00 A.M. Saturday and Sunday from Memorial Day through Labor Day. Also open weekends only in September. $, ages 2 and under Free.

A seasonal Mississippi River waterbus that resembles a large pontoon boat, the Channel Cat runs between four landings along the Mississippi. The two on the Iowa side are in East Davenport, a shopping area dating back to 1851, and in Bettendorf's Leach Park.

DAVENPORT RIVER BANDITS (all ages)
209 South Gaines Street, Davenport 52808; (563) 324–3000, www.river bandits.com. Season runs from early April to early September. $–$$, ages 2 and under Free.

This minor-league baseball team plays at a ballpark so picturesque it's often included on baseball stadium calendars. But beauty comes at a price. The park, which is right on the Mississippi, has had major flooding problems. The River Bandits are the Class A Midwest League affiliate of the Minnesota Twins.

Quad Cities Summer Weekend Fests The festival season begins the first weekend in July with the Mississippi River Blues Festival, followed the third weekend in July by the Bix Beiderbecke Memorial Jazz Festival. In early August it's the annual tug-of-war contest, waged from both sides of the river with a rope that's more than a half mile long.

MISSISSIPPI RIVER VISITOR CENTER (all ages)
Located on the western tip of Arsenal Island; (309) 788–6412. Open 9:00 A.M. to 5:00 P.M. daily from September through May, 9:00 A.M. to 9:00 P.M. from Memorial Day through Labor Day.

Watch boats pass through lock and dam #15 and learn about the Mississippi's lock and dam system.

Arsenal Island Attractions Located in the Mississippi River channel between Davenport and Rock Island, Arsenal Island is the upper Mississippi's largest island and the site of a former U.S. Army arsenal established in 1862. There is one entrance from Iowa, two from Illinois. Weapons and military parts are still made at the island's factory.

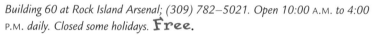

Eagle Watching on the Mississippi Quad Cities Bald Eagle

Days, held in mid-January, celebrates the 25,000-plus bald eagles that winter along the Mississippi near the locks and dams, including #15 in the Quad Cities. Eagles like dams because the turbulence provides open water and fish for eating. They also roost in wooded bluffs above the river. The celebration is held in Rock Island at the QCCA Expo Center, 2621 Fourth Avenue, and includes presentations with live wolves and river otters. Pick up a free map showing the best spots to see the eagles. Call (309) 794–5338.

ROCK ISLAND ARSENAL MUSEUM

Building 60 at Rock Island Arsenal; (309) 782–5021. Open 10:00 A.M. to 4:00 P.M. daily. Closed some holidays. **Free.**

This is the nation's second oldest U.S. Army museum and has one of the largest collections of military arms.

PUTNAM MUSEUM OF HISTORY AND NATURAL SCIENCE/IMAX THEATRE (ages 3 and up)

1717 West 12th Street, Davenport 52804; (800) 435–3701 or (563) 324–1933, www.putnam.org, museum@putnam.org. Open 9:00 A.M. to 5:00 P.M. Tuesday through Friday, 10:00 A.M. to 5:00 P.M. Saturday, and noon to 5:00 P.M. Sunday. $$, including IMAX.

Learn about Mississippi River history and natural science as well as cultures around the world at this 76,000-square-foot museum that recently went through a major $5 million expansion. Specifically designed for young children is the River Valley Discovery Room, which has hands-on interactive activities and games. Kids can play with old tools, touch a 200-million-year-old tree, and examine fossils. It's usually open from 9:00 A.M. to 4:00 P.M. Elsewhere, you can walk through a cave, watch river fish in a 718-gallon aquarium, and examine a diorama of lifelike African and Arctic animals. There's also a 3,000-year-old mummy and early Native American artifacts. The IMAX Theatre has several showtimes daily. One of the first museums west of the Mississippi, the Putnam was founded in 1867 and has more than 160,000 items.

FAMILY MUSEUM OF ARTS AND SCIENCE (all ages)

2900 Learning Campus Drive, Bettendorf 52722; (563) 344–4106, www.family museum.org. Open noon to 8:00 P.M. Monday, 9:00 A.M. to 8:00 P.M. Tuesday

through Thursday, 9:00 A.M. to 5:00 P.M. Friday and Saturday, and noon to 5:00 P.M. Sunday. $.

Hop through a rabbit hole, touch a 10-foot tornado, and make a cloud ring at this family museum with exhibits on weather, agriculture, the human heart, music, and sound. Preschoolers will enjoy The Garden, where they can play in a two-story Bear's Playhouse, build with foam blocks, and try out a climbing maze. The outdoor playground, for all ages, includes a picnic area and a water play area with buckets, funnels, and floating toys.

 BUFFALO BILL MUSEUM/THE SS *LONE STAR STEAMER* (ages 6 and up)
200 North River Drive, LeClaire 52753; (563) 289–5580. Open 9:00 A.M. to 5:00 P.M. Monday through Saturday and noon to 5:00 P.M. Sunday from mid-May to mid-October, 9:00 A.M. to 5:00 P.M. Saturday and noon to 5:00 P.M. Sunday from mid-October to mid-May. $, ages 5 and under **Free***.*

Showman Buffalo Bill Cody was born in LeClaire in 1846 and stayed until he was eleven years old. He earned his nickname after killing more than 4,000 buffalo to feed railroad workers. This small museum has memorabilia celebrating its native son, plus steamboat and pioneer artifacts. Also on display is the SS *Lone Star Steamer,* one of the few remaining wood riverboats, and a model of an airplane "black box," invented by an Iowan.

THE AMAZING MAIZE MAZE AT CARTER FARM (all ages)
28300 Great River Road, Princeton 52768; (563) 289–9999 or 289–3876, www.americanmaze.com/carterfarm.htm. Open (weather permitting) 10:00 A.M. to 6:00 P.M. Friday and Saturday and 1:00 to 6:00 P.M. Sunday from late July through early October. $$, ages 4 and under **Free***.*

The latest in "agritainment," this entertaining farm includes a four-acre corn maze, a mini maze, a petting zoo, and the Chuck Wagon Grill.

Where to Eat

Filling Station. *305 East 35th Street, Davenport; (563) 391–6954.* Burgers, sandwiches, and pizza are sold in this former west side gas station decorated with pinball machines and jukeboxes. $–$$

Happy Joe's. *2430 Spruce Hills Drive, Bettendorf; (563)359–5457 and 119 North Cody Road, Le Claire; (563) 289–3305.* Part of a Midwest chain, this pizza-and-ice-cream parlor has a game room where kids can win little prizes and serves a child-size pizza called a Little Joe. $

Iowa Machine Shed. *7250 Northwest Boulevard, Davenport; (563) 391–2427.* Decorated like a machine shed, this restaurant is famous for huge portions of hearty Midwestern fare, including pork chops, chicken-fried steak, and fried chicken. $$–$$$

Lagomarcino's. *2132 East 11th Street, Davenport; (563) 324–6137.* An old-fashioned soda fountain in the historic Village of East Davenport, Lagomarcino's serves a fantastic hot fudge sundae plus soup, sandwiches, and homemade chocolates. $

Rudy's Tacos. *4334 North Brady Street, Davenport; (563) 386–2475.* Part of a popular local chain, Rudy's is a Mexican restaurant with a children's menu. $

Waterfront Deli. *1020 State Street, Bettendorf; (563) 359–4300.* Right by the river, this small deli serves soups and sandwiches, including peanut butter and jelly. $

Where to Stay

The Abbey. *1401 Central Avenue, Bettendorf; (800) 428–7535 or (563) 355–0291.* Built in 1917, The Abbey is an elegant former Carmelite monastery on a bluff overlooking the Mississippi. It has nineteen rooms with Italian marble bathrooms, and an outdoor pool on manicured grounds. $$$$

Blackhawk Hotel. *200 East Third Street, Davenport; (563) 328–6000.* This classy 1915 hotel is listed on the National Register of Historic Places and owned by a nearby casino. It has 189 furnished rooms and suites, two restaurants, and an indoor pool. $$$

The Lodge. *900 Spruce Hills Drive, Bettendorf; (800) 285–8637 or (563) 359–7141.* Indoor and outdoor pools, a game room, suites, and a restaurant are among the attractions at this 210-room stone hotel with a nine-story tower that looks like a castle perched on the Mississippi. $$$–$$$$

For More Information

Quad Cities Convention and Visitors Bureau. *102 South Harrison Street, Davenport 52801; (800) 747–7800 or* *(309) 788–7800, www.visitquadcities.com, cvb@quadcities.com.*

Clinton

Continuing north along the Mississippi on US 67, you'll reach the old river town of Clinton, 13 miles north of Princeton.

CLINTON LUMBERKINGS (all ages)

Alliant Energy Field, junction of Sixth Avenue North and Riverview Drive, Clinton 52732; (563) 242–0727, www.clinton.net/~lkings, lumberkings@lumberkings. com. Season runs from April to September. $, ages 2 and under Free.

This single-A baseball club (a farm team for the Montreal Expos) plays in a wonderful 2,500-seat stadium built in 1937 by the Work Projects Administration. Clinton (population 28,000) is one of the smallest towns to have a minor-league baseball team. The LumberKings are part of the fourteen-team Midwest League, which includes teams from Burlington and Cedar Rapids.

FELIX ADLER MUSEUM (all ages)

501 11th Avenue South, Clinton 52732; (319) 243–3356, www.felixadler.com/ discovery.html. Open 10:00 A.M. to 4:00 P.M. Thursday through Saturday. $.

Clown around at this children's museum honoring longtime Ringling Brothers Circus clown Felix Adler, born in Clinton in 1895. You can dress up in funny clothes, get your face painted, and make animals out of balloons, plus play on a miniature golf course and see live bunnies in a rabbit house. Local legend has it that Frank "Felix" Adler's clowning around got him kicked out of Clinton High School. (He put a chicken in a teacher's muff.) Adler ran away from home and later joined the circus, eventually teaming up with a pig to become "Funny Felix and His Pig," a

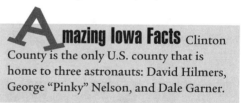

Amazing Iowa Facts Clinton County is the only U.S. county that is home to three astronauts: David Hilmers, George "Pinky" Nelson, and Dale Garner.

favorite of the grandchildren of Presidents Hoover and Roosevelt. There's an 11:00 A.M. story hour on Thursday, and 10:30 A.M. arts and crafts on Friday.

Where to Eat

Corner Deli. *246 Fifth Avenue South, Clinton; (563) 242–5545.* There's a children's play area in this downtown deli, located in a renovated brick building, serving sandwiches and ice cream. $

Rastrelli's. *238 Main Avenue, Clinton; (563) 242–7441.* North of downtown near Eagle Point Park, this family-owned Italian restaurant serves pasta and pizza. $

RJ Boars. *116 Fifth Avenue South, Clinton; (563) 243–0343.* A converted bowling alley, RJ Boars is known for barbecued ribs, chicken, and beef. $

Picnic Possibilities Try sixty-five-acre **Riverview Park** on Sixth Avenue North, overlooking the Mississippi.

Where to Stay

Country Inn and Suites. *2224 Lincoln Way West, Clinton; (563) 244–9922.* This centrally located chain hotel has sixty-three rooms (about one-third are suites) and an indoor pool. $$–$$$

Holiday Inn Express. *2800 South 25th Street, Clinton; (563) 242–5966.* On the outskirts of town in a commercial area, this sixty-seven-room chain hotel has an indoor pool. $$–$$$

For More Information

Clinton Area Convention and Visitors Bureau. *Fourth Avenue South, Clinton 52733; (800) 828–5702 or (563) 242–5702, cvbclinton@mcleodusa.net.*

Bellevue

Follow the Mississippi River along US 67 and US 52 north about 43 miles to the small river town of Bellevue, which, as its French name promises, offers beautiful views of the river from a riverfront park.

BELLEVUE BUTTERFLY GARDENS (all ages)
24668 US 52, Bellevue 52031; (563) 872–4019, www.state.ia.us/parks/ bttrfly.htm. Open 4:00 A.M. to 10:30 P.M. daily. **Free.**

Located in Bellevue State Park, this garden is planted to attract more than sixty species of butterflies, with nectar plants for adult butterflies and host plants for caterpillars. The best time to see butterflies is during the summer and fall, when the flowers are in bloom. The state park also has great Mississippi River views, a three-acre reconstructed prairie, five hiking trails, campsites, and an indoor visitor center with nature exhibits.

Amazing Iowa Facts

Iowa's only island city is Sabula, located in the Mississippi River between Clinton and Bellevue.

Where to Eat

Grandpa's Parlour. *306 South Riverview, Bellevue; (563) 872–4240.* A seasonal ice-cream shop near Bellevue State Park, Grandpa's also sells sand-wiches. $

Potter's Mill. *300 Potter's Drive, Belle-vue; (563) 872–3838.* Lunch and dinner served in a 1843 former gristmill that's also a bed-and-breakfast. $–$$

Richman's Maid-Rite. *602 South Riverview, Bellevue; (563) 872–3749.* This Iowa-born chain restaurant offers a loose-meat sandwich "made right" out of ground beef and spices. $

Where to Stay

Harbor Motel. *US 52 North, Bellevue; (563) 872–4644.* This brick motel is on the banks of the Mississippi on the north edge of town. $–$$$

Whispering Meadows Resort. *34452 100th Street, Spragueville; (877)* 968–9749 *or (563) 872–4430.* About 11 miles southwest of Bellevue near Springbrook, this resort has two full-service cabins (each sleeps four com-fortably, up to ten with sleeping bags), a fishing pond, and hiking trails. $$$$

For More Information

Bellevue Chamber of Commerce. *210 North Riverview, Bellevue 52031; (563) 872–5830, www.bellevueia.com.*

Maquoketa

Take State Highway 62 inland from Bellevue 20 miles southwest to Maquoketa, best known for its caves.

MAQUOKETA CAVES STATE PARK (all ages)

10970 98th Street, Maquoketa 52060; (563) 652–5833, Maquoketa_Caves@ dnr.state.ia.us. Open 4:00 A.M. to 10:30 P.M. daily. **Free.**

Located 6 miles northwest of Maquoketa off State Highway 428, this 272-acre park is a family favorite. Iowa's largest cave system, it includes one of Iowa's largest caves, Dancehall Cave, which leads more than 1,100 feet into the earth. You can explore thirteen limestone caves linked by sometimes rugged wooded trails. You'll pass a seventeen-ton balanced rock and a natural bridge rising almost 50 feet above Raccoon Creek. Bring a flashlight (only the two main caves are lit). Unfortunately, the stalactites and stalagmites were snatched long ago, but other rare formations remain. The park is also popular for picnicking and camping, with twenty-eight campsites nestled among mature pine trees with modern shower and toilet facilities. Eighteen sites have electrical hookups.

61 DRIVE-IN (all ages)

US 61, exit 153, Maquoketa 52060; (563) 674–4367, www.maquoketa.com/ 61drivein. Open May through October. Shows start at 8:30 P.M.; the box office opens at 6:30 P.M. $$, ages 12 and under **Free.**

Operating for more than fifty years, this small drive-in about 5 miles south of town is one of the last in Iowa. It can handle only about 200 cars, so bring along a portable radio and lawn chairs or a blanket. If the lot is full, you can park outside and walk in to watch the movie. The theater shows first-run family films. (The driver gets in free on Wednesday.)

Where to Eat

Decker Hotel & Restaurant. *128 North Main Street, Maquoketa; (563) 652–6654.* Lunch and dinner, from burgers to steaks, seafood (including superb trout amandine), and pasta are served in a pretty dining room with a stamped tin ceiling and antique wood booths. This family-friendly restaurant is inside a beautifully restored 1875 redbrick Italianate hotel downtown. $–$$

Where to Stay

Squires Manor Bed and Breakfast. *418 West Pleasant Street, Maquoketa; (563) 652–6961.* This 1882 Queen Anne–style mansion is packed with antiques (its owners are from nearby Banowitz Antique Mall, at the junction of US 61 and State Highway 64). It has eight rooms, including three suites, and

serves a delicious full breakfast. Our
infant son was warmly welcomed when
we visited years ago. $$$-$$$$

For More Information

Maquoketa Area Chamber of Commerce. *117 South Main Street, Maquoketa 52060; (563) 652–4602,* *chamber.maquoketa.net, chamber@maquoketa.net.*

Anamosa

Anamosa is a 34-mile drive west from Maquoketa along State Highway 64, known as the Grant Wood Scenic Byway. Driving on this highway, atop gentle rolling hills, feels like driving right through a Grant Wood landscape—and you probably are. Iowa's most famous painter, Wood was born on an Anamosa farm in 1891 and moved to Cedar Rapids at age ten. He later taught in the Cedar Rapids public schools and at the University of Iowa. He is buried in Anamosa's Riverside Cemetery.

GRANT WOOD ART GALLERY (ages 6 and up)
124 East Main Street, Anamosa 52205; (319) 462–4267. Open 10:00 A.M. to 4:00 P.M. Monday through Saturday and 1:00 to 4:00 P.M. Sunday. **Free.**

Kids will like the large display of amusing takeoffs on Grant Wood's most famous painting, *American Gothic,* in this small-town gallery that pays tribute to its famous son. (Spoof *American Gothic* couples include Hillary and Bill Clinton, Ingrid Bergman and Humphrey Bogart, Priscilla Presley and Michael Jackson, Nancy and Ronald Reagan, even Garfield and Odie.) Located in an old bank, the museum also features a twenty-minute video about the artist, plus original Grant Wood murals, prints, and memorabilia.

PENITENTIARY MUSEUM (ages 6 and up)
406 North High Street, Anamosa 52205; (319) 462–2386. Open noon to 4:00 P.M. Friday through Sunday from Memorial Day weekend through Labor Day weekend, or by appointment. $.

Opened in 2002, this tiny museum allows you to step inside a mock cell with heavy doors and see confiscated contraband plus old uniforms worn by prison inmates and guards. It's conveniently located next to the Iowa State Penitentiary, a remarkably grand nineteenth-century prison resembling a stone castle that houses over 1200 inmates. There's an interesting 20-minute video about prison life at Anamosa, which you watch while sitting on benches once used in cellblocks by inmates. The grand architecture, complete with landscaped gardens and stone lions at the door, was supposed to encourage prisoners' rehabilitation. Briefly known as "a reformatory," the prison is now a maximum-security penitentiary. The museum is in a former cheese shop where inmates used to work. Ask for a brochure to use during a self-guided architectural tour of the prison—from outside the prison walls.

NATIONAL MOTORCYCLE MUSEUM (ages 3 and up)

200 East Main Street, Anamosa 52205; (319) 462–3925. Open 9:00 A.M. *to 5:00* P.M. *Monday through Saturday and 11:00* A.M. *to 4:00* P.M. *Sunday. $, ages 11 and under* Free.

If you like bikes, this is motorcycle mecca. Moved in 2001 from the biker haven of Sturgis, South Dakota, to Anamosa, this two-story museum/hall of fame has 130 big and small motorcycles on display, some dating back to the early 1900s, plus old motorcycle toys and engines. Among the coolest bikes are military motorcycles (including one from the Gulf War), a 1919 olive brown Excelsior with a sidecar, and some peppy Hondas from the 1960s.   .

Stone City's Grant Wood Festival On the second Sunday in June, Stone City, a tiny little town a few miles east of Anamosa, throws a big party to honor artist Grant Wood, who hosted summer art colonies here during the 1930s. Activities and entertainment for children includes art projects, face painting, strolling musicians, and clowns. Area artists demonstrate and sell their work, and you can tour the town's limestone ruins (Stone City once had a thriving quarry). The town's picturesque rolling hills, round haystacks, rows of cornstalks, and church steeples were captured in the Grant Wood painting *Stone City*. Call (319) 462–4267 or visit the Web site www.grantwoodartfestival.org.

Where to Eat

City Limits. *101 Grant Wood Drive, Anamosa; (319) 462–3060.* On the eastern "city limits," this restaurant serves pork tenderloins and steaks, and has a children's menu and a weekend buffet. $$

McOtto's Family Restaurant. *100 Chamber Drive, Anamosa; (319) 462– 4200.* A children's menu is available at this downtown restaurant serving American, Italian, and Mexican food. $$

Where to Stay

Walnut Acres Campground. *Highway 38 North, Monticello 52310; (319) 465– 4665.* A ninety-acre privately owned campground about 11 miles north of Anamosa on the Maquoketa River, Walnut Acres has 200 campsites with modern facilities, two cabins (one sleeps four, another six), river swimming, a sandy beach, a fishing lake, basketball courts, and Saturday hayrides in the summer. $

Wapsipinicon State Park campgrounds. *21301 County Road E34, Anamosa; (319) 462–2761.* This shaded campground on the Wapsipinicon River ("The Wapsi") has thirty campsites, including half with electrical hookups, plus modern rest rooms and showers. $

For More Information

Jones County Tourism Association. *120 East Main Street, Anamosa 52205;* *(800) 383–0831, www.jonescountytourism. com, info@jonescountytourism.com.*

Cedar Rapids

From Anamosa, take US 151 about 20 miles west to Cedar Rapids, Iowa's second largest city. You may notice billowing white smoke and a sweet yeasty smell. An industrial center, Cedar Rapids provides the nation's grain markets with oats, corn, and cereal products. Looming above the skyline is the neon sign of homegrown Quaker Oats, whose cereal-making plant here is the world's largest. This city of 120,000 people also has leafy old neighborhoods and a pleasant downtown, with fun museums, minor-league sports, high culture, and a longtime Czech and Slovak community to explore.

Amazing Iowa Facts Cedar Rapids is the only city in the world with its government offices on an island. City hall, the courthouse, and the jail are on tiny May's Island in the Cedar River, across from downtown. Stop by City Hall to see a huge stained glass window designed by Grant Wood.

Amazing Iowa Facts Known as the "world's worst sister act," Iowa's infamous Cherry Sisters used to be pelted with eggs, tomatoes, and cabbages by audiences when they performed their vaudeville show in the late 1800s. The sisters—Addie, Jessie, and Effie—grew up on a farm near Marion and are buried in Cedar Rapids. They made legal history in 1901 after losing a libel suit against a newspaper critic who panned their act. The Iowa Supreme Court upheld the ruling—and critics have felt free to pan other performers ever since.

CEDAR VALLEY NATURE TRAIL (all ages)

Trailhead at Boyson Road, Hiawatha 52233; (319) 398–3505. Open dawn to dusk year-round. **Free**.

This 52-mile trail following an old railroad line between Cedar Rapids and Waterloo has an easy grade for hiking, biking, running, and cross-country skiing. The Hiawatha trailhead is just north of Cedar Rapids, near exit 25 of Interstate 380.

THE PLAY STATION (all ages)

200 Collins Road Northeast, Cedar Rapids 52402; (319) 373–1111. Open 10:00 A.M. to 8:00 P.M. Monday through Thursday, 10:00 A.M. to 9:00 P.M. Friday and Saturday, and 11:00 A.M. to 6:00 P.M. Sunday. $$ for children, adults and ages 1 and under **Free**.

Creep, crawl, climb, bounce, roll, and leap in this huge indoor playground for children.

SCIENCE STATION AND MCLEOD/BUSSE IMAX DOME THEATRE (ages 3 and up)

427 First Street Southeast, Cedar Rapids 52401; (319) 363–4629, www.science station.org. Open 9:00 A.M. to 4:30 P.M. Monday through Thursday, 9:00 A.M. to 9:00 P.M. Friday and Saturday, and 11:30 A.M. to 6:00 P.M. Sunday. Several IMAX shows daily. $$, including IMAX.

The coolest thing here is the state-of-the-art domed IMAX Theatre. Sitting in a reclining seat to watch a movie projected onto the domed ceiling feels like sitting inside a hollow egg. You're surrounded by sound and movement, which may be a little intense for young children and anyone prone to motion sickness. It also can be an enveloping, awesome experience. Most films last about fifty minutes. Housed in a former fire station, the two-floor science center also has hands-on exhibits about dinosaurs, simple machines, and weather. Especially fun is the mock television weather station, where you can pretend to be a meteo-rologist, and another station where you sit at a desk across from another person, separated by a sheet of lighted glass. You will see your-self in the glass *and* the other person's face superimposed on top of yours—an eerie experience for any kid who's been told he looks just like his dad.

CEDAR RAPIDS HISTORY CENTER (ages 5 and up)

615 First Avenue Southeast, Cedar Rapids 52401; (319) 362–1501. Open 10:00 A.M. to 4:00 P.M. Tuesday, Wednesday, Friday, and Saturday, and 10:00 A.M. to 7:00 P.M. Thursday, and noon to 4:00 P.M. Sunday. $, under age 6 Free.

At this history center, make a beeline to the TimeQuest attraction for a virtual tour of old Cedar Rapids. You sit in what looks like an open-air carnival ride compartment, with a front and back seat, in front of a large three-sided screen. The person in the driver's seat uses a stick shift to steer everyone through town, which is depicted in computer-driven three-dimensional images on the screen. It feels like you're traveling through Cedar Rapids circa 1926. (There's also a 1900 version.)

Culture for Kids

- **Cedar Rapids Symphony.** 205 Second Avenue Southeast, Cedar Rapids; (319) 366–8203. The symphony performs two annual forty-five-minute Saturday afternoon concerts for preschool through third-grade children and their families.

- **U.S. Cellular Center.** 370 First Avenue Northeast, and Paramount Theatre, 123 Third Avenue Southeast; (319) 398–5211, www.uscellular center.com. Major traveling children's shows are staged at both of these city venues.

- **Theatre Cedar Rapids.** 102 Third Street Southeast, Cedar Rapids; (319) 366–8592. This long-established community theater group performs downtown in a 1928 vaudeville and movie house.

- **Brucemore.** 2160 Linden Drive Southeast, Cedar Rapids; (319) 362–7375, www.brucemore.org. Music festivals and outdoor theater are among the offerings at this twenty-six-acre estate with a grand Queen Anne–style mansion.

CEDAR RAPIDS MUSEUM OF ART (all ages)

410 Third Avenue Southeast, Cedar Rapids 52403; (319) 366–7503, www. crma.org. Open 10:00 A.M. to 4:00 P.M. Tuesday through Saturday and noon to 4:00 P.M. Sunday. $, ages 17 and under Free.

Children can create designs with light and sand, plus try other activities at this fine-arts museum's Children's Hands-On Art Gallery. Featuring traditional and contemporary paintings, prints, photography, and sculpture, the museum also has the world's largest collection of work by Grant Wood.

CEDAR RAPIDS KERNELS (all ages)

950 Rockford Road Southwest, Cedar Rapids 52404; (319) 363–3887, www.kernels.com. Season runs from April through August. $$.

An affiliate of the Anaheim Angels, the Kernels' recently opened stadium includes the Jumbotron, a giant television screen for instant-replay broadcasts.

CEDAR RAPIDS ROUGH RIDERS HOCKEY TEAM (ages 4 and up)

1100 Rockford Road Southwest, Cedar Rapids 52404; (319) 247–0340, www.roughridershockey.com, crhockey@roughridershockey.com. Season runs from late September through early April. $$–$$$.

This is Cedar Rapids' United States Hockey League junior team.

Fun Cedar Rapids City Parks, most with swimming pools, picnic areas, tennis courts, and playgrounds include

- **Cherry Hill Park.** 341 Stoney Point Road Northwest.

- **Bever Park.** 2700 Bever Avenue Southeast. Includes a small zoo with barnyard petting animals, a wetland bird exhibit, and primate house.

- **Ellis Park.** 2000 Ellis Boulevard Northwest. Includes a lake, boat rentals, and interesting views of a neighborhood of houseboats.

- **Jones Park.** 201 Wilson Avenue Southwest. Includes a soccer field.

- **Noelridge Park.** 4900 Council Street Northeast. Includes a lagoon for ice-skating.

A Rubiner Family Adventure My Aunt Mary Ann called from Chicago with exciting news: She'd won a weekend stay in a fancy suite at a fancy hotel in Cedar Rapids. Could we join her? Sure thing. Our son Noah, then four, and daughter Lily, then three, were thrilled by our two-story hotel suite, which had a spiral staircase and a huge glass window overlooking the bright lights and billowing smoke of the Quaker Oats factory. But after staring out the window in fascination, Noah suddenly turned and looked at me with a concerned expression. "I don't see the rabbits," he said. Cedar Rapids has been known by my family as "see the rabbits" ever since.

CZECH VILLAGE (ages 5 and up)

16th Avenue Southwest, Cedar Rapids 52404; (319) 362–2846. Open 10:00 A.M. to 5:00 P.M. Monday through Saturday. ℱree.

This is a three-block neighborhood where Cedar Rapids' original Czech settlers lived during the nineteenth-century. (One-third of the city's population is of Czech or Slovak descent.) Located six blocks south of downtown along the Cedar River, it features old Czech-style buildings that house ethnic restaurants, bakeries, and specialty shops.

NATIONAL CZECH AND SLOVAK MUSEUM (ages 5 and up)

30 16th Avenue Southwest, Cedar Rapids 52404; (319) 362–8500, www.ncsml. org. Open 9:30 A.M. to 4:00 P.M. Tuesday through Saturday and noon to 4:00 P.M. Sunday. $$, ages 4 and under ℱree.

A highlight of Czech Village, this $2.9 million museum includes a restored nineteenth-century Czech immigrant home, antique national costumes, music, theater, and folk art. Periodic hands-on activities for children often include making kolace, a favorite Czech pastry.

DUFFY'S COLLECTIBLE CARS (all ages)

250 Classic Car Court Southwest, Cedar Rapids 52404; (319) 364–7000, www.duffys.com, duffys@duffys.com. Open 8:30 A.M. to 5:00 P.M. Monday through Friday and 8:30 A.M. to 4:30 P.M. Saturday. $.

Children (and some car-crazy parents) will be fascinated by this old-fashioned auto showroom with more than one hundred restored cars from the '40s, '50s, and '60s (most of which are for sale), plus old gas pumps, phone booths, and neon signs. Duffy's is a little tricky to find. If you're driving north on Interstate 380, take exit 17 (33rd Street) and make three right turns.

Revived 1930s Roadside Cafe

The Youngville Cafe, a 1931 rural roadside station/eatery along the famous Lincoln Highway (the nation's first transcontinental highway), recently reopened as a cafe and museum. A precursor of today's less charming convenience stores, the cafe (built by Joe Young, hence the name) is about 18 miles west of Cedar Rapids at the intersection of US 30 and US 218. Volunteers pitched in during the seven-year restoration of the cafe, which closed in 1967. The cafe serves locally produced food evocative of the 1930s. Call (319) 472–5545 or visit www.youngvillecafe.com.

Where to Eat

Al and Irene's BBQ. *2020 North Town Lane Northeast, Cedar Rapids; (319) 393–6242.* A kids' menu is available at Al and Irene's, an informal barbecue joint on the northeast known for its hickory-smoked ribs, chicken, and hot wings. $

Biaggi's. *320 Collins Road Northeast, Cedar Rapids; (319) 393–6593.* This white-tablecloth northern Italian restaurant serves steaks, pizzas, pasta, and fresh fish. A children's menu (with crayons) is available. $$

North Country Steak House. *1140 Blair's Ferry Road Northeast, Cedar Rapids; (319) 378–3970.* You can grill your own steak at this steakhouse with a wilderness lodge decor and a children's menu about a mile east of Interstate 380. $$

Sykora Bakery. *73 16th Avenue Southwest, Cedar Rapids; (319) 364–5271.* Czech pastries—including kolace, babovka, and houska—plus Czech staples like sauerkraut and dumplings are served along with American-style soup and sandwiches at this bakery that's been in Czech Village for ninety-eight years. $

The Vernon Inn. *2663 Mount Vernon Road Southeast, Cedar Rapids; (319) 366–7817.* This popular Greek restaurant doesn't have a children's menu, but it does have free entertainment: Every few minutes diners shout "Oopah!" as a server lights saganaki, a flamed cheese appetizer. The menu features traditional Greek favorites like

Picnic Possibilities

Try Seminole Valley Farm and Park, a 1900 farm on ten acres at the bottom of a quiet river valley in northeast Cedar Rapids. The farm's red weather-beaten buildings seem worlds away from the new suburban houses just up the hill. Nearby is Ushers Ferry Historic Village, a re-created turn-of-the-twentieth-century Iowa town with several old homes and buildings, including an old-time soda shop serving ice cream and candy.

moussaka, gyros, and souvlaki sandwiches, plus gourmet pizzas. $$

Willy Woodburn's. *836 First Avenue Northeast, Cedar Rapids; (319) 364–3321.* This greasy spoon near the History Center offers a no-frills breakfast and lunch menu, as well as popular kid fare like grilled cheese and hot dogs. (There's also a bucket of candy behind the counter for kids to rummage through after their meal.) $

Zindricks Czech Restaurant. *86 16th Avenue Southwest, Cedar Rapids; (319) 365–5257.* For authentic stick-to-your ribs Czech food, this Czech Village restaurant decorated with antiques and paintings is the place. Sunday brunch is also available. $-$$

Where to Stay

Belmont Hill. *1525 Cherokee Drive Northwest, Cedar Rapids; (319) 366–1343, www.belmonthill.com.* For a splurge, stay in this old brick carriage house, which has two single rooms and a two-bedroom suite decorated with antiques and exposed brick walls. A delicious full breakfast is served across the driveway in the owner's redbrick 1880s Victorian mansion. $$$$

Best Western Long Branch. *90 Twixt Town Road Northeast, Cedar Rapids; (800) 443–7660 or (319) 377–6386.* Located near the Play Station on the northeast side, this hotel has 106 rooms, including several with a pool view, and a restaurant. $$-$$$

Collins Plaza. *1200 Collins Road Northeast, Cedar Rapids; (800) 541–1067 or (319) 393–6600.* One of the nicest places to stay in town, this 221-room hotel across from Noelridge Park in north Cedar Rapids has a restaurant and an indoor pool. $$$-$$$$

Sheraton Four Points. *525 33rd Avenue, Cedar Rapids, (319) 366–8671.* This full-service hotel about five minutes south of downtown on a busy highway has 157 rooms, an indoor pool, and a dining room. $$-$$$

For More Information

Cedar Rapids Convention and Visitors Bureau, *119 First Avenue Southeast, Cedar Rapids 52406; (800) 735–5557 or* *(319) 398–5009, www.cedar-rapids.com, visitors@cedar-rapids.com.*

Other Things to See and Do in Eastern Iowa

- **Rock Creek State Park.** Grinnell, (515) 236–3722
- **Amana Arts Guild Center.** High Amana, (319) 622–3678
- **Lake MacBride State Park/MacBride Nature Area.** Solon, (319) 644–2200
- **Wildcat Den State Park.** Muscatine, (563) 263–4337
- **Davenport Museum of Art.** Davenport, (563) 326–7804
- **Ferjervary Park.** Davenport, (319) 326–7812
- **Vander Veer Botanical Park.** Davenport, (319) 326–7818
- **Splash Landing.** Bettendorf, (319) 344–4113
- **Bickelhaupt Arboretum.** Clinton, (563) 242–4771
- **Eagle Point Park/Nature Center.** Clinton, (563) 243–1260
- **Palisades-Kepler State Park.** Near Cedar Rapids, (319) 895–6039
- **Indian Creek Nature Center.** Cedar Rapids, (319) 362–0664
- **El Kahir Shrine Corn Maze.** Palo, (319) 851–2676

Southern Iowa

Southern Iowa has some of the state's best-known *and* little-known attractions. Here you'll find hot spots like the Dutch-American town of Pella and the Bridges of Madison County (made famous by the novel and movie of the same name). You can explore old Mississippi River ports and sleepy historic Van Buren County villages. You can fish, swim, and boat at popular recreation areas, including Lake Red Rock, Rathbun Lake, and Keo-Lacy Park.

Along the way there are surprises: actor John Wayne's birthplace in Winterset, a private toy museum in Chariton, a ballooning museum in Indianola, and a sprint car racing museum in Knoxville. Near the Amish farmers of Kalona are the New Age meditators of Fairfield. In tiny Eldon sits the farmhouse used as the backdrop for *American Gothic*, Grant Wood's famously dour farm couple. To make a meandering counter-clockwise loop, start in Kalona, located in the region's northeast corner. Dip south on State Highway 27/US 218 to Mount Pleasant, then drive west along US 34 to Ottumwa and northwest on US 63 and State Highway 163 to Pella and Knoxville. Continue west on State Highway 92 to Madison County. For the return trip, take Interstate 35 south to US 34 and travel east through Chariton and Ottumwa to State Highway 16. Continue southeast to Van Buren County and then east to the river cities of Keokuk, Fort Madison, and Burlington along US 61.

For More Information

Central Iowa Tourism Region. *P.O. Box 454, Webster City 50595; (800)* *285–5842 or (515) 832–4808, www.iowatourism.org, citr@netins.net.*

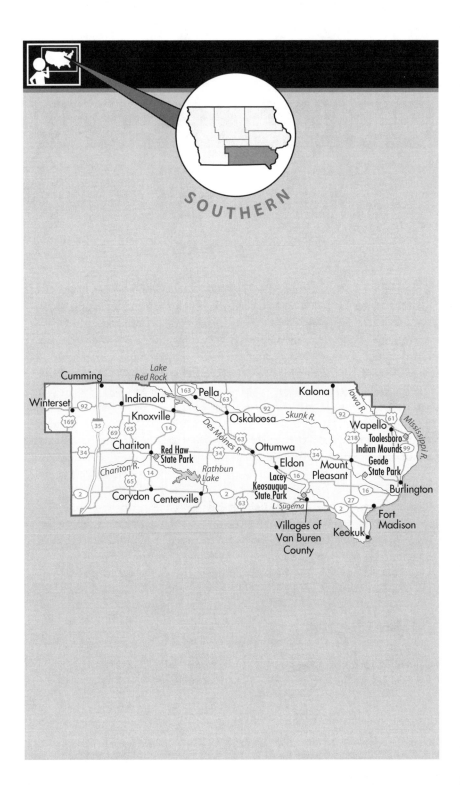

SOUTHERN

Cumming
Winterset
Lake Red Rock
Indianola
Pella
Kalona
Knoxville
Oskaloosa
Skunk R.
Wapello
Chariton
Red Haw State Park
Des Moines R.
Ottumwa
Toolesboro Indian Mounds
Geode State Park
Chariton R.
Rathbun Lake
Eldon
Mount Pleasant
Burlington
Corydon
Centerville
Lacey
Keosauqua State Park
L. Sugema
Fort Madison
Villages of Van Buren County
Keokuk

Iowa R.
Mississippi R.

Betsy's Top Ten Picks for Fun in Southern Iowa

1. Tulip Time, Pella

2. Eagle spotting at Lake Red Rock, Knoxville

3. Dan-D Farms Corn Maze, Knoxville

4. Snake Alley, Burlington

5. The National Balloon Classic, Indianola

6. The Northside Cafe, Winterset

7. Old Fort Madison

8. Cumming Orchard in the fall, Cumming

9. Geode State Park, Danville

10. Belinda Church Toy and Antique Museum, Chariton

Kalona

Located about 20 miles south of Iowa City, on State Highways 1 and 22, Kalona has the largest Amish Mennonite settlement west of the Mississippi. Amish and Mennonite farm families live here quietly, the bearded men in dark clothing and straw hats driving horse-drawn buggies, the women wearing bonnets and long dresses with aprons. Respectful visitors are welcome in local

Shoppers' Alert The kids may not get a kick out of quilt shopping, but parents might still want to see some of the nation's finest quilts during Kalona's annual spring quilt show and sale, held the last Friday and Saturday of April at the **Kalona Community Center,** 307 Sixth Street. Admission is charged. Call (319) 656–2660.

Other popular Kalona shops:

- **The Stringtown Grocery,** 2266 540th Street SW, which sells food in bulk.

- **The Community Country Store,** 5757 James Avenue SW, is a general store.

- **Sister's Garden,** 4895 Highway 1, sells garden items.

shops that sell baked goods, antiques, and hand-stitched quilts. The annual Fall Festival, with homemade bread and apple butter for sale and craft demonstrations of wood sawing, spinning, and cornmeal grinding, is held the last Friday or Saturday in September.

KALONA HISTORICAL VILLAGE AND MUSEUMS (ages 6 and up)

Highway 22 East and Ninth Street, Kalona 52247; (319) 656-3232. Open 9:30 A.M. to 4:00 P.M. Monday through Saturday from April through mid-October, 11:00 A.M. to 3:00 P.M. Monday through Saturday from mid-October through March. $, ages 6 and under Free.

Located about four blocks from town on State Highway 22, this small historic village has several restored nineteenth-century buildings as well as a welcome center and two museums celebrating Amish Mennonite life. A guide dressed in period clothing leads a one-hour walking tour that stops at a two-story wood train depot, a one-room schoolhouse, and a general store that sells trinkets, candy, and polished rocks. The **Quilt and Textile Museum** has exhibits on farm women's handiwork and a rock and mineral collection. The **Mennonite Museum** has displays on early culture and life in town.

Amazing Iowa Facts Attention *Star Trek* fans! Riverside, just east of Kalona, is the future (yes, future) birthplace of Captain James T. Kirk. Enterprising townspeople convinced *Star Trek* creator Gene Roddenberry to designate Riverside as Kirk's hometown after reading in a Roddenberry book that the captain was "born [in the year 2228] in a small town in Iowa." A rather dinky replica of the Starship *Enterprise* was duly erected in a downtown park. On the last Saturday in June, the town throws a Trek Fest, featuring videos of the television show, a parade, and swap meet. Call (319) 648-5475.

Where to Eat

Columns and Chocolate. *811 Fourth Street, Kalona; (319) 656-2992.* This tearoom behind an antiques and gift shop in an old house serves great brown sugar cookies and nice lunches. $

Kalonial Townhouse. *110 First Street, Kalona; (319) 656-2514.* This long-established downtown restaurant serves a family-style breakfast and a lunch buffet, and specializes in weekend evening buffets featuring broasted chicken and catfish. There's also a children's menu. $

Parlor Cafe. *125 Fourth Street, Kalona; (319) 656-2550.* Homemade soups, deli sandwiches, and hot meals are served at this lunch spot in a pretty house near downtown. $

Picnic Possibilities Pick up some cheese curds at the **Kalona Cheese House,** 2206 540th Street NW, and head to the **Kalona City Park,** off State Highway 22 near the Kalona Historical Village, which has a playground and public pool.

Where to Stay

The Carriage House Bed and Breakfast. *1140 Larch Avenue, Kalona; (319) 656-3824, www.carriagehousebb.net, chouse@kctc.net.* Located on a fifteen-acre Mennonite farm, the Carriage House includes a 1918 farmhouse and a 1996 carriage house. There are four guest rooms with private bath, two with a pull-out bed. A full breakfast is served, and a family-style Mennonite lunch or dinner meal is available by reservation. $$

Pull'r Inn Motel. *110 East Avenue, Kalona; (319) 656-3611.* This twenty-nine-room motel is off State Highways 1 and 22 in a quiet rural area. $$

Windmill Ridge Campground. *2110 140th Street, Kalona; (319) 656-4488.* A few miles outside town off State Highway 1, this private campground offers tent and RV camping in quiet countryside from April through mid-November. $

For More Information

Kalona Area Chamber of Commerce, *514 B Avenue, Kalona 52247; (319) 656-2660, www.kalonachamber.org.*

Mount Pleasant

This town of 8,500 welcomes more than 100,000 people during the Midwest Old Threshers Reunion, its annual Labor Day celebration of old-fashioned agriculture. Mount Pleasant is about 45 miles south of Kalona at the junction of US 34 and US 218.

MIDWEST OLD THRESHERS HERITAGE MUSEUMS
(ages 7 and up)

405 East Threshers Road, Mount Pleasant 52641; (319) 385–8937, www. oldthreshers.org, info@oldthreshers.org. Open 8:00 A.M. to 4:30 P.M. Monday through Friday and 9:00 A.M. to 4:30 P.M. Saturday and Sunday from Memorial Day through Labor Day, weekends only from mid-April to Memorial Day and from Labor Day to mid-October. $, ages 14 and under **Free.**

For your first stop at this rural museum, try a ride on the steam-operated 1894 carousel. Then get a glimpse of old-fashioned farming by visiting the museum's collection of antique trailers, buggies, and wagons, plus steam engines and farm implements. The museum also has interpretive exhibits on water, electricity, and farming, as well as women's contributions to family farms. Also on the grounds is the **Museum of Repertoire Americana,** boasting the nation's largest collection of rural show business memorabilia (costumes, scrapbooks, even opera house curtains) from traveling theater companies that once performed in small Iowa towns. (It's open 1:00 to 4:00 P.M. Tuesday through Saturday.) The buildings aren't heated, so bundle up on a cold day. Get a feel for what life was once like in Iowa farm communities during the five-day Midwest Old Threshers Reunion that ends on Labor Day. Started in 1950, the annual event features ancient farm tractors and trucks, a horse-pull competition, live entertainment, homemade food, and fun stuff for children, including soap-making and trolley rides. In the working log village, circa 1846, you'll be greeted by costumed guides. Admission is charged. Call (319) 385–8937.

Where to Eat

Iris Restaurant. *915 West Washington Street, Mount Pleasant; (319) 385–2241.* Steaks are the star of this restaurant on US 34 west of downtown, which also serves seafood for lunch and dinner, plus a Sunday buffet brunch. $–$$$

Jerry's Restaurant. *2105 East Washington Street, Mount Pleasant; (319) 385–4412.* Jerry's, a lunch and dinner spot on US 34, serves everything from pizza to taco salad and is known for its salad bar, turkey tenderloin, hot buffets, and daily specials. $

Where to Stay

AmeriHost Inn and Suites. *1100 North Grand Avenue, Mount Pleasant; (800) 434–5800 or (319) 385–2004.* This sixty-three-room motel north of town on US 218 has an indoor pool. $$

Heartland Inn. *810 North Grand Avenue, Mount Pleasant; (800) 334-3277 or (319) 385-2102.* There's an indoor pool at this fifty-eight-room chain motel about 2 miles north of town. $$

For More Information

Mount Pleasant Chamber of Commerce. *124 South Main Street, Mount Pleasant 52641; (319) 385-3101, www.mtpleasantiowa.com/chamb.html.*

"Maharishi U" Fairfield, 22 miles west of Mount Pleasant, is home to Iowa's most unique educational institution, Maharishi University of Management, which combines traditional academics with transcendental meditation. Twice a day, students and faculty meditate in two giant domes on what otherwise looks like a typical Midwestern college campus. The university opened in 1972, when representatives of Maharishi Mahesh Yogi bought a 262-acre defunct college campus. Nearby is another TM stronghold, Vedic City, Iowa's first new city in twenty years. All buildings follow a Maharishi-recommended design, with atria, an east-facing entrance, and a swirl-shaped roof. Some children here go to a private school that conducts meditation sessions in the "Hall of Bliss."

Eldon

Artist Grant Wood put the tiny town of Eldon on the map. It's on State Highway 16 about 43 miles west of Mount Pleasant and 13 miles east of Ottumwa.

AMERICAN GOTHIC HOUSE (all ages)
301 American Gothic Street, Eldon 52554; (641) 652-3406, gothicman@lisco.com. Open year-round. **Free.**

You can't go inside, but you can strike an American Gothic pose in front of the small white house Grant Wood used as the backdrop for his famous 1930 painting *American Gothic,* which now hangs in the Art Institute of Chicago. Listed on the National Register of Historic Places, the house is owned by the state's historical society. There are special festivities during Gothic Day, held the second Saturday in June. Wood spotted the Eldon house in the late 1920s. Intrigued by the contrast between the house's modest design and its fancy Gothic-style windows, he sketched the house on the back of an envelope. Fun Fact: The couple in *American Gothic* weren't husband and wife. Wood intended them to be father and daughter. In real life, the models were Wood's sister and dentist.

Where to Eat

Jones Cafe. *419 Elm Street, Eldon; (641) 652-7516.* This little cafe on Eldon's main drag serves home-cooked breakfasts and lunches. $

Ottumwa

About 17 miles west of Eldon is Ottumwa, at the junction of US 34 and US 63.

AIRPOWER MUSEUM (ages 5 and up)
22001 Bluegrass Road, Ottumwa 52501; (641) 938-2773. Open 9:00 A.M. to 5:00 P.M. Monday through Friday, 10:00 A.M. to 5:00 P.M. Saturday, and 1:00 to 5:00 P.M. Sunday. Closed August 31 through September 4 and major holidays. Free.

This 20,000-square-foot museum located on a thirty-acre antique airfield showcases twenty vintage planes, including World War II models.

THE BEACH OTTUMWA (ages 3 and up)
101 Church Street, Ottumwa 52501; (641) 682-7873. Outdoor pool open 11:00 A.M. to 7:00 P.M. daily during the summer. Indoor pool open year-round. $.

This water park's outdoor attractions include a wave pool, speed slide, 340-foot body slide, kayaks, paddleboats, and a play area. Inside is a competition-size pool with a tube slide.

Where to Eat

Fisherman's Bay. *221 North Wapello Street, Ottumwa; (641) 682-6325.* Big fish tanks and old ship replicas adorn this lunch and dinner seafood restaurant northeast of town. $-$$

The Greenbriar. *1207 North Jefferson Street, Ottumwa; (641) 682-8147.* This casual fine dining restaurant north of downtown serves prime rib, seafood, chicken dishes, and steak. It has a children's menu with burgers, shrimp, and chicken strips. $-$$$

Picnic Possibilities Visit 340-acre **Ottumwa Park,** at the junction of US 63 and US 34, which has playgrounds, hiking trails, lagoons for fishing and ice-skating, baseball diamonds, a campground, and a pond where you can feed the birds.

Where to Stay

The Fairfield Inn by Marriott. *2813 North Court Road, Ottumwa; (800) 228-2800 or (641) 682-0063.* North of town, this sixty-three-room chain motel has an indoor pool. $-$$$

Heartland Inn. *125 West Joseph Avenue, Ottumwa; (800) 334-3277 or (641) 682-8526.* This ninety-one-room hotel with an indoor pool occasionally serves free evening snacks. $$

For More Information

Ottumwa Convention and Visitors Bureau. *217 East Main Street, Ottumwa 52501; (800) 564-5274 or (641) 682-*

3465, www.ottumwachamber.com/business.htm.

Oskaloosa

Oskaloosa is located on US 63 and State Highway 92 about 25 miles northwest of Ottumwa.

NELSON PIONEER FARM MUSEUM (ages 5 and up)
2294 Oxford Avenue, Oskaloosa 52577; (641) 672-2989, www.nelsonpioneer. org. Open 10:00 A.M. to 4:30 P.M. Tuesday through Saturday from May through early October; closed Sunday and Monday. $, ages 5 and under Free.

Just north of town, this nineteenth-century restored farm has fifteen buildings, including a brick home and barn the Nelsons built in the 1850s. Children may enjoy the one-room schoolhouse and the mule cemetery, where two mules are buried. A tour includes visits to a log cabin meetinghouse, post office, blacksmith shop, and stagecoach stop. Several picnic tables are available. The annual Pioneer Festival, featuring musical entertainment, a country dinner, and demonstrations of pioneer skills, is usually held the third Saturday in September.

Where to Eat

The Peppertree. *2274 US 63, Oskaloosa; (641) 673-9191.* A children's menu with five selections at $3.25 is offered at The Peppertree, a large restaurant specializing in certified Black Angus steaks, pasta, fresh seafood, baked potato soup, over-the-top desserts, and Sunday brunch. $$

Rock Island Grill. *206 Rock Island Avenue, Oskaloosa; (641) 672-1180.* Near the town square in a former depot with a corkscrew-twisted chimney and antique train decorations, this restaurant serving everything from steaks to seafood has a children's menu. Ask to try out the grill's old train whistle. $-$$$

Picnic Possibilities Visit **Edmondson Park,** south of town, which has a fun wooden playground. To get there, take US 63 south and turn right on 11th Avenue. Another option is **Lake Keomah State Park,** a 366-acre wooded park with shaded picnic areas near an eighty-three-acre man-made lake with a sandy beach for swimming, fishing, and boating (rentals available), plus a nature trail and modern campsites. To get there, drive 4 miles east of Oskaloosa on State Highway 92, then 1 mile south on State Highway 371. The park is located at 2720 Keomah Lane. Call (641) 673-6975.

Where to Stay

Red Carpet Inn. *2278 US 63, Oskaloosa; (800) 251-1962 or (641) 673-8641.* There's an outdoor pool, a basketball court, and horseshoe pits at this forty-room motel with large flowerbeds on three and a half acres north of downtown. $-$$

For More Information

Oskaloosa Area Chamber. *124 North Market Street, Oskaloosa 52577; (641) 672-2591.*

Pella

Is this Iowa? Or is it Holland? It's hard to tell in Pella, a small town that proudly celebrates its Dutch heritage. Located off State Highway 163 just west of Oskaloosa, Pella was founded in 1847 by a small group of Hollanders. Today this mini Holland offers all things Dutch, from a town square filled with pretty tulip beds to an animated Klokkenspel, a musical clock with moving figurines built into a brick archway. There's also an imported Dutch windmill, a 100,000-square-foot Dutch canal ("the Molengracht") lined with Dutch buildings with gabled and stepped roofs, and a European-style hotel. Most shops are closed on Sunday.

Tulip Time The first full weekend in May is Pella's famous annual **Tulip Time Festival,** when thousands of tulips bloom and townspeople dress in colorful Dutch costumes. Kids are everywhere: sitting on the big cannon in the square, eating Dutch letters (an S-shaped pastry filled with almond paste), and playing in town parks. The three-day event includes folk dancing, craft demonstrations, and the crowning of the Tulip Queen. Especially fun is the Volks Parade, held twice daily—in the afternoon and evening (with lighted floats). Pella residents parade by in heavy wooden clogs, the women in long floral dresses, lace shawls, and pointy white bonnets, the men in black fisherman's caps, billowing black pants, and red sashes. Many participants push babies, also costumed, in antique carriages. As the floats, "street scrubbers," and old-time street vendors pass by, an announcer helpfully explains the Dutch customs they reflect. For a good view, sit on the grass in front of the Pella Library.

PELLA HISTORICAL VILLAGE (ages 5 and up)

507 Franklin Street, Pella 50219; (641) 628-4311, www.pellatuliptime.com. Open 9:00 A.M. to 5:00 P.M. Monday through Friday from January through March, 9:00 A.M. to 5:00 P.M. Monday through Saturday from April through December. $$ for adults, $ for ages 5 through 12, ages 4 and under **Free.**
Plan to spend at least two hours at this re-created old-fashioned Dutch village. The large courtyard is lined with twenty-two buildings,

some more than 140 years old, including one of the nation's tallest working windmills, imported from Holland in 2002. You can also climb partway up the 135-foot 1850s-style windmill to watch grain being ground. (The first few flights are dull, but the top floor is worth the trip.) Other village highlights include a miniature-scale Dutch village that fills an entire room, plus pottery, blacksmithing, and clog-making workshops. There's also an interpretive center with exhibits on Dutch history, heritage, and culture, as well as the childhood home of Wyatt Earp, the nineteenth-century western marshal who grew up in Pella.

Pella Playgrounds There's a wonderful, whimsical wooden playground at **West Market Park,** plus a puppet theater, butterfly garden, picnic tables, and a pretend castle and boat. It's three blocks west of the town square. Three blocks *north* of the square is **Sunken Gardens Park,** with a sunken pond shaped like a wooden shoe. It's lined with tulips during the spring, and popular with ice-skaters during the winter.

PELLA OPERA HOUSE (ages 5 and up)

611 Franklin Street, Pella 50219; (641) 628–8628, www.pellaoperahouse.com, boxoffice@pellaoperahouse.com. Season runs from September through May. Self-guided tours available 11:00 A.M. to 4:00 P.M. Monday through Saturday.

Family-friendly performances by traveling children's theater troupes, puppeteers, and nationally known musicians are offered at this beautifully restored opera house built in 1900.

A Rubiner Family Adventure The four kids (our two and our friends' two) were starting to squirm. So were the parents. We'd been waiting—remarkably patiently—for more than an hour at a crowded Pella restaurant for food. I finally flagged down our frazzled waitress and begged for some bread. When she returned with a tiny loaf and practically threw it onto the table, something snapped. Everyone (except the waitress) burst into laughter. It was either laugh or cry. Our dining disaster continued with missed orders, messed-up orders, and my favorite, a handwritten check smeared with butter. (Perhaps the butter that never arrived with our bread?) Lesson learned. During our next Tulip Time trip, we'll do what the locals do. We'll eat on the street at the many stands that sell burgers, brats, fries, homemade root beer, ice cream, Dutch letters, and funnel cake. I might even dare to try a "Dutch taco" (made with Pella bologna).

Where to Eat

Inn't Veld Meat Market. *820 Main Street, Pella; (641) 628-3440.* Also on the town square, this longtime meat shop offers casual sit-down service featuring soups and sandwiches with smoked meats, including fresh-made ring bologna and delicious beef jerky. $

Jaarsma's. *727 Franklin Street, Pella; (641) 628-2940.* One of two well-known bakeries on the square famous for Dutch letters, Jaarsma's has no seating and long lines during Tulip Time. (The other bakery is **Vander Ploeg,** at 711 Franklin.) $

Olde Town Eatery. *719 Franklin, Pella; (641) 628-4042.* Try the Dutchman's Classic (a hot bologna and melted Gouda grinder), Dutch Lettuce (an iceberg lettuce salad with creamy mustard dressing), the potato soup, and apple cobbler at this small-town cafe. $

Scoops n' Loops. *606 Oskaloosa Street, Pella; (641) 628-8558.* This '50s-style retro diner serves malts, sandwiches, and fries. $

Where to Stay

AmeriHost Inn and Suites. *2104 Washington Street, Pella; (641) 628-0085.* Opened in 2001, this sixty-room hotel on the west edge of town has an indoor pool and a few suites. $$

Dutch Mill Inn. *205 Oskaloosa Street, Pella; (800) 647-6684 or (641) 628-1060.* This twenty-five-room hotel is well located near popular Caldwell

Park, which has a skateboard park and outdoor public pool. $$

Royal Amsterdam Hotel and Grand Cafe. *705 East First Street, Pella; (877) 954-8400.* Located on the new canal a block from downtown, this European-style hotel has thirty-eight rooms. $$$-$$$$

For More Information

Pella Convention and Visitors Bureau. *518 Franklin Street, Pella 50219;* *(888) 746-3882 or (641) 628-2626, www.pella.org, pellacvb@pella.org.*

Knoxville

Knoxville bills itself as the "sprint car racing capital of the world." Located at the junction of State Highways 92 and 14 just southwest of Pella, it has one of the nation's fastest dirt racetracks as well as a sprint car racing museum.

NATIONAL SPRINT CAR HALL OF FAME AND MUSEUM (ages 8 and up)

At the Marion County Fairgrounds, 1 Sprint Capital Place, Knoxville 50318; (800) 874-4488 or (641) 842-6176, www.sprintcarhof.com, sprintcarhof@ sprintcarhof.com. Open 10:00 A.M. to 6:00 P.M. Monday through Friday, 10:00 A.M. to 5:00 P.M. Saturday, and noon to 5:00 P.M. Sunday from April through September, 10:00 A.M. to 6:00 P.M. Monday through Friday and noon to 5:00 P.M. Saturday and Sunday from October through March. $.

This is the world's only museum dedicated to sprint car racing, with twenty-five restored cars and tributes to champion drivers. Check out the sprint car simulator, a computerized game mounted onto a sprint car chassis, which makes you feel like you're zooming around the Knoxville raceway.

LAKE RED ROCK (all ages)

Visitor Center at 1105 Highway T15, Knoxville 50138; (641) 828-7522, www. lakeredrock.org. Lake open year-round. Visitor center open daily 9:30 A.M. to 6:00 P.M. from Memorial Day through Labor Day, noon to 4:00 P.M. weekdays in May; open weekends only, with varying hours, most other months. Closed December and January. Free. *Beach admission, $; under 12* Free.

One of Iowa's largest lakes, Red Rock is between Knoxville and Pella. Popular for swimming, boating, fishing, bicycling, and animal viewing, Red Rock includes sandy beaches, woods, rocky bluffs, and wetlands. With more than 50,000 acres, this is Iowa's largest expanse of public land. Start at the visitor center, which has a film about bald eagles, a butterfly garden, and outdoor deck with great lake views. For hiking, try the Volksweg Trail, a 13-mile paved trail that starts in Pella and goes below the dam area to the lake's north side and Fifield Recreation Area. On the north side at Cordova County Park are seven popular cabins available year-round. Red Rock also has seven campgrounds and many perfect picnic spots.

CORDOVA OBSERVATION TOWER (ages 7 and up)

1378 Highway G28, Otley (Lake Red Rock) 50214; (641) 627-5935. Open 7:00 A.M. to 8:00 P.M. daily, weather permitting. $.

For an awesome view, climb 170 steps to the viewing platform of this 106-foot converted water tower overlooking the Des Moines River Valley and Lake Red Rock. Located in Cordova Park on the north side of Red Rock, this is one of the Midwest's tallest observation towers.

*E*agle Watching at Red Rock Bald eagles have made a big

comeback in Iowa. In 2001 there were 130 bald eagle nests in Iowa. In 1990, there were eight. At Red Rock, you'll see the most in December through early March, especially at Horn's Ferry Bridge near the North Tailwater Recreation Area. It's right below the dam, which eagles like because the rushing water stuns fish, making them easy picking. Biologists say eagles have returned across the nation after a seventy-year absence because of a 1972 federal ban on the pesticide DDT that thinned eagle eggshells.

 DAN-D FARMS CORN MAZE (ages 3 and up)
2043 Highway 14, Knoxville 50138; (641) 842–2829, www.dandfarms.com. Open weekends 1:00 to 7:00 or 9:00 P.M. in August and September, 1:00 P.M. to 5:00 P.M. in October. Open some weekdays. $, ages 4 and under Free.

Each year, Dan-D Farms comes up with a dandy Iowa-inspired design for its fourteen-acre corn maze. (Grant Wood's *American Gothic,* a portrait of John Wayne, an Iowa map with a sprint car—you name it.) Located 5 miles south of Knoxville, the maze has 4 miles of twists and turns plus two bridges over the corn. Staff is usually inside the maze to help out. There are also farm animals and hayrack rides. Fall is the best time to visit. The last two Friday and Saturday nights in October, from 7:00 to 10:00 P.M., the maze is "spooked" with family-friendly but scary stuff. FYI: there's a $1.00 off coupon on the Web site.

*S*mall-town Eats The Marion County town of Pleasantville has

only 1,539 residents. But it also has three locally owned restaurants.

- **Benoni's,** 1004 North Highway 5 (515–848–3986), is known for its steaks and theme buffets, from seafood to Mexican. $–$$

- **Checkerboard Restaurant,** 108 East Monroe Street (515–848–3742), is famed for its onion rings and pizza and is filled with antiques (also sold in the basement). $

- **Smokey Row Coffee House,** 111 East Monroe Street (515–848–5959), serves soup in bread bowls, sandwiches, and cheesecake. $

Where to Eat

Farley's Lazy Dog Cafe. *112 South Second Street, Knoxville; (641) 828-8983.* Farley's, a coffee shop decorated with local artwork, serves light items, including soups, salads, and baked goods. Closed on Sunday. $

Kin Folks Eatin' Place. *1731 High Street, Attica; (641) 943-2362.* Down-home barbecue beef brisket and ribs,

hand-cranked ice cream, and homemade fruit cobblers are highlights at this small-town restaurant near Knoxville. $$

Udder's Steak House. *1265 Hayes Drive, Knoxville; (641) 828-7821.* Get it? This grill-your-own steak joint is in the country between Knoxville and Red Rock's Mile Long Bridge. $$–$$$

Where to Stay

Cordova Park Cabins at Lake Red Rock. *1378 Highway G28, Otley; (641) 627-5935 or 828-2213, www.mvr.usace. army.mil/RedRock/recreation/cabins.htm, cordovapark@hotmail.com.* Located in Cordova County Park, these seven quaint cabins offer lake views and modern amenities and sleep up to ten each (four have two bedrooms and a loft sleeping area; three newer ones have three bedrooms with a deck and electric fireplace). Open year-round,

they're so popular there's a lottery to handle requests, and they're often booked for the summer by December. Cabins are rented on a weekly basis during the summer and for a two-night minimum off-season. You can send in your request in November. $$

Red Carpet Motel. *1702 North Lincoln, Knoxville; (641) 842-3191.* This forty-two-room motel is two blocks from the Knoxville raceway on State Highway 14 North. $$

For More Information

Marion County Development Commission. *214 East Main Street,*

Knoxville 50138; (641) 828-2257, www.redrockarea.com.

Amazing Iowa Facts The small southern Iowa town of Carlisle is home to a big family: the first septuplets born in the United States. The McCaughey septuplets (Kenneth, Alexis, Natalie, Kelsey, Brandon, Nathan, and Joel) were born on November 19, 1997. They live with their parents, Bobbi and Kenny, and their older sister, Mikayla, in a seven-bedroom house built with donations from Iowans.

Indianola

About 17 miles south of Des Moines on US 65/69, Indianola hosts the National Balloon Classic, an annual summer hot air balloon competition.

NATIONAL BALLOON MUSEUM (ages 5 and up)

1601 North Jefferson Street, Indianola 50125; (515) 961–3714, www.balloon. weather.net. Open 10:00 A.M. to 2:00 P.M. Monday through Saturday and 1:00 to 4:00 P.M. Sunday from February through April, 9:00 A.M. to 4:00 P.M. Monday through Friday, 10:00 A.M. to 4:00 P.M. Saturday, and 1:00 to 4:00 P.M. Sunday from May through December; closed some holidays and in January. Free.

Entering this museum feels like you're walking into an upside-down hot air balloon. Inside are ballooning artifacts, memorabilia and exhibits about the history and mechanics of hot air and gas ballooning. In early August the sky above Indianola is filled with beautiful hot air balloons during the annual National Balloon Classic, which attracts more than one hundred professional balloonists. The nine-day event kicks off with a parade, bathtub races, and an art fair in the town square, but the real action is at the Balloon Launch Field, 2 miles east of Indianola on State Highway 92, where balloons (some resembling dinosaurs and pandas) go up twice daily, at about 7:00 A.M. and 7:00 P.M., weather permitting. Food is sold on-site. Bring blankets and lawn chairs. Other events include fireworks, live entertainment, and inflatable rides for children. Admission is charged. Call: (800) 690–1287 or (515) 961–8415 or log on to www.nationalballoonclassic.com.

If you'd like to ride in a beautiful balloon, one-hour rides are offered twice daily during the Classic. They cost $140 to $150 per person. Children must be at least age six *and* more than 4 feet tall. Another option is a tethered balloon ride. Call On the Fly Inc. at (800) 690–1287 or onthefly250@yahoo.com.

DES MOINES METRO OPERA (ages 5 and up)

Simpson College's Blank Performing Arts Center, 106 West Boston Avenue, Indianola 50125; (515) 961–6221, www.dmmo.org.

Located in Indianola on the Simpson College campus, this opera company puts on one of the nation's largest opera festivals each summer. For children, there's a special June family event, Peanut Butter and Puccini, which includes a forty-five-minute production and backstage tour.

Exotic Chicks Ever seen a Pekin duck or a Buff Orpington? You may be able to find them—and about thirty other varieties—at Reynolds Feed Service, 2612 West Second Street in Indianola. A good time to visit is on a designated "Chick Day" in April, May, and June. Call (515) 961–6300.

Where to Eat

Corner Sundry. *101 North Buxton Street, Indianola; (515) 961–9029.* Who needs real food when you can have ice-cream sundaes, sodas, malts, and flavored cokes? They've been served for decades at this old-fashioned soda fountain on the town square. $

Cottage Inn. *302 South Jefferson Street, Indianola; (515) 961–3137.* This down-home cafe serves home-cooked food, from onion rings to beef tenderloin and pies for lunch. $

Harvest. *107 East Salem Avenue, Indianola; (515) 962–0466.* Open for weekend dinner and occasional Sunday brunch, this grown-up restaurant specializes in innovative American bistro fare from pasta to seafood, plus Midwestern mainstays like barbecued pork ribs. $$–$$$

Where to Stay

Apple Tree Inn. *1215 North Jefferson Street, Indianola; (800) 961–0551 or (515) 961–0551, www.appleinn.qpg.com.* Located on US 65/69 atop a hill overlooking town, the Apple Tree Inn is a locally owned and operated brick hotel with sixty rooms including king suites with sofa sleepers. $–$$

For More Information

Indianola Chamber of Commerce. *515 North Jefferson Street Suite D, Indianola 50125; (515) 961–6269,* *www.indianolachamber.com/community guide/default.asp.*

Amazing Iowa Facts George Washington Carver, who discovered hundreds of ways to use peanuts, soybeans, and sweet potatoes, attended Indianola's Simpson College (and later Iowa State University).

Cumming

Cumming is located about 21 miles northwest of Indianola off of Interstate 35.

CUMMING ORCHARD (all ages)

284 R45 Highway, Cumming 50061; (515) 981–4413. Open 8:00 A.M. to 6:00 P.M. Monday through Saturday and 10:00 A.M. to 6:00 P.M. Sunday from August through October. Free. Hayrack rides, $.

Pick your own or pick up ready-picked apples at this orchard that includes seasonal entertainment, hayrack rides, a pumpkin patch, farm animals to feed, and a snack bar with caramel apples, apple pie, and apple crisp.

A Rubiner Family Adventure

They're called "Iowa Moments"—occasions when Iowans perform acts of old-fashioned generosity. One of our best Iowa Moments occurred on a glorious autumn day when my bicycle tire suddenly went flat, prematurely halting a family ride on a rural trail. A young boy who'd been watching us quietly from a small town park suddenly piped up: "We have a bike you can use." He ushered us over to his house and introduced us to his mother who wheeled out a bicycle from her garage (a John Deere bicycle, this being Iowa). Before I took off on her bike, I asked if she wanted my name and phone number. "No, I trust you," she replied. Two hours later, after a great ride, I put the bike back in her garage.

HOWELL TREE FARM/HOWELL FLORAL AND GREENHOUSE (all ages)

3129 Howell Lane, Cumming 50061; (515) 981–4762 or 981–0863. Floral barn and greenhouse open 10:00 A.M. to 7:00 P.M. daily year-round. Tree Farm open the Saturday before Thanksgiving through December 23 from 9:00 A.M. to 5:00 P.M. daily except for Thanksgiving Day. Fall hayride and pumpkin patch visit, available late September through Halloween. $, ages 2 and under Free.

This pretty farm about 20 miles south of Des Moines is home to two family businesses: a tree farm and a dried flower and greenhouse operation. Children will especially enjoy the petting zoo, which has goats, lambs, bottle calves, and a miniature donkey, plus a play area. In the fall there are hayrides and a pumpkin patch. Santa visits the Saturday before and after Thanksgiving. This is also a great place to buy a Christmas tree. Concessions are available. The Howells started their tree business in 1963 to earn money to send their seven children to college. The kids helped plant, trim, and weed the trees, then began cutting and selling them seven years later. Check out the beautiful dried flower arrangements in the old dairy barn.

Winterset

Located near the junction of State Highway 92 and US 169 about 23 miles southwest of Cumming, this small town with its pretty square and domed limestone courthouse is best known for its nineteenth-century covered bridges that dot the countryside. They starred in Robert Waller's 1992 novel *The Bridges of Madison County* (the best-selling hardcover novel of all time) and the 1995 movie with Clint Eastwood and Meryl Streep, which was filmed here.

🏛 BRIDGES OF MADISON COUNTY (all ages)
Start at the Roseman Covered Bridge Shop off Highway G47 at 2451 Elderberry Lane, Winterset 50273; (888) 999-2902 or (515) 462-4368, www.roseman bridge.com. **Free.**

Even if you hated the novel (or the movie), these pretty old bridges are worth a visit. Sadly, the most famous of the six bridges—the Cedar Bridge where Oprah did her 1993 television show about the Bridges novel and the only one you could drive through—burned down in fall 2002. The five remaining bridges are tucked away in quiet, somewhat hard-to-find rural locations. So start by picking up a map at the Madison County Chamber of Commerce/Welcome Center on the town square. Roseman Bridge, where Eastwood and Streep kissed passionately in the movie, is the most well known and developed, with a nearby gift shop. Stick around long enough for a picnic near the Cutler-Donahue Bridge.

The Madison County Covered Bridge Festival
On the second full weekend in October, when the autumn leaves are in full glory, Madison County throws a party featuring old-time craft demonstrations, live music, lots of food, a spelling bee, talent shows, and an antique car parade. Guided bus tours of the bridges are also offered. Admission is charged.

JOHN WAYNE BIRTHPLACE (ages 5 and up)

216 South Second Street, Winterset 50273; (515) 462-1044, www.johnwayne birthplace.org. Open 10:00 A.M. to 4:30 P.M. daily except some holidays. $.

This tiny four-room house is where Marion Morrison (later John Wayne) was born in 1907. The house has been restored to the way it was when Marion—err, John—was a child, and includes memorabilia about "the Duke's" movie career.

Home of the Delicious Apple

In 1872, Madison County farmer Jesse Hiatt discovered a strange seedling in his apple orchard. The seedling grew into a tree with apples that were described as "delicious" by a judge of the 1873 Missouri State Fair's apple contest. A star was born. A descendant of the original Delicious apple tree still stands just north of Peru, where residents each year host an Apple Daze festival.

Where to Eat

Expresso Yourself. *122 North First Avenue, Winterset; (515) 462-5962.* Located on the west side of the town square, this quaint coffee shop serves a light lunch with delicate sandwiches on interesting breads. $

Northside Cafe. *61 Jefferson Street, Winterset; (515) 462-1523.* Cheap, hearty dinner plates and sandwiches are served in the cozy Northside Cafe, which has been around since the mid-1800s and was featured in the movie *The Bridges of Madison County*. (Clint Eastwood sat at the counter on the fourth seat from the front door.) $

Picnic Possibilities

Try **Winterset City Park,** at the intersection of South and Ninth Street, a shady seventy-five-acre park with a playground, public pool, and an unusual English-style maze made of high hedges (at its peak from June through September). For a great view, also visit Clark's Tower, a 25-foot high limestone memorial. To get to the park, start at the town square on the southeast corner, take Court Street east to Ninth Street, then go south two blocks.

Where to Stay

Village View Motel. *711 East Highway 92, Winterset; (800) 862-1218 or (515) 462-1218.* This sixteen-room motel on the north edge of town on State Highway 92 is about a mile from the town square. $

For More Information

Madison County Chamber of Commerce. *73 East Jefferson Street, Winterset 50273; (800) 298-6119 or (515) 462-1185, www.madisoncounty.com, chamber@dwx.com.*

Chariton

Chariton is at US 34 and State Highway 14, about 60 miles southeast of Winterset.

 BELINDA CHURCH TOY AND ANTIQUE MUSEUM (all ages)
11 miles south of Knoxville on Highway 14, Chariton 50049; (641) 862-4439. Open 9:00 A.M. to 8:00 P.M. daily (but call ahead to make sure someone's there). $, ages 4 and under Free.

This 1846 country church perched above a two-lane rural state highway is packed with thousands of dolls and toys. Owner George Piershbacher, a former farmer and coal miner, has collected toys since he was a kid (he's now in his seventies). What used to be the altar is now densely stocked with dolls: Barbies, Spice Girls, Sesame Street characters, Ronald McDonald, you name it. Where the church pews once were are high shelves stuffed with dusty toy trucks, tractors, corn pickers, steam shovels, NASCAR race cars, planes, World War II army tanks, wind-up stuffed animals, and circus toys, some dating back to the early 1900s. A white sheet metal addition to the old church is also filled with toys. There are 1930s pedal tractors and three vintage cars, including a 1950 Chevy and a 1959 Edsel. Ask George to show you his Volkswagen Beetle toy cars (he has a "Herbie" VW bug from the movie of the same name), the cast-iron toy-size Russian *Sputnik,* and a toy tractor made from a corn cob.

CINDER PATH TRAIL (all ages)

Catch the trail off the main square in downtown Chariton; (641) 774–2438. Open year-round. **Free.**

Iowa's first Rails-to-Trails project, Cinder Path is a 13½-mile walking and cycling trail from Chariton to Humeston built on the old CB & Q railroad that ran for more than a century. The trail winds through wooded areas and farmland over the Chariton River. The surface is cinders, so don't try it with narrow racing bike tires.

PIERCE'S PUMPKIN PATCH (all ages)

2491 Highway 14, Chariton 50049; (641) 862–3398. Open 8:00 A.M. to 8:00 P.M. daily from the last weekend in September through October. **Free.**

Pierce's has thousands of pumpkins, gourds, squash, and Indian corn, plus special activities, including a flea market, hayrides, country crafts, and a threshing machine demonstration. The hay bale maze is another favorite. An annual Pumpkin Festival in mid-October features chainsaw carving, oats thrashing, and fall food favorites (pumpkin pie, caramel apples, apple cider). Pierce's is across from the Belinda Church Toy and Antique Museum.

Amish Meals Drive south from Chariton on State Highway 14 and chances are you'll see a farmer in a broad-brimmed hat riding across the rolling fields in a horse-drawn wagon. Since 1993, several Amish families have moved onto area farms. Learn more about the Amish way of life by visiting some Amish homes where baked goods, wooden toys, and handmade quilts are sold. Some Amish families also welcome visitors to their homes for a traditional Amish buffet-style meal. Advance reservations and payment are required. Call (515) 774–4059.

PIPER'S GROCERY STORE (ages 5 and up)

901 Braden Avenue, Chariton 50049; (800) 479–1343 or (641) 774–2131. Open 8:00 A.M. to 5:30 P.M. Monday through Saturday. **Free.**

A cheerful red-and-white striped awning and old-fashioned red lettering on a white marquee welcome you to this 1905 grocery store famous for homemade chocolates. Walk inside, across the scuffed wood-planked floor, to find not just groceries but homemade pies and doughnuts, handmade pottery and baskets by Iowa artisans, and a glass-enclosed wooden display case with delicious chocolates (try the caramel turtles). A regular stop for bus tours, the store's guest book has signatures from all over the world.

Where to Eat

Donna's Place. *126 North Grand Avenue, Chariton; (641) 774-8597.* Old-fashioned home cooking, from pork tenderloin and burgers to beef and noodles, chicken fried steak, and liver and onions, is served at this cozy cafe. $

Double Dip and More. *400 North Main Street, Chariton; (641) 774-3413.* Homemade ice cream is the main attraction, but there's also pizza and sit-down tables at this little ice-cream shop north of the square. $

L&L European Delight. *213 North Main Street, Chariton; (641) 774-2104.* Run by a Ukrainian family, this ethnic restaurant and food shop features Ukrainian food like borscht and cucumber soup, plus a good croissant sandwich with chicken salad or smoked turkey. $

Tasos Steakhouse. *123 North Main Street, Chariton; (641) 774-8192.* Right on the town square, Tasos has a full menu, from pizza to garden salads, steaks, burgers, and Greek specialties. $

Picnic Possibilities Get some carryout broasted chicken, pork tenderloin, and seasoned potato wedges from **TGI Chicken and Tenderloin,** one block south of the town square at 114 South Grand Avenue, then head to **Red Haw State Park,** off of US 34. The 420-acre park has a 72-acre lake, a sandy beach for swimming, a stone shelter house, picnic areas, and a nicely shaded campground overlooking the lake. Visit in the spring to see the spectacular red bud trees or during fall foliage season.

Where to Stay

Ralph and Norma's. *Route 1, Box 28, Lucas; (641) 766-6770.* Located on a farm with a fruit orchard about 9 miles west of Chariton, this B&B in a 1918 farmhouse has two guest rooms with shared bath. It creatively accommodates families by offering discounts and, if need be, use of a downstairs hideaway bed. A country breakfast is included. $$

Royal Rest Motel. *137 East Grace Avenue, Chariton; (641) 774–5961.* This twenty-seven-room motel is just east of town on US 34 near Red Haw State Park. $–$$

For More Information

Tourism Lucas County (TLC) Chariton Chamber. *104 North Grand, Chariton 50049; (641) 774–4059.*

Corydon

Corydon is 17 miles south of Chariton off State Highways 14 and 2.

 PRAIRIE TRAILS MUSEUM OF WAYNE COUNTY (ages 5 and up)
515 East Jefferson (State Highway 2), Corydon 50060; (641) 872–2211. Open 10:00 A.M. to 5:00 P.M. Monday through Saturday and 1:00 to 5:00 P.M. Sunday from June through August, 1:00 to 5:00 P.M. daily from mid-April through May and September to mid-October. $, ages 4 and under **Free.**

Walk along a re-created turn-of-the-twentieth-century Main Street that includes an actual bank safe robbed by Jesse James (he robbed a Corydon bank). There are exhibits about the history of the prairie and about the Mormon Trail (featuring a real oxen-drawn wagon). The Heritage Barn is filled with old-time farm implements.

Where to Eat

C.J.'s Food and Spirits. *201 West Anthony Street, Corydon; (641) 872–3544.* North of the town square, this former tearoom in a renovated house serves burgers and other light fare for lunch, plus steak and fish entrees for dinner. $–$$

For More Information

Wayne County Economic Development Corporation. *P.O. Box 435, Corydon 50060; (641) 872–1536.*

Centerville

Drive about 23 miles east from Corydon on State Highway 2 to Centerville.

RATHBUN LAKE (all ages)

20112 Highway J5T, Centerville 52544; (641) 647–2464, www.nwk.usace. army.mil/rathbun/rathbun_home.htm. Lake open daily year-round. Information center open 8:00 A.M. to 4:00 P.M. daily from Memorial Day through Labor Day. **Free.**

The information center is a good jumping-off spot for exploring one of Iowa's largest lakes, created in the 1970s as part of a flood-control project. The center has displays on coal mining and lake history, plus a wildlife diorama. With 34,000 acres of public land and water, Rathbun is good for bird-watching, fishing, boating, camping, hiking on nature trails, and picnicking at seven lakeside parks. There are three designated swimming beaches in the Island View and Buck Creek areas, plus eight campgrounds with playgrounds. For on-line reservations, visit www.reserveusa.com. Pontoon and fishing boat rentals are available at Rathbun and Southfork Marinas.

RATHBUN FISH HATCHERY (all ages)

15053 Hatchery Place, Moravia 52571; (641) 647–2406. Open 7:45 A.M. to 3:45 P.M. Monday through Friday year-round. **Free.**

This modern warmwater fish hatchery is open for self-guided tours along an elevated observation walkway through the hatchery and aquariums. There are also films on fish productions and a mile-long nature trail. The best time to see fish is mid-April to mid-August. The hatchery is about 7 miles north of Centerville, directly below the Rathbun Reservoir Dam.

Where to Eat

The Green Circle. *22984 Highway 5, Centerville; (641) 437–4472.* Sandwiches, steaks, and a children's menu are available at this restaurant just past the city limits. $

Lakeside Restaurant at Rathbun Marina. *21646 Marina Place, Moravia;* *(641) 724–3212.* The lake view from the outdoor deck or through the big windows inside is the star of the Lakeside Restaurant, which serves steaks, ribs, and sandwiches. $$

The Manhattan Steak House. *24256 Highway 5, Centerville; (641) 856–8565.*

Just south of town, this restaurant serves steaks, burgers, and fried chicken. It also has a buffet and a children's menu. $-$$

The Skean Block Restaurant. *11 Benton Street, Albia; (641) 932-2159.* About 21 miles north of Lake Rathbun in a high-ceilinged Victorian building on Albia's restored town square, this award-winning restaurant with large storefront windows, cherry-colored wood, and posters of old Paris serves creative cuisine for lunch and dinner, from a garlic pesto burger to raspberry pork tenderloin and beef Oscar, plus a (less creative) children's menu with chicken nuggets, burgers, and grilled cheese. $$-$$$

Where to Stay

Buck Creek Cabins. *20787 Highway J5T, Moravia; (641) 724-9588, buckcreek @jetnetinc.net.* Near Rathbun Dam in a wooded rural area, each of these modern cabins has a double bed and hideaway bed, a shower, kitchenette, dishes, linens, air-conditioning, and heating. Reservations, deposit, and a two- to four-night minimum stay are often required. $$

The Grey Goose Inn. *12063 Overturf Drive, Moravia; (641) 724-3265, www.greygooseinn.com.* Recently opened in a new building in the country near Rathbun Lake, the Grey Goose has six rooms, each with private bath and some with several beds. Breakfast and dinner available through advance reservations and at additional cost, although children age five and under eat breakfast free. $$-$$$

Lakeside Inn. *21646 Marina Place, Moravia; (641) 724-3212, www.lake rathbunia.com.* This small, seasonal, multistory hotel at Rathbun Marina promises a deck and lake view with every room, from singles to suites with kitchens. Reservations, deposit, and two- to three-night minimum sometimes required. A campground, the Lakeside Restaurant, and boat rental are nearby. $$-$$$$

For More Information

Centerville Area Chamber of Commerce, *128 North 12th Street, Centerville 52544; (800) 611-3800 or (641) 437-* *4102, www.centerville-ia.com, cntrvlle@lisco.net.*

Villages of Van Buren County

From Centerville, it's about a 45-mile drive east to Van Buren County and its historic villages: Keosauqua, Bentonsport, Bonaparte, Cantril, and Farmington. These five small, sleepy communities thrived during the mid-nineteenth century and are now home to artists and craftspeople who sell their work in the Bentonsport and Bonaparte historic districts, which are lined with old brick buildings. The most action is during peak fall foliage season; the annual Forest Craft Festival and Scenic Drive, held the second full weekend of October, features arts and crafts, a parade, carnival, and lumberjack show (complete with log rolling and ax throwing). The fastest way to get to Van Buren County is along State Highway 2. The most scenic route is on County Highway J40 through Amish farm country.

LACEY-KEOSAUQUA STATE PARK (all ages)

22895 Lacey Trail, Keosauqua 52565; (319) 293–3502, www.state.ia.us/dnr/ organiza/ppd/laceykeo.htm, lacey_keosauqua@dnr.state.ia.us. Open 4:00 A.M. to 10:30 P.M. year-round. **Free.**

This is one of Iowa's largest parks, with 1,653 acres of hills, bluffs, and valleys hugging the Des Moines River for hiking and camping on the historic Mormon Trail. Thirty-acre Lacey Lake has a sandy beach for swimming, plus a bathhouse and lifeguards. There are also hiking trails (try the River and Lake Trails), a shaded campground with 113 campsites (about a third with electrical hookups), and six family cabins with modern facilities. For reservations call (319) 293–3502.

BENTONSPORT NATIONAL HISTORIC DISTRICT (all ages)

Scenic Byway J40, Bentonsport 52565; (319) 592–3579, www.bentonsport.com. Most shops are open 10:00 A.M. to 5:00 P.M. daily from April through October, weekends only in November and December. Some businesses are open daily or for a longer season.

This tiny unincorporated town of 55 residents near State Highway 1 has an old-world feel, with original 1800s homes adorned with historical markers. The two-block business district along the river has antique and craft shops. There are weekend demonstrations by a blacksmith and potter at Iron and Lace, 21909 Marion Street. Two doors down, sample free fudge at Greef General Store. The riverside park with a century-old iron bridge is a good picnic spot.

BONAPARTE NATIONAL HISTORIC DISTRICT (all ages)

Scenic Byway J40, Bonaparte 52620; (319) 592–3400, www.bonaparte-iowa. com. Open 10:00 A.M. to 5:00 P.M. daily except Monday.

Located about 20 miles southeast of Keosauqua, this historic district along the Des Moines River features thirty-seven old buildings converted into shops selling antiques and collectibles, plus the well-known Bonaparte Retreat Restaurant.

Can-U-Canoe? The second full weekend in July is when Canoe Van Buren, a casual 23-mile canoe float down the Des Moines River, takes place. It starts in Selma on Saturday morning, with an overnight stop in Keosauqua, and finishes on Sunday in Farmington. Call (800) 868-7822 or (319) 293-7111.

Where to Eat

Bonaparte Retreat Restaurant. *713 Front Street, Bonaparte; (319) 592-3339.* This former nineteenth-century redbrick gristmill with exposed brick walls, 2-foot-thick wooden beams, and antiques serves steak, seafood, and pork chops for lunch and dinner. $-$$

Bridge Cafe and Supper Club. *101 Olive Street, Farmington; (319) 878-3315.* The cafe serves three meals daily (from burgers and fries to daily specials), while the pricier supper club has a

piano bar and serves dinner only, including rib eyes, prime rib, and a salad bar. $-$$

Red Barn Bistro. *21268 Fir Avenue, Keosauqua; (319) 293-6154.* Inside a barn on a gravel road in a ghost town outside Keosauqua, this home cookin' restaurant serves dinner Thursday through Saturday, offering steaks, shrimp, chicken strips, and a salad bar, plus Sunday brunch. $-$$

Picnic Possibilities Try **Bonaparte's Riverfront Park**, which has a butterfly garden, old lock walls, and nice views of the Des Moines River.

Where to Stay

Hotel Manning B&B and Motor Inn. *100 Van Buren Street, Keosauqua; (800) 728-2718 or (319) 293-3232.* This well-known nineteenth-century hotel with eighteen rooms has a wide veranda overlooking the sleepy Des Moines River. The adjacent motor inn has nineteen rooms. $-$$

Red Fox Lodging, *24418 Lacey Trail, Keosauqua; (877) 293-3224 or (319)*

293-6329, www.redfoxlodging.com, info@redfoxlodging.com. Each of these modern cabins on Lake Sugema, a 574-acre lake popular for fishing, hiking and boating, has a queen-size bed and full-size futon, furnished kitchen, air-conditioning and heat, towels, and linens. Nearby is a playground, shelter pavilion, boat ramp, and campground. The cabins are south of Keosauqua off State Highway 1. $$.

For More Information

Villages of Van Buren Inc. *P.O. Box 9, Keosauqua 52565; (800) 868-7822 or* *(319) 293-7111, www.800-tourvbc.com, villages@800-tourvbc.com.*

Keokuk

Tucked in Iowa's southeastern heel, Keokuk, an old Mississippi River town with Victorian architecture, is known for eagle watching. Samuel Clemens (alias Mark Twain) sold his first written material to the *Keokuk Post*. He lived in Keokuk for about two years during the 1850s, working in his brother's printing shop. From Van Buren County, Keokuk is about 35 miles southeast on State Highway 2, US 218, and US 61.

*B*ald Eagle Watching Keokuk has the largest concentration of wintering eagles along the Mississippi. See them the third weekend in January during Keokuk's Bald Eagle Appreciation Days, when observation points are set up along the river and a local mall has activities that include a live eagle show (with injured eagles). Call (800) 383-1219.

 GEORGE M. VERITY RIVERBOAT MUSEUM (ages 8 and up)
In Victory Park, 101 Mississippi Drive, Keokuk 52632; (319) 524-4765. Open 9:00 A.M. to 5:00 P.M. daily from Memorial Day through Labor Day. $.
   Step aboard a 1927 paddle wheel steamboat, which was retired in 1960, to see the original boiler, machinery, crew quarters, and pilot house. A self-guided tour of the dry-docked boat takes about forty-five minutes. Afterward, picnic at Victory Park, which has a playground.

*C*ivil War Reenactment During the last weekend in April at Keokuk's Rand Park, more than 1,000 costumed people, many dressed in soldiers' uniforms, reenact the two-day Battle of Pea Ridge. This 1862 Civil War battle took place in Arkansas, not Iowa, but the winning Union Army general was Samuel R. Curtis, a former Keokuk mayor.

Where to Eat

The Cellar. *29 South Second Street, Keokuk; (319) 524-4040.* A downtown eatery near the bridge across the Mississippi, The Cellar serves huge hamburgers and homemade onion rings. $

The Hawkeye. *105 North Park Street, Keokuk; (319) 524-7549.* Right off US 218, this lunch and dinner spot has good pork tenderloins and steak. $–$$

No Wake Cafe. *201 Water Street, Montrose; (319) 463-7701.* Dine inside an old towboat on the Mississippi known for its barbecued ribs, steak, prime rib, and seafood. Lunch is available only on weekends, dinner Wednesday through Sunday, and there's a children's menu. $$

Picnic Possibilities Head to Keokuk's riverfront and the observation deck of the **Swing Span Bridge** over the Mississippi, First and Lucas Streets, which has a great view and picnic tables. Or try **Rand Park,** at Seventeenth and Orleans Streets, on a bluff with an overlook, picnic tables, a playground and the grave of the city's namesake, Sauk/Fox Chief Keokuk.

Where to Stay

Fairfield Inn. *3404 Main Street, Keokuk; (319) 524-9000.* There's an indoor pool at this sixty-two-room chain hotel on the north end in a commercial area. $$$

Holiday Inn Express. *Fourth and Main Street, Keokuk; (319) 524-8000.* Across from the Keossippi Mall (headquarters for Bald Eagle Appreciation Days), this eighty-room chain hotel a short walk from the riverfront has an indoor pool. $$$

For More Information

Keokuk Area Convention and Tourism Bureau. *329 Main Street, Keokuk 52632; (800) 383-1219 or (319)* *524-5599, www.keokuktourism.com, keokukia@interl.net.*

Fort Madison

Travel north 25 miles from Keokuk along US 61 to Fort Madison, home of the first U.S. Army fort west of the upper Mississippi. Now home to a maximum-security penitentiary, it's also the birthplace of the first white child born in Iowa, Rozanna Stark, who was born here in 1810.

Famous Mormon Community

Famous Mormon Community Across the Mississippi on Fort Madison's Swing Span Bridge is Nauvoo, Illinois, a fascinating, reconstructed nineteenth-century Mormon community. The grand Nauvoo Temple, which opened in 2002, is a reconstruction of an 1846 temple that was burned down by arsonists. In Nauvoo visit more than two dozen restored homes and shops with guides in period clothing and artisans demonstrating tinsmithing, printing, and brick making. Horse-drawn wagon rides and evening musicals are also offered from Memorial Day through Labor Day. Learn about the sad history of Mormons in Nauvoo at the Latter Day Saints Visitors Center and at the Joseph Smith Historical Center, which includes the homestead, mansion, and grave site of the Mormon leader who brought his followers to Nauvoo in 1839. Today the town has 1,500 residents, but in Smith's day, it was the nation's tenth largest city, with 12,000 residents. By 1846 it was all over. After Smith was assassinated, persecuted church members fled west to Utah. For more information see the Web site www.nauvoo.net.

OLD FORT MADISON (ages 5 and up)

*On US 61 at Riverview Park, Fort Madison 52627; (319) 372–6318, www.
fort-madison.net/oldfort. Open 9:00 A.M. to 5:00 P.M. daily from Memorial Day
through August, weekends during May, September, and October. $, ages 5 and
under* **Free.**
*Family day pass
available.*
Take a
ninety-minute
tour led by a
costumed inter-
preter through
this recon-
structed fort on

Amazing Iowa Facts Fort Madison has the world's longest double-decker swing span bridge. Built in 1927, the 525-foot-long bridge at the foot of Second Street stretches across the Mississippi, connecting Iowa and Illinois. The top level is for cars, the bottom for trains. The bridge lifts in a half circle to let barges pass.

the Mississippi that looks like the one built in 1808. The original fort was destroyed in 1813 after being abandoned. The tour winds through the blockhouses and gardens, where you might see bread baking, candle dipping, and even musket shooting and cannon firing.

Tri-State Rodeo For more than fifty years, Fort Madison has hosted a huge rodeo at Rodeo Park, beginning the Wednesday after Labor Day and ending the following Saturday. Children will especially enjoy the Saturday morning parade featuring hundreds of horses. There are also weekend concerts by top country music performers. For tickets call (800) 369-3211.

Where to Eat

Alpha's On the Riverfront. *709 Avenue H, Fort Madison; (319) 372-1411.* Eat off glass-topped tables that display memorabilia from Fort Madison's past at this downtown restaurant with exposed brick walls in the Kingsley Inn. Specialties include sandwiches, steak, salad, and fried strawberries. $$

Ivy Bake Shop. *622 Seventh Street, Fort Madison; (319) 372-9939.* This downtown gourmet breakfast and lunch spot with a screened-in porch serves baked goodies and rich desserts plus quiche, pastas, soups, sandwiches, spinach salad, homemade lemonade, and fancy coffees. $–$$

Sorrento's Pizza. *2515 Avenue L, Fort Madison; (319) 372-6465.* Authentic Italian pizza sauce is the star attraction at this neighborhood pizza joint downtown on US 61. $

Where to Stay

Kingsley Inn. *707 Avenue H, Fort Madison; (800) 441-2327 or (319) 372-7074, www.virtualcities.com/ons/ia/z/iaz3601. htm, kingsley@interl.net.* This nineteenth-century redbrick and smoked-glass Victorian Inn near the old fort has fourteen rooms, each with private bath, including a two-bedroom, two-bathroom apartment with a kitchen, living room, and dining area. A full hot breakfast at Alpha's Restaurant, off the lobby, is included. $$$–$$$$

Madison Inn Motel. *3440 Avenue L, Fort Madison; (319) 372-7740, www.madisoninnmotel.com.* Just east of downtown, the Madison has twenty rooms, each with one or two queen-size beds, and is near several shops and restaurants. $–$$

For More Information

Fort Madison Area Convention and Visitors Bureau. *614 Ninth Street, Fort Madison 52627; (800) 210–8687 or* *(319) 372–5472, www.visitfortmadison. com, tourism@visitfortmadison.com.*

Burlington

Drive 16 miles north from Fort Madison along the Mississippi on US 61 to Burlington, another old river port famous for its bluffs, which used to provide flints for Native Americans, and its curvy Snake Alley, once dubbed the World's Crookedest Street by *Ripley's Believe It or Not.*

BURLINGTON BEES BASEBALL (all ages)

2712 Mount Pleasant Street, Burlington 52601; (888) GOBEES8 or (319) 754–5705, www.gobees.com. Season runs from early April through early September. $$ for adults, $ for children, ages 5 and under **Free.**

Burlington is one of the smallest towns to have a minor-league team, a Class A affiliate of the Kansas City Royals.

SNAKE ALLEY (all ages)

Sixth Street between Washington and Columbia Streets, Burlington 52601; (319) 752–6365. **Free.**

Walk, drive, or dare to cycle down this Burlington landmark, a 275-foot-long street that drops 58 feet, with five half-curves and two quarter-curves.

STARR'S CAVE NATURE CENTER AND PRESERVE (all ages)

11627 Starr's Cave Road, Burlington 52601; (319) 753–5808, www.interl. net/~starcave/SCNCpg.html, starcave@interl.net. Preserve open 6:00 A.M. to 10:30 P.M. daily. Cave open from April through October. Nature Center open 9:00 A.M. to 3:00 P.M. Monday through Friday. **Free.**

Hike and explore caves at this 200-acre preserve just outside Burlington that includes three caves hidden in limestone bluffs along Flint Creek. The largest and only natural cave is Starr's Cave, best suited for ages eight and up. The other two are dynamited holes and are fine for younger children. Remember to bring flashlights and a sweatshirt (it's 55 degrees inside), wear clothes you don't mind getting covered in mud, and be prepared to encounter bats. There are also 2 miles of hiking trails through bluffs, forests, and patches of prairie, including a paved trail good for baby strollers. The nature center has interactive exhibits and educational programs. To get there, take US 61 to Sunnyside Road and turn east. Go a half mile and then turn north onto Irish Ridge Road. Continue a half mile to the entrance on the left.

GEODE STATE PARK (all ages)

3249 Racine Avenue, Danville 52623; (319) 392–4601; www.state.ia.us/parks/ geode.htm. Open year-round, 4:00 A.M. to 10:30 P.M. **Free.**

Henry County's Geode State Park about 10 miles west of Burlington is one of the best places to find examples of the Iowa state rock—the geode. Found in limestone deposits, geodes are round hollow stones lined with glittering crystals. The 1,640-acre state park also includes a lake for swimming, fishing, and boating, plus hiking trails, campgrounds with modern showers, and picnic areas. To get to the park from Burlington go east on US 34 and State Highway 79.

Steamboat Days Special events for children, including a kid's karaoke contest, are part of the fun at Burlington's annual Steamboat Days festival in mid-June. There are also evening rock, country, pop, and blues concerts on an outdoor stage at the Port of Burlington, plus food, fireworks, parades, and carnival rides. Ticket prices vary. Call (319) 754–4334, visit www.steamboatdays.com, or e-mail sales@steamboatdays.com.

Where to Eat

Big Muddy's. *710 North Front Street, Burlington; (319) 753-1699.* Inside a former 1898 railroad freight station, Big Muddy's serves lunch and dinner, offering sandwiches, barbecued ribs, steak, and shrimp. Sunday brunch and a children's menu are available. $

Jefferson Street Cafe. *300 Jefferson Street, Burlington; (319) 754-1036.* In an old downtown building with big windows near Snake Alley, this restaurant serves everything from steak to sandwiches. $

Martini's Grille. *3001 Winegard Drive, Burlington; (319) 753-2291, www.martinis grille.com.* Located in the uptown business area, inside the Best Western Pzazz Motor Inn, this lively restaurant features "free-style American cuisine," including char-grilled pizzas, steaks, and seafood, plus uniquely named entrees like Chicken Lips (chicken strips marinated in hot sauce), a children's menu, and takeout. $$

Picnic Possibilities Visit **Crapo and Dankwardt Parks,** downtown near Main Street, with more than one hundred acres on a bluff overlooking the river. There are playgrounds, an outdoor public pool, horseshoe courts, nature trails, and baseball diamonds.

Where to Stay

Best Western Pzazz Motor Inn.
3001 Winegard Drive, Burlington; (800) 373-1223 or (319) 753-2223. A full-service hotel with a sports bar that serves tenderloins, a takeout pizza place, and Martini's Grille, this motor inn on a commercial strip west of downtown on US 61 has 151 rooms, including fourteen rooms and one suite that overlook an indoor pool. $$$

Holiday Inn Express. *1605 North Roosevelt Avenue, Burlington; (319) 752-0000.* Located in a commercial area on US 61 west of downtown, this seventy-six-room chain motel has an indoor pool. $$-$$$

For More Information

Burlington Convention and Visitors Bureau. *807 Jefferson, Burlington 52601; (800) 827-4837 or (319) 752-6365, www.visit.burlington.ia.us/.*

Port of Burlington Welcome Center. *400 North Front Street, Burlington 52601; (319) 752-8731.*

Wapello

Wapello is on US 61 about 25 miles north of Burlington.

🏛 TOOLESBORO INDIAN MOUNDS (ages 5 and up)
5788 Toolesboro Road, Wapello 52653; (319) 523-8381. Open noon to 4:00 P.M. daily from the third weekend in May through Labor Day, on weekends from Labor Day through October. **Free.**

Located off State Highway 99 about 24 miles north of Burlington between Oakville and Wapello, these ancient Indian burial mounds are on a bluff overlooking the Iowa River. The five-acre site, a National Historical Landmark, includes an education center. The cone-shaped earthen mounds were built between 100 B.C. and A.D. 200 to bury important people (and their precious trade items). A short video explaining the mound-building tradition and displays of excavated items are in the education center.

Other Things to See and Do in Southern Iowa

- **Dumont's Museum of Dreamworld Collectibles.** Sigourney, (641) 622-2592

- **Wapello County Historical Museum.** Ottumwa, (641) 682-8676

- **Pioneer Ridge Nature Area/Center.** Ottumwa, (641) 682-3091

- **Scholte House.** Pella, (641) 628-3684

- **Knoxville Raceway.** Knoxville, (641) 842-5431

- **Lake Ahquabi State Park.** Indianola, (515) 961-7101

- **John L. Lewis Museum of Mining and Labor.** Lucas, (641) 766-6831

- **International Center for Rural Culture and Art.** Allerton, (641) 872-2667

- **Historical and Coal Mining Museum.** Centerville, (641) 856-8040

- **Honey Creek State Park.** Moravia, (641) 724-3739

- **Lake Sugema.** Keosauqua, (319) 293-7111

- **The Secret Garden Flower Farm.** Danville, (319) 392-8288

Central Iowa

For a rural state, central Iowa is surprisingly urban and urbane, in a relatively gentle way. The region includes Des Moines, surrounding Polk County, and bits of neighboring counties. With a population of about 200,000, Des Moines is Iowa's largest city. It's also the state capital and a major financial and cultural hub. Ringing the city (and boosting the metro population to 456,000) are the ever growing suburbs, with new housing developments, corporate campuses, and shopping malls. Beyond that is countryside.

In central Iowa, you'll find big-city culture and attractions: art, music, theater and opera, plus minor-league sports, a zoo, a science center, a botanical center, and the Iowa Historical Building. You'll also find reminders of Iowa's proud agrarian soul: the Iowa State Fairgrounds, historic farms, bountiful farmers' markets, and a reconstructed prairie with buffalo. Here you can see the latest musical imported from Broadway *and* take a bike ride past idyllic farms.

Driving west on Interstate 80 from Newton toward Des Moines, cropland gradually dissolves into urban sprawl. Rising above corn and soybean fields is a sign of the big city ahead, the forty-four-story 801 Grand, Iowa's tallest building. Continue west onto Interstate 235 through the city and you can't miss Des Moines's other dominant landmark, the gold-leaf dome of the elegant Iowa State Capitol. State Highways 415 and 141 take you northwest into the suburbs and the countryside.

For More Information

Central Iowa Tourism Region. *P.O. Box 454, Webster City 50595; (800)* *285–5842 or (515) 832–4808, www.iowatourism.org, citr@netins.net.*

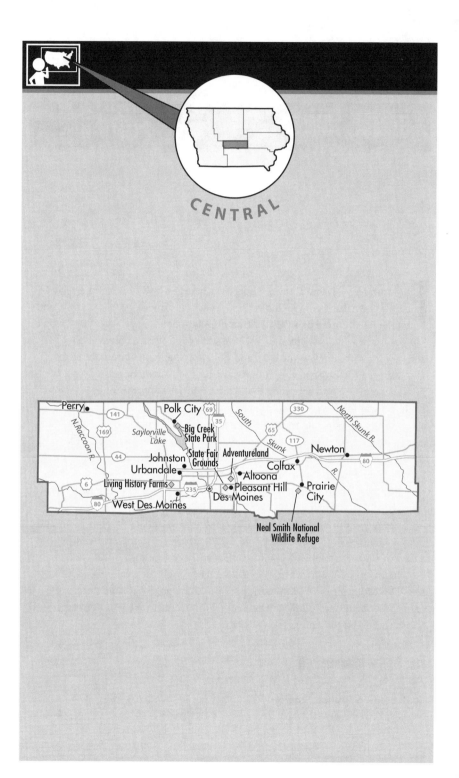

CENTRAL

Betsy's Top Ten Picks for Fun in Central Iowa

1. Iowa State Fair, Des Moines
2. Iowa Cubs Baseball, Des Moines
3. Living History Farms, Urbandale
4. Downtown Farmers' Market, Des Moines
5. Blank Park Zoo, Des Moines
6. Neal Smith National Wildlife Refuge and Prairie Learning Center, Prairie City
7. A Drake Bulldogs women's basketball game, Des Moines
8. Adventureland, Altoona
9. Whitewater University, Des Moines
10. A Des Moines Menace soccer game, Des Moines

Newton

Remember that lonely Maytag repairman? He got his start in Newton, home of Maytag Corporation, one of the world's largest appliance makers. Maytag has made washing machines since 1907—and lots of other things, from home appliances to World War II aircraft parts. The Maytag family also makes cheese (yes, cheese . . . see entry later in this section). Newton is north of Interstate 80 at exit 164.

AMBOY TRAIL RANCH (all ages, trail riding ages 10 and up)

4423 Iowa Street, Newton 50208; (641) 792–9932, www.amboyranch.com. Open 10:00 A.M. to 6:00 P.M. Monday through Saturday year-round, daily in October. $$–$$$$, depending on length of ride. Reservations are required.

At this one-hundred-acre recreational ranch just outside Newton, you must be at least ten years old to go on the forty-five- or ninety-minute guided trail ride, but anyone can do the twenty-minute ride in the corral. Hayrides are also available. Between late March and early July, great blue herons nest in the ranch's woods. Lodgings include one log cabin with a kitchenette and whirlpool, and two large tipis that sleep six.

INTERNATIONAL WRESTLING INSTITUTE AND MUSEUM (all ages)

1690 West Nineteenth Street South, Newton 50208; (641) 791–1517, www. wrestlingmuseum.org. Open 10:00 A.M. to 5:00 P.M. Tuesday through Saturday; closed Sunday and Monday. $, ages 6 and under **Free.**

In Iowa, high school and college wrestling matches draw large crowds. So what better place for this tribute to the world's oldest sport? Opened in 1998, the museum pays homage to Iowa's wrestling super-stars Cael Sanderson and Dan Gable. In 2002 Iowa State wrestler Sanderson finished his college career with a record of 159 wins and no losses. Gable won an Olympic gold medal in 1972, coached two gold-winning U.S. Olympic teams, and compiled the all-time winning record as wrestling coach at the University of Iowa. The museum has Gable's 1972 Olympic uniform and his 1971 World Championship gold medal. There's also a time line tracing wrestling from ancient Greece to Abe Lincoln's day, film clips of Tom Cruise and Kirk Douglas wrestling, and nineteenth-century wrestling cards.

MAYTAG DAIRY FARMS (all ages)

2282 East Eighth Street, Newton 50208; (800) 247–2458 or (641) 792–1133. Open 8:00 A.M. to 5:00 P.M. Monday through Friday and 9:00 A.M. to 1:00 P.M. Sunday. **Free.**

Sample one of the world's best blue cheeses, Maytag Blue, during a visit to a cheese shop near the farm and plant where it's made. Plan on spending about a half hour here, watching a twelve-minute video about the history of Maytag Blue and visiting the cheese-packing room (closed to the public on Saturday). Fred Maytag II, son of the Maytag Appliance Company's founder, started producing cheese in 1941 using a new Iowa State University method. Today, Maytag Blue is still made the same time-consuming way, in small batches from the milk of the Maytag Farms' prize Holstein-Friesian cows and aged for months in curing caves. Warning: Maytag Blue is strong stuff.

VALLE DRIVE-IN (all ages)

4074 Highway F48, Newton 50208; (641) 792–3558. Open daily from May through Labor Day, weekends through October. Gates open at 7:30 P.M. The first show is at 8:30 P.M. $$, ages 11 and under (accompanied by a parent) **Free.**

During the 1950s Iowa had almost seventy drive-in movie theaters. Today, only a handful remain, including the Valle Drive-In, which opened in Newton in 1948. It shows first-run films.

Where to Eat

LaCabana. *2002 First Avenue, Newton; (641) 791–1932.* Popular with locals, LaCabana is a Mexican restaurant on Newton's east side. $-$$

Uncle Nancy's CoffeeHouse and Eatery. *214 First Avenue West, Newton; (641) 787–9709.* Just west of the town square, this coffeehouse serves fresh made soups, sandwiches, and salads. $

Where to Stay

La Corsette Maison. *629 First Avenue East, Newton; (614) 792–6833.* Located in a 1911 Arts and Crafts home, this elegant downtown inn has five rooms and two suites, including one suitable for a family, and serves a complimentary gourmet breakfast. Gourmet dinner is available by reservation. $$-$$$$

For More Information

Newton Convention and Visitors Bureau. *113 First Avenue West, Newton 50208; (800) 798–0299 or (641) 792–0299, www.visitnewton.com.*

Colfax

Colfax is 9 miles west of Newton, off Interstate 80.

TRAINLAND U.S.A. (all ages)

3135 Highway 117 North, Colfax 50054; (515) 674–3813. Open 10:00 A.M. to 6:00 P.M. daily from Memorial Day through Labor Day. $, under age 2 **Free**.
This operating toy-train museum traces the history of American rail travel and includes many Lionel frontier, steam, and diesel trains.

Prairie City

From Colfax, take State Highway 117 7 miles south to Prairie City.

NEAL SMITH NATIONAL WILDLIFE REFUGE AND PRAIRIE LEARNING CENTER (all ages)

9981 Pacific Street, Prairie City 50228; (515) 994–3400, www.tallgrass.org. Open 9:00 A.M. to 4:00 P.M. Monday through Saturday and noon to 5:00 P.M. Sunday. **Free**.

The prairie's quiet beauty comes alive when you hike in this 5,000-acre park and visit its indoor Prairie Learning Center.

Amazing Iowa Facts About 150 years ago, tallgrass prairie covered 85 percent of Iowa's 36 million acres. Today, less than one-tenth of 1 percent of Iowa's native prairie remains.

Opened in 1991 about 20 miles east of Des Moines, the refuge is the federal government's most ambitious effort to restore and reconstruct the prairie. More than 200 varieties of seeds collected from tiny remnants of prairie found in south-central Iowa's old cemeteries and abandoned railroad tracks have been planted. The goal is to bring back hundreds of native plants and animals that greeted Iowa's first settlers in the mid-1880s. It's already happening. During the spring the refuge's 5 miles of trails wind through 12-foot-high prairie grasses and a colorful variety of native prairie flowers. Helpful signs explain what you're seeing. You may also spot pheasant, badgers, elk, white-tailed deer, and buffalo. If you can't find the buffalo on foot, try driving, following a marked auto tour. Don't forget to visit the Learning Center, an attractive modern building that has several interactive exhibits, including the popular prairie maze, with tunnels kids scurry through like gophers. An annual Buffalo Day Festival in early June celebrates the birth of buffalo calves, with activities including buffalo hair spinning, storytelling, buffalo chip throwing, Native American music, and buffalo burgers (not made from the refuge's thirty-six resident buffalo).

Where to Eat

Coffee Cup Cafe. *616 Fourth Street, Sully; (641) 594–3765.* Try the homemade pancakes, sausage, Dutch salad, and pie at this small-town cafe about 15 miles east of Prairie City that's been featured in *Gourmet* magazine. $

Altoona

Altoona is located near the intersection of Interstates 80 and 35, just east of Des Moines. Iowa children know it as the home of the state's largest amusement park, Adventureland. Iowa adults know it as the home of the large gambling casino, Prairie Meadows.

ADVENTURELAND (all ages)

3225 Adventureland Drive, Altoona 50316; (800) 532–1286 or (515) 266–2121, www.adventureland-usa.com. Open daily from mid-May to late August, weekends only from late April to mid-May and in September. Doors open at 10:00 A.M.; closing times vary between 6:00 and 10:00 P.M. $$$$, ages 3 and under Free.

One of Iowa's top tourist attractions, Adventureland is a 180-acre amusement park with more than one hundred rides including four roller coasters. Other popular rides include the Inverter (which swings riders 50 feet in the air, repeatedly flipping them 360 degrees), the Giant Sky-wheel (a gentle gondola ride across the park), and the Raging River (a white-water raft ride). For no extra charge, watch the small circus that performs daily under a big top, and an entertaining magic show. The park, which is off exit 142A of Interstate 80 at US 65, also has a hotel and campground.

Where to Eat

The Big Steer. *1715 Adventureland Drive, Altoona; (515) 967–6933.* Complete with ranch decor, the Big Steer is famous for steak and potatoes. $$

Where to Stay

Adventureland Campground. 3200 *Adventureland Drive, Altoona; (800) 532–1286 or (515) 265–7384.* Open year-round, this full-service campground has 281 RV campsites with electricity, modern showers and rest rooms, an outdoor pool, tent camping, and a free shuttle to the amusement park. $

Adventureland Inn. *I–80 at US 65, Altoona; (800) 910–5382 or (515) 265–7321.* Part of the Adventureland complex, this hotel has an indoor pool. About half of the 130 rooms are poolside; four are suites. $$–$$$$

Settle Inn. *2101 Adventureland Drive, Altoona; (888) 222–8224 or (515) 967–7888.* Three blocks from Adventureland, the Settle Inn has sixty-seven rooms, an indoor pool, and a mini arcade. $–$$$$

For More Information

Altoona Area Chamber of Commerce. *119 Second Street Southeast, Altoona 50009; (515) 967–3366.*

Des Moines

Des Moines is growing both downtown and in its suburbs, which include Pleasant Hill, Ankeny, West Des Moines, Clive, Urbandale, and Johnston. Cranes and construction sites dot the downtown area, where more than $1 billion worth of new development is under way, including construction of a new science center, events center, and public library. In the suburbs, new homes, apartment complexes, and a huge new shopping mall are sprouting in what were once cornfields.

The Des Moines and Raccoon Rivers meet downtown. East of the Des Moines River are the state fairgrounds, the state capitol complex, and the East Village, a newly vibrant commercial area with chic renovated brick buildings. To the west is the business

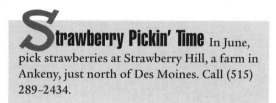

Strawberry Pickin' Time In June, pick strawberries at Strawberry Hill, a farm in Ankeny, just north of Des Moines. Call (515) 289-2434.

district, a tight cluster of office buildings connected by indoor skywalks that shelter pedestrians from harsh weather. Surrounding downtown, especially to the west and north, are old leafy neighborhoods with elegant homes, comfortable middle-class areas, pockets of urban poverty, and some lively commercial streets, including Ingersoll and Beaverdale Avenues.

During the weekday Des Moines bustles with state government and insurance company workers. (With more than sixty insurance companies, this is the world's third largest insurance center.) On weekends and at night, areas of activity include the Court Avenue entertainment district and the Sherman Hill National Historic District, plus West Des Moines's Valley Junction. In the summer the city comes alive with outdoor farmers' markets, festivals, ball games, and concerts.

WHITEWATER UNIVERSITY FUN PARK (all ages)

5401 Northeast 12th Avenue, Pleasant Hill 50317; (515) 265–4904. Park open 11:00 A.M. to 7:00 P.M. daily from Memorial Day through Labor Day. Mini golf and go-carts available 10:00 A.M. to 10:00 P.M. daily from June through August and on weekends in March, April, May, September, and October. $$, children under 42 inches tall Free.

Located in an eastern bedroom community of Des Moines, this popular water park has a wave pool, water slides, lazy river, children's play pool, miniature golf, and twin-engine go-carts.

IOWA STATE FAIR (all ages)

East 30th Street and University Avenue, Des Moines 50317; (515) 262–3111. $$, ages 5 and under ꟻɾₑₑ. *Advance purchase tickets are cheaper.*

The Iowa State Fair is one of the nation's oldest, biggest, and best state fairs, packed with people, animals, rides, food, entertainment, farm machinery, you name it. Held each year for eleven days in August, it's a major event that draws almost a million visitors. Some Iowans make this their summer vacation, camping nearby.

Tackling the Iowa State Fair

There are always fresh surprises at "The Fair." (In 1999, the surprise was a life-size depiction of the Last Supper, sculpted out of 1,700 pounds of butter.) Even so, it's wise to arrive with a game plan:

- To avoid crowds, go on a weekday morning. Wear hats, sturdy shoes, and sunblock. Carry bottled water, tissues, and an ATM card. Study the daily events schedule you receive at the gate.

- First stop: the livestock barns to see the astonishing Big Boar (more than 1,000 pounds) and the even more astonishing Big Bull (more than 3,000 pounds). There are also baby pigs, sheep, chicken, cows, horses, even elk and reindeer.

- Second stop: the dairy barn for a big ice-cream cone, then on to the agriculture building to see the Butter Cow, a 600-pound cow sculpted out of butter. Check out the prize-winning produce and get free samples from pork, beef, and dairy producers.

- Third stop: the Bill Riley Stage for live entertainment, from pint-size tap dancers competing in the famous "talent sprouts" concert to the ninety-nine teen-age girls (one from each of Iowa's ninety-nine counties) competing in the Miss Iowa State Fair contest.

- With small children, ride the toy train that chugs through the park. With bigger kids, try the giant slide.

- For lunch, devour classic fair food: corn dogs, grilled turkey tenderloins, curly fries, fresh squeezed lemonade, and funnel cakes dusted with powdered sugar.

- Last stop: the noisy chaos of the Midway, for carnival rides and games.

SLEEPY HOLLOW SPORTS PARK (ages 5 and up)

4051 Dean Avenue, Des Moines 50317; (515) 262–4100, www.sleepyhollow sportspark.com. Open 4:00 to 9:00 P.M. Tuesday through Friday, 9:00 A.M. to 9:00 P.M. Saturday, and 11:00 A.M. to 9:00 P.M. Sunday from mid-December through mid-March; 8:00 A.M. to 6:00 P.M. daily in spring and fall; 8:00 A.M. to 10 P.M. daily in summer. $$$.

Sand volleyball, swimming, miniature golf, go-carts, a driving range, and batting cages are among the offerings at this sixty-acre sports park and family recreation center. In the winter there's snow tubing, snowboarding, and skiing. In the autumn take a hayrack ride and visit a haunted house.

HERITAGE CAROUSEL IN UNION PARK (all ages)

East Ninth and Thompson Streets, Des Moines 50316; (515) 362–5958, www.heritagecarousel.org. Open noon to 7:00 P.M. Tuesday through Thursday, 11:00 A.M. to 8:00 P.M. Friday through Sunday from May through mid-September. $, adults ride **Free** *when accompanying a child.*

Located in a hilly city park on the east side, this colorful wooden carousel with hand-painted scenes of Des Moines landmarks has thirty carved animals and two chariots that revolve to the music of a Stinson band organ. Don't miss the nearby Rocket Slide, a winding slide that resembles a space rocket.

The Weather Beacon Wondering about the weather tomorrow? Check out the color of the lights on the "Weather Beacon," a 500-foot television broadcast tower rising above downtown Des Moines. Then remember this popular local rhyme: *Weather beacon red, warmer weather ahead. Weather beacon white, colder weather in sight. Weather beacon green, no change foreseen. Weather beacon flashing night or day, precipitation on the way.*

Like many kids, my stepdaughter Emma loved the Weather Beacon when she was little. Once when we visited Kansas City, she asked us with a puzzled expression, "Where's the weather beacon in this town?"

IOWA STATE CAPITOL (ages 5 and up)

East Ninth Street and Grand Avenue, Des Moines 50319; (515) 281–5591. Open for tours 9:30 A.M. to 3:00 P.M. Monday through Saturday. Tours are generally every half hour, but call ahead. **Free.**

Completed in 1886, Iowa's state capitol looks like something out of St. Petersburg, Russia. Its twenty-three-karat gold-leafed dome looms 275 feet above the ground and is flanked by four small green copper domes. Inside, the capitol is just as grand. For a self-guided tour, pick up a brochure sheet at the information desk. Better yet, take a free one-hour guided tour. The guides tell interesting tales about the capitol's colorful history and point out hidden decorative details (like the mysterious optical illusion in the intricate Italian mosaic on the second floor). They'll also take you up to the main dome's rim, by climbing up a hidden spiral staircase through a dingy attic. Other highlights include the ornate Senate and House chambers, the Governor's outer office, the Iowa Supreme Court Chambers (where, during the guided tour, children may get to stage a courtroom drama), and the law library with its iron catwalks and spiraling staircases. Another favorite is the collection of First Lady dolls, each dressed in her inaugural gown.

Amazing Iowa Facts Every four years, Iowans expect (and often get) up-close-and-personal contact with presidential candidates, thanks to the Iowa Caucuses, the first major political event of the country's presidential race.

IOWA HISTORICAL BUILDING (ages 5 and up)
600 East Locust Street, Des Moines 50319; (515) 281–5111. Open 9:00 A.M. to 4:30 P.M. Tuesday through Saturday and noon to 4:30 P.M. Sunday; also open on Monday from June through August. **Free.**

Three vintage airplanes dangle above the four-story atrium of this dramatic modern granite and glass building that houses a treasure trove of Iowa historical artifacts and exhibits. Plan on spending at least two hours exploring the museum's first two floors, which have permanent exhibits showing how Iowa's natural resources have been used since prehistoric times and what life was like for Native Americans and various waves of settlers. Another interesting exhibit, *Honor the Colors,* highlights Iowans who fought in the Civil War and the state's recent efforts to preserve 138 Iowa regiment battle flags. The fragile flags, some blood-stained and with cannon holes, were painstakingly removed in 2002 from the State Capitol where they'd been displayed for more than a century. The museum also has a restaurant and an excellent gift shop.

A Rubiner Family Adventure

In a stroke of luck, my two children recently went to school for six weeks at the Iowa Historical Building while their elementary school was under construction. They fell in love with the place, and one day they gave me a guided tour. We had lots of fun walking inside a mock coal mine and a mock Native American bark hut. We scraped a pretend buffalo hide and learned how to play ancient Native American games. Playing pioneer farmer, we pushed a plow, pulled a two-person saw, and carried two buckets of water using a shoulder harness. I felt like a kid again . . . until we got to a permanent exhibit called *A Few of Our Favorite Things*. On display, among one hundred relics from the twentieth century, was a pair of hot pants just like the ones I wore as a teenager in the 1970s. My kids were astonished when I told them this, and I felt like a kid no more.

DES MOINES BOTANICAL CENTER (all ages)

909 East River Drive, Des Moines 50316; (515) 323–8900. Open 10:00 A.M. to 5:00 P.M. daily, until 9:00 P.M. Friday. $, under age 6 Free.

For a pick-me-up during a cold Iowa winter, stroll through the botanical center's moist indoor tropical forest, past a waterfall and brightly colored birds. Located on fourteen acres along the Des Moines River's east bank, the Botanical Center has a glass-domed conservatory containing one of the Midwest's largest collections of tropical, subtropical, and desert plants. It also has a cafe and an interesting gift shop. Check for special events and activities for children, especially during the winter holidays.

IOWA CUBS BASEBALL (all ages)

Sec Taylor Stadium, 350 Southwest First Street, Des Moines 50309; (800) 464–2827 or (515) 243–6111. Open 9:00 A.M. to 5:00 P.M. Monday through Friday from April through September. $.

Even if you don't like baseball, there's nothing like a clear summer night at this comfortable modern ballpark overlooking the Des Moines and Raccoon Rivers, with the gold dome of the Iowa State Capitol shimmering on the horizon. The Iowa Cubs ("Cubbies") are the farm team for the Chicago Cubs. The games are a lot of fun, with goofy entertainment including trivia contests, pitching contests, gregarious mascots, and a portable cannon that shoots hot dogs up into the stands. Some Friday night games are followed by fireworks.

BLANK PARK ZOO (all ages)

7401 Southwest Ninth Street, Des Moines, 50315; (515) 285–4722, www.
blankpark.com. Open 10:00 A.M. to 5:00 P.M. daily except Thanksgiving, Christ-
mas Eve, and Christmas. $$ for adults, $ for ages 3 through 11, under age 3
Free.

There are bigger, maybe even better zoos, but if you're used to
sprawling, crowded, expensive big-city zoos, you'll be delighted and
relieved after a visit to Des Moines's zoo. There are no long lines, elbow-
to-elbow crowds, or parking hassles. Located a few miles south of
downtown, the zoo is small (a cozy twenty-two acres), manageable (you
can be in and out in two-and-one-half hours), and the kids see animals
up close. There are more than 1,000 animals and 90 species from
flamingos to bongos, camels to crocodiles. As children race along a
path in front of a woodland landscape, a snow leopard runs with them
behind a fence. As they stand atop a wooden tree house, a giraffe nib-
bles hay dangling from a tall pole. They can watch penguins waddle and
sea lions dive—from only a few feet away. After thirty-five years, the zoo
recently became a year-round attraction, with two new indoor spaces.
The Discovery Center re-creates the water-fed habitats of more than 200
animals, including lynx, marmosets (monkeys), dwarf caimans (small
crocodiles), geckos, scorpions, boa constrictors, and Egyptian fruit bats.
There's a chilly Alpine mountain forest with cold snow, a humid rain for-
est with a rickety suspension bridge, and a dark damp cave with drip-
ping stalactites and stalagmites. The *Great Cats* exhibit is home to
Himalayan snow leopards, Siberian tigers, and African lions. It's also fun
to feed carp and goats in the farm area, wander among emus and pea-
cocks in the Australian area, watch the seals being fed, and crawl
through a short tunnel into a chamber where you're surrounded by
prairie dogs. There's an outdoor grill for summer months and an indoor
cafe open year-round.

DES MOINES DOWNTOWN FARMERS' MARKET (all ages)

Court Avenue in downtown Des Moines; (515) 243–6625. Open 7:00 A.M. to
noon Saturday from early May through late October. **Free**.

For proof that Des Moines has street life and diversity, visit this lively
farmers' market that resembles an international street fair. Next to
stands overflowing with fresh tomatoes, lemongrass, zucchini, and zin-
nias are imported Polish pottery, Hmong crafts, jugglers, Peruvian pipe
musicians, and magicians. It's a feast for the eye and the stomach, with
an array of classic American food—apple cider, mustards, breads, pies,

goat cheese, and sticky buns—and interesting ethnic food, including Middle Eastern hummus, Indian potato cakes,

Amazing Iowa Facts Des Moines is home to the Downtown School, a public elementary school that is one of the nation's largest "work-site schools," specifically located near where parents work.

and Mexican breakfast burritos. This is *the* place to see and be seen. And where else can you have Laotian egg rolls and homemade root beer for breakfast?

TERRACE HILL (ages 8 and up)

2300 Grand Avenue, Des Moines 50312; (515) 281–3604, www.terracehill.org. Open 10:00 A.M. to 1:30 P.M. Tuesday through Saturday from March through December. Closed January and February. $ for tours.

Now the home of Iowa's governor, this fancy 1869 Victorian mansion was built high on a grassy hill by Iowa's first millionaire, Benjamin F. Allen. During the forty-five-minute tour, you'll see elegant nineteenth-century public rooms, the carriage house, and a brief video. (The governor lives on the third floor.)

Summer in the City Des Moines offers a variety of popular family-friendly concerts and programs, including:

- **Saturday in the Park,** a family-style gathering at Gray's Lake with children's activities, food, crafts, and live music on weekends in May and June.

- **Jazz in July,** more than thirty free jazz concerts throughout the city.

- **ShowMotion,** a traveling stage with family performances.

- **Nightfall on the River,** evening concerts at the Simon Estes Amphitheater south of City Hall at East First and Locust Streets.

- **The Des Moines Arts Festival,** a three-day arts and crafts show in late June with live entertainment, food, and children's art activities held on the bridges downtown.

Call (515) 280–3222 or visit www.metroarts.org.

SALISBURY HOUSE (ages 8 and up)

4025 Tonawanda Drive, Des Moines 50312; (515) 274–1777, www.salisbury house.org. Tours available at 11:00 A.M. and 2:00 P.M. Tuesday through Saturday in March, April, October, and November; 11:00 A.M. and 2:00 P.M. Tuesday through Friday in May; 11:00 A.M., 1:00 P.M., and 2:00 P.M. Monday through Friday and 1:00, 2:00 and 3:00 P.M. Sunday from June through September; 2:00 P.M. Tuesday through Friday in December. Closed January and February. $ for tours.

Children will be particularly captivated by the knights' armor on display in this forty-two-room castlelike mansion modeled after the King's House in Salisbury, England. Set on a ten-acre wooded estate, Salisbury House was built in the 1920s by Carl and Edith Weeks. Featuring Tudor, Gothic, and Carolean architectural details and real sixteenth-century English oak rafters dating back to Shakespearean days, the mansion is filled with art, paintings, and tapestries.

Renaissance Festival During the third weekend in May, the Salisbury House hosts an annual Renaissance Festival at Water Works Park on the Raccoon River near downtown Des Moines. There are children's activities, jousting on horseback, craftspeople, food, period music, and dancing. Admission is charged; ages 5 and under get in **Free.**

DES MOINES ART CENTER (all ages)

4700 Grand Avenue, Des Moines 50312; (515) 277–4405, www.desmoinesart center.org. Open 11:00 A.M. to 4:00 P.M. Tuesday through Saturday, until 9:00 P.M. Thursday, and noon to 4:00 P.M. Sunday. **Free.**

Children who are regulars at this nationally known contemporary art museum often rush right to "The Butter Cow," an amusing sculpture of a famous Iowa State Fair attraction, a huge cow sculpted in butter. Press a button and the cow bats her heavy eyelashes, flaps her lips, and talks with a glamorous foreign accent. Officially titled *Agricultural Building,* this Red Grooms sculpture is among the highlights at the Art Center, which openly courts children with art classes and family-friendly open houses. Ask at the information desk for a free family backpack filled with fun educational activities for children three and older. Some are tailored to temporary exhibits, others to the permanent collection of nineteenth- through twenty-first-century paintings, sculpture, and video installations. The art center is also known for its architecture, with three distinct wings, each designed by a famous architect: Eriel Saarinen, I. M. Pei, and Richard Meier. Other highlights for children include an enclosed stone spiral staircase, a giant electrical plug by Claes Oldenburg, and an installation called *Jewelry Display Window* that creates a miniature world out of jewelry store boxes. There's a stylish cafe with grown-up food and a terrific selection of children's educational toys in the gift shop.

SCIENCE CENTER OF IOWA (all ages)

Greenwood-Ashworth Park, 4500 Grand Avenue, Des Moines 50312; (515) 274–4138, www.sciowa.org. Open 10:00 A.M. to 5:00 P.M. Monday through Saturday and noon to 5:00 P.M. Sunday. $$ for adults, $ for ages 2 through 12, under 2 **Free**.

A $60 million science center at a new downtown site off Court Avenue is scheduled to open in 2005. For now, this small interactive museum on the edge of a leafy park offers permanent exhibits on the physical and environmental sciences, a small planetarium with daily free shows and laser light matinees ($1.50 per person), and the Challenger Learning Center, two rooms that simulate a space station and mission control. There is also usually a fun traveling exhibit. When you arrive, check the schedule of free demonstrations; they're typically brief and interesting. For ages seven and under, a play space (*Small Discoveries*) with toys, games, and crafts is open weekday afternoons and all day on weekends. (An adult must accompany children.) Older children will enjoy the turtles, snakes, and fossils in the environmental exhibit. On Saturdays and Sundays, families can take a forty-five-minute simulated "Flight to Mars" or rendezvous with a comet in the Challenger Learning Center. A fifth-grade reading ability and reservations are recommended.

Presidential Sportscaster
The nation's 40th president, Ronald Reagan, worked in Des Moines in the 1930s as a radio sports announcer. Today, a plaque commemorating his four-year stay is in Des Moines's Court Avenue entertainment district.

DRAKE UNIVERSITY BULLDOGS BASKETBALL AND FOOTBALL (all ages)

Drake's Knapp Center and Drake Stadium on Forest Avenue, Des Moines 50311; ticket office, (515) 271–3791, www.drakebulldogs.org. $$, ages 15 and under usually **Free** *when accompanied by a paying adult.*

For family fun on a cold winter weekend, don't miss a Drake women's basketball game. The men also play basketball at the sparkling modern Knapp Center, but the women's games—often on Thursday evenings and Sunday afternoons—are especially popular with families. Kids are everywhere, and not just in the stands. Some perform as cheerleaders (with their parents). Some hang out near the baskets, ready to rush out with brooms to sweep off the court. In addition to fiercely competitive basketball, there's a festive, fun atmosphere. Free T-shirts and balls are thrown into the stands as Spike, Drake's bulldog mascot, offers handshakes and hugs. The halftime show is often a lively high school dance team. Bulldog football, played at Drake's 18,000-seat red-brick stadium next to the Knapp Center, is also a fun fall family outing.

The Drake Relays One of the world's top track-and-field meets, the Drake Relays are held the last weekend in April at Drake's stadium. Sellout crowds attend the three-day event to watch some of the nation's best college and Olympic athletes compete. For tickets call (515) 271-DOGS. Also fun is the Beautiful Bulldog Contest, usually held a few days before the relays in downtown Des Moines's Nollen Plaza. Bulldog owners dress their cherished pets in goofy outfits and vie for the honor of being Drake's mascot.

DES MOINES MENACE SOCCER (all ages)

Cara McGrane Memorial Stadium at Hoover High School, 50th Street and Aurora Avenue, Des Moines 50310; (515) 226–9890, www.dmmenace.org. $$ for adults, $ for ages 14 and under.

Soccer is very popular in Des Moines, and so is the Menace, a minor-league team that has been playing for years at a local high school. A new 6,000-seat stadium with a state-of-the-art field—the first of its kind in Iowa—is scheduled to open sometime in 2004 at 138th Street and Urbandale Avenue in Urbandale.

Amazing Iowa Facts More than 10,000 players and up to 73,000 spectators flock to Des Moines in March for the weeklong Iowa Girls State High School Basketball Tournament, held continuously since 1920.

Des Moines Area Culture for Kids

- **The Des Moines Civic Center,** 221 Walnut Street (515–243–1140, www.civiccenter.org), is the city's downtown performing arts center, offering professional touring theater productions, some specifically for children.

- **The Des Moines Symphony,** 221 Walnut Street (515–280–4000, www.dmsymphony.org), performs several annual family concerts, including the popular Snowflake Celebration at the Civic Center and the Yankee Doodle Pops concert, a free July 3rd performance on the State Capitol grounds.

- **Ingersoll Dinner Theater,** 3711 Ingersoll Avenue (515–274–4686, www.dinnertheater.org), offers several children's programs.

- **Iowa Youth Chorus,** 1011 Locust Street (515–262–8312, www.iowa youthchorus.org), has sixteen choirs with more than 400 children ages six to eighteen. The choruses have two annual concerts at the Civic Center, plus an international children's choir festival every other year.

- **Des Moines Metro Opera,** 106 West Boston Avenue in Indianola (515–961–6221, www.dmmo.org), presents one of the nation's largest opera festivals each summer. This company, based 15 miles south of Des Moines at Simpson College, holds an annual June family event called Peanut Butter and Puccini, which includes a forty-five-minute production and backstage tour.

- **Temple for the Performing Arts,** 1011 Locust Street (515–288–4700), opened in 2002 in a former Masonic temple with an elegant ballroom. After undergoing a $7.5 million renovation, this new cultural enter-tainment center offers concerts, theater, music lessons, shops, and restaurants. It's also the new home of the Iowa Youth Chorus and Iowa Youth Symphony.

- **Veterans Memorial Auditorium,** 833 Fifth Avenue (515–323–5400), is the city's major arena and exhibit area. It hosts sports events, ice shows, concerts, circuses, rodeos, and motor sports, and will become part of the new $201 million Iowa Events Center in 2004.

GRAY'S LAKE PARK (all ages)

1700 Fleur Drive, Des Moines 50309; (515) 237–1386. Open 6:00 A.M. to 10:00 P.M. daily from November through March, 5:00 A.M. to midnight from April through October. **Free.**

This small lake south of downtown with a view of the Des Moines skyline has blossomed, thanks to a recent multimillion dollar face-lift. By day, walkers, joggers, in-line skaters, and bicyclists enjoy the new Kruidenier Trail, a 1.9-mile trail around the lake. There are also picnic tables, boat rentals, a playground, and a beach for swimming and fishing. By night, a quarter-mile pedestrian footbridge that stretches across the lake lights up in a rainbow of color.

Other Popular Des Moines Parks

- **Greenwood Park,** behind the Des Moines Art Center off Grand Avenue at 45th Street, has a lovely rose garden and pond with an environmental art project by Mary Miss.

- **Waterworks Park and Arboretum,** 2201 Valley Drive, near downtown.

- **Waveland Park,** 49th Street and University Avenue.

- **Yellow Banks Park,** 6801 SE 32nd Avenue.

KATE GOLDMAN CHILDREN'S THEATER AT THE DES MOINES PLAYHOUSE (ages 5 and up)

831 42nd Street, Des Moines 50312; (515) 277–6261. Performances usually at 7:00 P.M. Thursday and Friday, 1:00 and 4:00 P.M. Saturday, and 3:00 P.M. Sunday. $$.

This modern children's theater in one of the nation's oldest community theaters stages several family productions, each lasting one to two hours, with matinees and evening performances.

HISTORIC VALLEY JUNCTION (all ages)

Fifth Street, West Des Moines 50265; (515) 222–3642, www.valleyjunction. com. **Free.**

A quaint historic district perfect for wandering, Valley Junction has 120 antique shops, boutiques, art galleries, and restaurants. With children, check out three stores: Winnie's Toy Orphanage, A Small World, and Whatta' Dish, a paint-your-own-pottery place. From mid-May through mid-September, a farmers' market is held Thursday from 4:00 to 8:00 P.M., offering children's activities, entertainment, and quick-and-easy dinner options. Valley Junction also hosts annual art fairs with a children's art area in May and September, plus two Holiday Open Houses at Thanksgiving, featuring Santa and Mrs. Claus (on a West Des Moines fire engine), carolers, free hot cocoa and baked goodies in the shops, and more than 100,000 Christmas lights.

JORDAN HOUSE (ages 8 and up)

2001 Fuller Road, West Des Moines 50265; (515) 225–1286. Open 1:00 to 4:00 P.M. Wednesday and Saturday and 2:00 to 5:00 P.M. Sunday from May through October. $.

Not only can you tour this stately Victorian home that was once an Underground Railroad stop, your guide may be a descendant of James C. Jordan, Iowa's first white settler, who built this house in 1850. The oldest structure in West Des Moines, Jordan House has sixteen period rooms and an Underground Railroad museum. The guided tour lasts about an hour and includes a ten-minute video. Ask about the ghost of Eda, one of the settler's eleven children.

A Rubiner Family Adventure During our many rides on Iowa bike trails, we've seen a wide variety of animals—cows, horses, birds, dogs, snakes, turtles—usually at a comfortable distance. But one blustery spring day on the Chichaqua Valley Trail near Bondurant, our family was pedaling along when we spotted a distressed sow and several of her piglets running right toward us. After we got over our initial shock, my husband and I quickly got the kids over to the side of the trail and tried to stay as calm and still as possible. The pigs ran right by us (and all the way home, we hope).

DES MOINES BUCCANEERS HOCKEY (ages 5 and up)

Metro Ice Sports Arena, 7201 Hickman Road, Urbandale 50322; (515) 278–9757, www.bucshockey.org. Friday and Saturday night games (sometimes Sunday) from September through April. Reservations are required. $–$$ for adults, $ for ages 12 and under.

A junior A team in the United States Hockey League, "the Bucs" play thirty-two home games a year.

Outdoor Fun

Favorite Central Iowa trails for biking, hiking, jogging, walking, and in-line skating include:

- **Clive Greenbelt Trail,** a 7-mile paved trail through suburban Des Moines.

- **Great Western and Bill Riley Trails,** a 16.5-mile paved trail from Des Moines south to Martensdale.

- **Neal Smith Trail,** a 24-mile paved trail from Des Moines north past Saylorville Lake to Big Creek State Park.

- **Raccoon River Valley Trail,** a 57-mile paved trail from suburban Des Moines northwest to Jefferson.

- **Chichaqua Valley Trail,** a 20-mile paved trail from Bondurant east to Baxter.

LIVING HISTORY FARMS (all ages)

2600 111th Street, Urbandale 50322; (515) 278–5286, www.livinghistory farms.org. Open 9:00 A.M. to 5:00 P.M. daily from May through late October. $$ for adults, $ for ages 4 through 12, under age 4 **Free**.

For a hands-on introduction to Iowa's agricultural heritage, visit this open-air museum in a western suburb. It features three period farms—an Ioway Indian Village (1700), a Pioneer Farm (1850), and a 1900 farm—each painstakingly re-created to look, feel, sound, and smell like the real thing. "Interpreters" in period dress demonstrate chores, from sheep sheering to harvesting corn, and answer questions. Plan on at least a three-hour visit, and don't dawdle at the first stop, a re-created 1875 frontier town with wooden boardwalks lined with clapboard shops. It's interesting, and the General Store sells tasty lemon drops, but the farms are the real attraction. A ten-minute ride on a tractor-drawn cart brings you to a gentle three-quarters-of-a-mile woodland trail linking the three farms. At the Ioway Village, a small dirt clearing in the forest, you'll learn how Iowa's first farmers, Native Americans, planted lush gardens of pumpkin, squash, corn, and beans. At the forty-acre 1850s farm, you'll see the all-important oxen that do the heavy farm work, plus hogs, a milk cow, sheep, and chickens. Corn, wheat, and potatoes grow in the fields. Step inside a simple one-room log cabin to experience firsthand the cramped quarters shared by a large pioneer family. The 1900 farm is much bigger (120 acres) and the livin' is a little easier, thanks to horses that help with the farm work. The farmhouse is a pretty white frame building with a picket fence, a cozy parlor, and a huge iron stove. Outside, beyond the windmill and the big red barn, you might see a horse-drawn plow in the field. For a meal visit the nearby Iowa Machine Shed, a restaurant that bills itself as "a tribute to the hardworking American farmer" with "homestyle, made-from-scratch cookin' with all the fixin's," including huge portions of beef and pork. The decor is rough wood paneling and old farm machinery. The restaurant is at 11151 Hickman Road in Urbandale; call (515) 270-6818.

SAYLORVILLE LAKE AND VISITOR CENTER (all ages)

5600 Northwest 78th Avenue, Johnston 50131; (515) 276–4656, www.saylor villelake.org. Open daily, generally during daylight hours. Visitor center open 10:00 A.M. to 4:00 P.M. Saturday and noon to 4:00 P.M. Sunday from January through March, 10:00 A.M. to 4:00 P.M. Monday through Friday, 10:00 A.M. to 5:00 P.M. Saturday, and noon to 5:00 P.M. Sunday in April, May, September, and October; closed November and December. **Free**. *Camping, $.*

The 26,000-acre Saylorville Lake project stretches for more than 50 miles up the Des Moines River Valley. The 5,950-acre man-made lake with two sand beaches is popular for camping, boating, swimming, hiking, fishing, picnicking, disk golf, and bike trails. The visitor center is a great place to visit with children, especially when you're feeling cooped up during the winter. It has hands-on exhibits of native wildlife, a fifteen-minute nature film, and live reptiles and fish. Nearby is a half-mile woodland hiking trail and a butterfly garden (prime butterfly viewing is July through September). Saylorville has several campgrounds. Cherry Glen campground, with 125 sites on a thirteen-acre wooded ridge, is the oldest and most popular. To reserve on-line, visit www.reserveusa.com, or call (888) 448–1474.

JESTER PARK (all ages)

11407 Northwest Jester Park Drive, Granger 50109; (515) 323–5300. Open 6:30 A.M. to 10:30 P.M. daily from mid-April through mid-October, during daylight hours the rest of the year. **Free**. *Camping, $.*

This sprawling county park bordering Saylorville Lake is popular for camping and family gatherings, with picnic areas, five shelters, three fishing ponds, a fun playground, hiking and bike trails, boat ramps, and real live buffalo. A nearby riding stable offers horseback riding and hayrack rides from April through October; call (515) 999–2818.

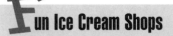un Ice Cream Shops

- **Bauder Pharmacy.** 3802 Ingersoll Avenue, Des Moines, (515) 255–1124.

- **Blue Sky Creamery.** 107 Northeast Delaware Street, Ankeny, (515) 964–4366.

- **Classic Frozen Custard.** 4000 Southeast 14th Street, Des Moines, (515) 287–1194, and 1248 Eighth Street, West Des Moines, (515) 457–8295.

- **Culver's Frozen Custard and ButterBurgers.** 8650 Plum Drive, Urbandale, (515) 270–8699.

- **Dairy Zone.** 2219 East University, Des Moines, (515) 265–7824.

- **Fifth Street Fountain.** 115 Fifth Street, West Des Moines (Valley Junction), (515) 279–3716.

- **Granny's Sweet Freeze.** 3417 Hubbell Avenue, Des Moines, (515) 266–0887.

- **Maggiemoo's Creamery.** 2000 University, West Des Moines, (515) 225–1065.

- **Snookie's Malt Shop.** 1810 Beaver Avenue, Des Moines, (515) 255–0638.

Where to Eat

B-Bop's. *1105 73rd Street, Windsor Heights; (515) 279–5757.* This drive-thru joint with outdoor tables serves the best fast-food charbroiled burgers and fries in town. There are several other Des Moines and Central Iowa locations. $

Chat Noir. *644 18th Street, Des Moines; (515) 244–1353.* Adventurous young diners will like the muffuletta sandwich, whole wheat crepes, soups, and dessert crepes at this hip, European-style cafe in a restored house in the Sherman Hill historic district. $–$$

Drake Diner. *1111 25th Street, Des Moines; (515) 277–1111.* A popular family spot near Drake University, this retro diner serves burgers, great shakes, and blue-plate specials, and has a children's menu with fun activities. Try also the **North End Diner,** 5055 Merle Hay Road, Johnston (515–276–5151) and the **West End Diner,** 3535 Westtown Parkway, West Des Moines (515–222–3131). $–$$

Java Joe's. *214 Fourth Street, Des Moines; (515) 288–5282.* This funky downtown coffeehouse with exposed brick walls and a hidden playroom for young children serves homemade soups, snacks, and sandwiches, including PB&J, Pop-Tarts, and Rice Krispies Treats. $

The Royal Mile. *210 Fourth Street, Des Moines; (515) 280–3771.* This pub feels like the real thing, with a lively bar downstairs and a family-friendly restaurant upstairs that serves pub grub, from delicious fish and chips to shepherd's pie (a meat and mashed potato pie) and ploughman's lunch (a cheese plate). $

Stella's Blue Sky Diner. *3289 100th Street, Urbandale; (515) 278–0550.* Have a sassy server pour a milk shake into a glass you hold on your head at this 1950s-style diner with burgers and sandwiches. $

The Tavern. *205 5th Street, West Des Moines; (515) 255–9827.* Pizza and huge bowls of pasta are served in a casual family dining room in the historic Valley Junction district. You'll find the same at the two other Taverns, 1755 50th Street in West Des Moines (515–223–6700) and 1106 Army Post Road in Des Moines (515–285–8050). $$

Thai Flavors. *1254 East 14th Street, Des Moines; (515) 262–4658.* Diners pick their level of spiciness, from mild to very very hot, at this superb Thai restaurant in an East Side shopping plaza. A mean Pad Thai and intricately flavored hot-and-sour chicken soup (Tom Ka Kai) are served. $

Waveland Cafe. *4708 University Avenue, Des Moines; (515) 279–4341.* You won't be the only family waiting in line for a weekend breakfast at this popular neighborhood cafe. The eggs, sausage, hash browns, and pancakes are worth the wait. $

Where to Stay

Carter House Inn. *640 20th Street, Des Moines; (515) 288–7850.* Located in the historic Sherman Hill district, this Victorian home with antiques has four rooms, each with private bath. $$

Comfort Suites at Living History Farms. *11167 Hickman Road, Urbandale; (800) 395–7675 or (515) 276–1126.* Next to Living History Farms in the western suburbs, Comfort Suites has 101 rooms and a large indoor pool. $$$–$$$$

Embassy Suites on the River. *101 East Locust Street, Des Moines; (515) 244–1700.* Overlooking the Des Moines River, this downtown hotel with a fancy lobby, restaurant, and indoor pool has 234 rooms, all suites. $$$–$$$$

Fairfield Inn by Marriott. *1600 114th Street, Clive; (515) 226–1600.* Just off Interstates 80 and 35 in the western suburbs, this 135-room chain hotel has an outdoor pool. $–$$

Holiday Inn Express at Drake. *1140 24th Street, Des Moines; (515) 255–4000.* This is a 52-room easy-in-and-out hotel near Drake University. $$

Wildwood Lodge. *11431 Forest Avenue, Clive; (800) 728–1223 or (515) 222–9876.* This attractive lodge-themed hotel has ninety-four rooms and ten suites, including a family suite, and a pool. The lobby has a huge stone fireplace and rustic furniture. $$$–$$$$.

For More Information

Greater Des Moines Convention and Visitors Bureau. *405 Sixth Avenue, Suite 201, Des Moines 50309;* *(800) 451–2625 or (515) 286–4960, www.seedesmoines.com.*

Polk City

Polk City is 11 miles northwest of Des Moines off State Highway 415.

BIG CREEK STATE PARK AND LAKE (all ages)
Located on State Highway 415, 2 miles north of Polk City; (515) 984–6473. Open year-round, 4:00 A.M. to 10:30 P.M. **Free.**

This 3,550-acre state park is dominated by an 866-acre man-made lake. Big Creek has a popular beach for swimming, plus shelters and three playgrounds, including a whimsical wooden castle playground. It's also popular for boating and fishing.

Where to Eat

Rascal's. *211 West Broadway, Polk City; (515) 984–6681.* On the town square, this popular ice-cream and sandwich shop specializes in hamburgers, pork tenderloins, chicken fingers, and malts. $

Perry

From Polk City, pick up State Highway 141 and drive about 20 miles northwest to Perry. An unassuming city 30 miles from Des Moines, Perry had some incredible luck in the 1990s. Roberta Green Ahmanson, a Perry native who became a California philanthropist, returned to revitalize her hometown. She has poured millions into buying and renovating buildings in town.

HOTEL PATTEE (ages 5 and up)
1112 Willis Avenue, Perry 50220; (515) 465–3511, www.hotelpattee.com. Tours usually available at about 2:00 P.M. Sunday and Monday. **Free.**

The crown jewel of Roberta Green Ahmanson's revitalization of her hometown, this once faded hotel got a $10 million face-lift in 1997. Each of its forty rooms is individually and impeccably decorated to highlight an aspect of small-town Iowa. Usually about six guest rooms are open during the tour. Fun rooms for kids to see include the R. M. Harvey Room, decorated with circus memorabilia (it honors a Perry resident who was a circus agent), the Afton School Room, decorated to resemble a one-room school, and the Marching Band Room, with light fixtures and a headboard made from band instruments. Children will especially enjoy staying in the "Suite for Kids," which has a hand-carved and painted bunk bed, a fanciful tiled bath, and cookies and milk served at bedtime. (Be forewarned, it's about $200 a night.) If you don't want to stay overnight, visit for a meal and a room tour. For kids, the hotel is definitely a put-on-a-nice-shirt, brush-your-hair kind of place, requiring good behavior. That said, families won't feel uncomfortable. The charming hotel restaurant has a thoughtful, reasonably priced children's menu. Be sure to stroll through the lobby, ballroom, surprisingly elegant bowling alley (for overnight guests only, and at additional cost), and the neighboring gift shop.

Where to Eat

David's Milwaukee Diner at the Hotel Pattee. *1112 Willis Avenue, Perry; (515) 465–3511.* Tasty children's meals with a wide selection of entrees, half portions of main entrees at a reduced price, and endless refills of Shirley Temples are highlights for children at this classy restaurant decorated in a railroad motif. David's serves inventive Midwestern and international cuisine. $$$–$$$$

Where to Stay

The Hotel Pattee. *1112 Willis Avenue, Perry; (515) 465–3511.* This gorgeous art-filled hotel has thirty-four rooms and six suites, a bowling alley, a cozy library, and a gourmet restaurant. $$$$

For More Information

Perry Chamber of Commerce. *1226 Second Street, Perry 50220; (515) 465–4601.*

Other Things to See and Do in Central Iowa

- **Jasper County and Maytag Historical Museums.** Newton, (641) 792–9118

- **Fred Maytag Park.** Newton, (641) 792–1470

- **Heritage Village.** Des Moines, (515) 262–3111

- **Brown's Woods.** Des Moines, (515) 323–7612

- **Des Moines Equestrian Center.** Des Moines, (515) 243–4777

- **Pearson Park.** West Des Moines, (515) 222–3444

- **Grand Slam USA.** Urbandale, (515) 278–1070

- **Metro Ice Sports Facility and Urbandale Winter Park.** Urbandale, (515) 276–7200

- **Bob Feller Hometown Exhibit.** Van Meter, (515) 996–2808

- **Glazed Expressions paint-your-own-pottery.** Clive, (515) 224–4700

North-Central Iowa

Blessed with deep black soil, North-Central Iowa is not just farm country, it's among the world's richest, most productive farm country, and it has helped make Iowa the nation's leading producer of corn and pork. Here you'll find one of the nation's top agriculture colleges, Iowa State University in Ames, offering families not only earthy attractions like a farmhouse museum and a children's garden, but children's theater, ISU Cyclones games, and hands-on activities at the University's art museum.

With little towns named Fertile and Swaledale, this region also offers old-fashioned small-town fun: an antique carousel in Story City, a giant tree house in Marshalltown, a steam-powered excursion train in Boone. You can also hike in Ledges State Park or ride a boat on Clear Lake. Or visit the birthplaces of former First Lady Mamie Doud Eisenhower and Meredith Willson of *Music Man* fame. For something a little different, stop by the strange grotto in West Bend and the Hobo Museum in Britt.

To begin a clockwise tour, start in the region's southeast corner in Marshalltown, then drive west on US 30 through the Ames, Boone, and Jefferson areas. Go north on US 169 to Fort Dodge and northwest to West Bend, located on State Highway 15, before heading back east via US 18 toward Clear Lake and Mason City.

For More Information

Central Iowa Tourism Region. *P.O. Box 454, Webster City 50595; (800) 285–* *5842 or (515) 832–4808, www.iowa tourism.org, citr@netins.net.*

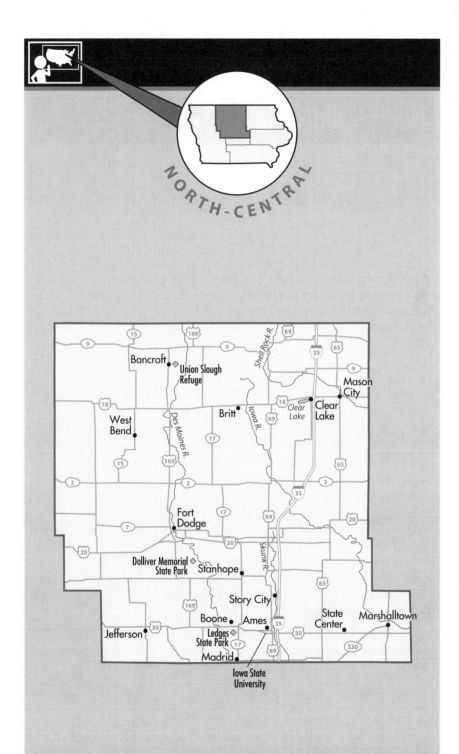

NORTH-CENTRAL

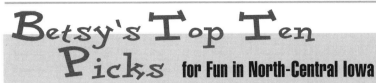

Betsy's Top Ten
Picks for Fun in North-Central Iowa

1. Story City Antique Carousel
2. Big Treehouse, Marshalltown
3. A hike in Ledges State Park, Boone
4. Riding the Boone and Scenic Valley Railroad, Boone
5. The Grotto, West Bend
6. An ISU Cyclones game, Ames
7. Stone's Restaurant, Marshalltown
8. Reiman Gardens, Ames
9. Ribs and a sundae at Hickory Park Restaurant, Ames
10. A *Lady of the Lake* cruise, Clear Lake.

Marshalltown

Located off US 30 and State Highway 14 about 45 miles northeast of Des Moines, Marshalltown calls itself the "Go-Kart Capital" because it has weekly summer races and hosts a national championship.

IOWA INTERNATIONAL RACEWAY (all ages)

2002 East Anson Street, Marshalltown 50158; (641) 753–6362. Races held Sunday at 1:00 P.M. from April through October. **Free.**

This is the place to see go-cart races, with kids and adults from across Iowa competing. Sit in the bleachers or set up lawn chairs and blankets on the grass. Bring a picnic or visit the concession stand for snack food. Every other year, for a week in August, this premier Midwest go-cart track hosts a national championship featuring drivers from across the country.

BIG TREEHOUSE (ages 3 and up)

2370 Shady Oaks Road, Marshalltown 50158; (641) 752–2946, www.marshall net.com/mcbigg/treehouse.html, bigtreehouse@mchsi.com. Open by appointment only, daily from mid-May through mid-October, weather permitting. Reservations are required. $. Camping is available at a neighboring private campground.

Located in the countryside east of Marshalltown, this remarkable twelve-level tree house complete with running water, electricity, porch swings, and piped-in music sits on a six-acre campground owned by Mary Gift, a spry older woman who enthusiastically leads visitors on a tour. The 55-foot-high tree house wraps up and around a sprawling old maple tree behind Mary's house. It's the ongoing hobby of Mary's grandson Mick Jorgenson, who first started building it in 1983 when he was in college. He's now a local school principal. Equipped with kitsch (sensor-operated croaking frogs and chirping birds) and high-tech (a computer and a microwave), the tree house is surrounded by elevated walkways and gardens. From the upper reaches, shaded by leafy branches, you look out on a glorious meadow. At the end of the tour, Mary pulls out a box of old-fashioned toys for kids to play with. Expect to stay at least an hour—it's a refreshing break from modern-day children's entertainment. Preschoolers need to be well supervised; the tree house's upper levels have railings with wide openings.

To get to the tree house, take US 30 3 miles east of Marshalltown, turn north on Shady Oaks Road, and drive a quarter mile.

APPLEBERRY FARM (all ages)

2402 West Main Street, Marshalltown 50158; (641) 752–8443, www.apple berryfarm.com. Open 8:00 A.M. to 6:00 P.M. daily from August through October, reduced hours the rest of the year. **Free.**

This twenty-acre orchard with fourteen different apple varieties, including the popular Honey Crisp, is a good place to pick your own. Located in a residential area twenty-four blocks west of the county courthouse, the orchard also sells already picked apples, pumpkins, homemade cider, and crafts.

Where to Eat

Stone's Restaurant. *507 South Third Avenue, Marshalltown; (641) 753–3626.* This nationally known local favorite with an old-fashioned oval counter, wood wainscoting, and a stamped tin ceiling has served down-home meals since 1887. Hidden below the State Highway 14 South viaduct, Stone's serves chicken and noodles, fried chicken, pork loin, and roast beef meals for lunch and dinner, plus a salad bar and delicious pies, including its infamous "mile-high lemon chiffon pie," a four-inch-high wedge of pale yellow wet-spongy pie. There's also a hearty Sunday brunch. $

Taylor's Maid-Rite. *106 South Third Avenue, Marshalltown; (641) 753–9684.* Get your loose-meat sandwich—a hamburger bun filled with steamy ground hamburger and onions—at one of the most well-known and oldest (seventy years!) franchises in the Iowa-born Maid-Rite chain. $

Zeno's Pizza. *109 East Main Street, Marshalltown; (641) 752–1245.* Try the taco pizza or the Zeno's special (with sausages, green peppers, and olives) at this longtime family-owned pizza parlor east of the courthouse. $

Picnic Possibilities Visit **Riverview Park,** on Marshalltown's north side at North Third (State Highway 14) and Woodland Avenues. The seventy-acre park along the Iowa River has a playground, outdoor pool, campground, picnic tables, and an 8-mile paved "bike-walk-and-jog" trail.

Where to Stay

AmericInn and Suites. *115 Iowa Avenue West, Marshalltown; (800) 634–3444 or (641) 752–4844.* There are four "grand suites" (with two rooms, a fireplace, kitchen, and hot tub) plus forty-four rooms at this new motel. Situated in a commercial area just west of State Highway 14 on Marshalltown's south side, it has an indoor pool and free freshly baked cookies nightly. $$–$$$$

Best Western Regency Inn. *3303 South Center Street, Marshalltown; (800) 241–2974 or (641) 752–6321.* Located 5 miles south of downtown near the busy intersection of US 30 and State Highway 14, this hotel has 106 rooms and suites, a restaurant, and an indoor pool. $$–$$$

Comfort Inn. *2613 South Center Street, Marshalltown; (641) 752–6000.* Behind the Marshalltown Center mall south of downtown, this sixty-two-room motel has an indoor pool. $$

For More Information

Marshalltown Convention and Visitors Bureau. *709 South Center Street, Marshalltown 50158; (800) 697–3155 or*

(641) 753–6645, www.marshalltown.org, aust@marshalltown.org.

State Center

Not everyone agrees that this small town *is* exactly the state's center, but it's close enough. Located 15 miles west of Marshalltown off US 30, State Center also bills itself as the state's rose capital. Visit between mid-June and August to see the roses in bloom in the garden at the intersection of Third Street and Third Avenue SE. (It's also lit up at night.) The annual rose festival is held the third weekend in June, featuring a parade and carnivals with rides and games.

WATSON'S GROCERY STORE (ages 7 and up)
106 West Main Street, State Center 50247; (641) 483–2110. Open 1:00 to 4:00 P.M. Saturday and Sunday from Memorial Day through Labor Day, or by appointment. **Free.**

Wonder what shopping was like for Iowa pioneers? Then visit this restored 1895 mercantile and grocery store, which is owned by the local historical society. It has original oak bins and light fixtures, a hand-powered elevator, and period dry goods.

MAXWELL MUSEUM (ages 7 and up)
81 Main Street, Maxwell 50161; (641) 385–2376. Open 1:00 to 4:00 P.M. Sundays and holidays from Memorial Day through late September, or by appointment. **Free.**

This local history museum in a small town southwest of State Center has some interesting stuff, including an Ice Age mastodon scapula bone and a foot-long leech floating in a jar of formaldehyde. Located downtown, the three-building museum also has a remnant of a B-17 bomber that crashed nearby en route to England for the D-Day invasion, the elaborately painted stage curtain from Maxwell's 1892 Opera House, and replicas of small-town businesses, from a dentist's office to a post office.

Where to Eat

Baileys. *121 West Main Street, State Center; (641) 483–2920.* Try the pizza and broasted chicken for dinner. $

For More Information

State Center Commerce Club. *201 West Main Street, State Center 50247; (641) 483–2081.*

Ames

Ames is home to Iowa State University, founded in 1868 as the nation's first land-grant college. This bustling college town off US 30 offers many attractions, from college sports to topflight museums, concerts, theater, and dance. There are two main shopping areas with restaurants: Campustown, south of campus, and the historic downtown area along Main Street. (While you're there, also check out the independent bookstore, Big Table Books.)

 BRUNNIER ART MUSEUM (ages 4 and up)
290 Scheman Building, Ames 50011; (515) 294–3342, www.museums.iastate. edu, museums@adp.iastate.edu. Open 11:00 A.M. to 4:00 P.M. Tuesday through Friday, 5:00 to 8:00 P.M. Thursday, and 1:00 to 4:00 P.M. Saturday and Sunday; closed when Iowa State is not in session. **Free.**

Iowa State University's fine-arts museum, the Brunnier is also well known for its decorative art collection, which includes dolls, glass, ceramics, ivory, and jade. Kids can do hands-on activities connected to a specific exhibit during Family Day, held four Sundays during the year. The Brunnier is part of the Iowa State Center arts complex.

 FARM HOUSE MUSEUM (ages 4 and up)
Knoll Road, Ames 50011; (515) 294–7426, www.museums.iastate.edu, museums@adp.iastate.edu. Open noon to 4:00 P.M. Monday through Friday and Sunday; closed when Iowa State is not in session. **Free.**

This 1860 three-story gray stucco farmhouse—Iowa State's first building—sits right in the middle of campus. It's a restored National Historic Landmark with period Victorian furnishings. You can walk around on your own or request a guide. On the first three Sunday afternoons in December, there's a Victorian Holiday celebration with horse-drawn carriage rides, live music, crafts, and refreshments.

IOWA STATE CENTER (all ages, depending on show)

Suite 4, Scheman Building, Ames 50011; tickets, (877) THE–CENTER or (515) 294–3347, www.center.iastate.edu, sbarr@center.iastate.edu.

This sprawling modern performing arts and conference center on the south end of campus has three main stages. Stephens Auditorium hosts mostly family-friendly performances, including national traveling theater, music, and dance shows. The more intimate Fisher Theater often features university productions. Hilton Coliseum is best known for hosting big-name concerts and ISU sports, but also offers some entertainment children will enjoy, including traveling ice-skating companies.

IOWA STATE UNIVERSITY CYCLONES (all ages)

Hilton Coliseum and Jack Trice Stadium, on Elwood Drive near South Fourth Street, Ames 50011; tickets, (888) 478–2925 or (515) 294–1816, www.center.iastate.edu/athletics, athletics@iastate.edu. Ticket prices vary depending on the sport and specific game.

Veishea In mid-April Iowa State throws itself a big party: the annual Veishea celebration, a tradition that's more than eighty years old. Although sometimes marred by excessive drinking and rowdiness, the three-day student-run event offers some fun stuff for children, especially the big Veishea parade and an international food fair. (Veishea is an acronym composed of the first letters of ISU's original five colleges: Veterinary, Engineering, Industrial Science, Home Economics, and Agriculture.)

Call (515) 294–1026 or log on to www.veishea.org for more information.

When you meet Iowans, chances are they're either a Cyclone or a Hawkeye (the University of Iowa) fan. The ISU Cyclones men's and women's basketball, gymnastics, volleyball, and wrestling teams compete in Hilton Coliseum. Football is at nearby Jack Trice Stadium. Both are just south of campus. The sports ticket office is next to the stadium in the Jacobson Building, located at 1800 South Fourth Street.

Amazing Iowa Facts Iowa State University senior Cael Sanderson had a banner year in 2002. *Sports Illustrated* dubbed Sanderson's perfect college wrestling career (159–0) "the second most impressive college sports feat ever." And the four-time national champion's photo appeared on a Wheaties cereal box.

Cyclones Maze Find your way through a corn maze shaped like the Iowa State Cyclones logo. Right off the Interstate 35 Ames–Nevada exit on US 30, a mile east of Ames, the maze is open 4:00 to 10:00 P.M. Friday, 1:00 to 10:00 P.M. Saturday, and 1:00 to 7:00 P.M. Sunday from the last week in August through October. It's also open in July during the Iowa Summer Games, an annual three-day sports festival. Admission is charged, ages 4 and under free. Call (641) 842–2829.

REIMAN GARDENS (all ages)

1407 Elwood Drive, Ames 50011; (515) 294–2710, www.reimangardens.ia state.edu. Open 9:00 A.M. to 4:30 P.M. Monday through Wednesday, 9:00 A.M. to 8:30 P.M. Thursday through Saturday, and noon to 6:00 P.M. Sunday from May through October 1; 9:00 A.M. to 5:00 P.M. daily from October 2 through April. $.

Young children can race up hills, peek through a covered bridge, hide in an open-air grass house, and watch carp swim in a pond at this fourteen-acre spread filled with trees, shrubs, roses, and gardens on the south end of the ISU campus. There's also a lovely children's garden where kids can crank an old water pump and watch the water come spitting out of the mouth of a frog lawn ornament. The flowers are at their peak from June through August, but a new conservatory with a cafe and indoor butterfly flight house is fun year-round. Special events include summer concerts, children's programs, and brown bag lunch tours. There are also herb, wetland, and pond gardens.

MCFARLAND PARK (all ages)

56461 190th Street, Ames 50010; (515) 232–2516, www.storycounty.com/ conservation/mcfarland.html, conservation@storycounty.com. Open 5:00 A.M. to 10:30 P.M. daily. **Free.**

This 200-acre area 5 miles northeast of Ames is a good place to picnic, fish, hike, and cross-country ski. It includes a conservation center with exhibits, a butterfly garden, wildlife habitat, stargazing observatory, "touch-a-life" nature trail, and 5½ miles of hiking/off-road biking trail. There's also a six-and-a-half-acre lake stocked with bluegill, catfish, bass, and two swans named Elaine and Lancelot. (No swimming is allowed.) Primitive camping is also available. A half-mile walk through restored prairie leads to the Bauge Log Home, a pioneer farmstead museum open Sunday afternoons. When something big is happening in the sky, the observatory throws a "star party," which includes a presentation and a look through a huge telescope.

Where to Eat

Hickory Park Restaurant. *1404 South Duff Avenue, Ames; (515) 232–8940.* You may have a wait at Hickory Park, a large popular barbecue joint located south of downtown and decorated with highway memorabilia. But the food—huge portions of barbecued ribs and chicken, plus burgers and an extensive list of ice-cream concoctions—is worth it. $–$$

Pizza Kitchens. *120 Hayward Avenue, Ames; (515) 292–1710.* A good place for grown-ups and kids, this Campustown favorite has pasta and designer pizzas (including a ninja pizza and a PB&J pizza on the kids' menu), plus salads and homemade soup. Also try the "crock pizza," which is baked upside down in a crock then turned over onto a plate and served gooey. Kids get crayons and a menu with connect-the-dots and word jumbles. $–$$

Ruttles. *531 South Duff Avenue, Ames; (515) 233–1952.* This retro 1950s diner with neon signs and old photos serves hearty American food, including corn dogs and a "burger bar" with twenty-six toppings. For dessert, try the infamous "ramalama dingdong," a humungous 3,000-calorie banana split. (Your name goes on a plaque if you eat it all.) $

Where to Stay

The Hotel at Gateway Center. *2100 Greenhills Drive, Ames; (800) 367–2637 or (515) 292–8600, www.thehotelatgate waycenter.com.* A former Holiday Inn on seventeen acres south of campus near US 30 and Elwood Drive, this full-service hotel popular with ISU visitors has 188 rooms, a restaurant, indoor pool, and landscaped gardens. $$$–$$$$

Iowa State Memorial Union. *Lincoln Way at Lynn Avenue, Ames; (515) 292–1111, www.mu.iastate.edu.* Plunge into college life by staying in one of the fifty-one cozy European-style rooms and suites at the graceful old student union on campus, which also has a parking garage, bookstore, restaurant, food court, and convenience store. $$

MonteBello Bed and Breakfast Inn. *3535 South 530th Avenue, Ames; (515) 296–2181, www.montebellobandbinn.* This unusual Mexican-themed "prairie hacienda" on a nineteen-acre farm overlooking a pond with gardens is located just south of the ISU campus (take Elwood Drive south). It has four colorful guest rooms decorated with authentic Mexican arts, crafts, and furniture, each with a private bath featuring hand-painted tiles. A full Mexican breakfast is served by gracious hosts, as well as an evening treat. $$$–$$$$

For More Information

Ames Convention and Visitors Bureau, *1601 Golden Aspen Drive, Suite 110, Ames 50010; (800) 288–7470 or (515) 232–4032, www.acvb.ames.ia.us, amescvb@netins.net.*

Story City

Kids know Story City as the place with the carousel. This small town about 17 miles north of Ames near Interstate 35 celebrates its heritage during its annual Scandinavian Days. Usually held the first full weekend in June, the festival features a parade, carnival, talent show, and tractor pull.

STORY CITY ANTIQUE CAROUSEL (all ages)

North Park on Broad Street, Story City 50248; (515) 733–4214. Open noon to 6:00 P.M. daily, until 9:00 P.M. Wednesday and Friday through Sunday from Memorial Day through Labor Day; noon to 8:00 P.M. weekends in May and September. $. There's a Friday night two-for-one special.

Young children love this restored 1913 Herschell-Spillman antique carousel with hand-carved wooden animals and tunes from a 1936 Wurlitzer band organ. It's in a small, pretty town park with a fun playground, picnic tables, and a nearby public pool. A short walk away is an 1859 one-room schoolhouse, a small redbrick city museum, and a Depression-era stone pedestrian "swinging bridge" crossing the Skunk River in neighboring South Park.

Where to Eat

Dairy Queen. *1533 Broad Street, Story City; (515) 733–2840.* If you need an ice-cream cone after riding the carousel, this is your place, just off Interstate 35. There's a Subway sandwich shop nearby at 1631 Broad. $

Royal Cafe. *625 Pennsylvania Avenue, Story City; (515) 733–9074.* The Royal Cafe has a children's menu and serves burgers, sandwiches, grilled cheese, burritos, and nachos. $

Valhalla Restaurant and Lounge. *1513 Broad Street, (515) 733–4884.* Off Interstate 35, this longtime family restaurant serves three meals daily, with burgers, fries, nachos, steaks, and seafood, plus occasional Norwegian specialties. $

For More Information

Story City Chamber of Commerce. *618 Broad Street, Story City 50248; (515) 733–4214, www.storycity.net, chamber@storycity.net.*

Stanhope

Stanhope is about 19 miles northwest of Story City at the junction of State Highways 17 and 175.

COUNTRY RELICS VILLAGE (all ages)

3280 Briggs Woods Road, Stanhope 50245; (515) 826–4386, www.country relicsvillage.com. Open 10:00 A.M. to 5:00 P.M. Monday through Saturday and 12:30 to 5:00 P.M. Sunday from May through mid-October. $, ages 2 and under Free.

Everything is one-half to two-thirds its normal size at this elaborate scaled-down version of an early 1900s village, which has sixteen buildings, including a homestead. Located on Varlen and Fern Carlson's farm off State Highway 17 about 1½ miles north of Stanhope, the village also has 113 "dummies" (or pretend villagers). There's a show of scale-model engines, tractors, and machines on the fourth Saturday in June. At Christmastime the village is closed, but you can drive through a half-mile lighting display and see decorated Christmas trees in a barn hayloft. The drive is open 5:30 to 8:00 P.M. daily from the Friday before Thanksgiving through the last Sunday of December.

Where to Eat

Princess Sweet Shop/Cafe. *607 Washington Avenue, Iowa Falls; (641) 648–9602.* About 42 miles northeast of Stanhope, this amazing restaurant/ice-cream shop is worth the drive, serving good burgers and great ice cream sundaes in a fantastic 1935 art deco building with the original neon sign outside. Inside are the original 25-foot-long marble soda fountain and deco wooden booths. $

Worth a Road Trip Iowa Falls has several beautifully restored historic downtown buildings worth exploring (pick up a guide from the local chamber of commerce), including the old opera house, and an excursion boat along the Iowa River from May through October. Call (641) 648–5549.

Boone

About 15 miles south of Stanhope off State Highway 17, Boone is the place to go for a cool train ride. A good time to visit is during the annual Pufferbilly Days, held the first weekend after Labor Day, celebrating Boone County's heritage as the railroad center of Iowa. One of Iowa's largest festivals, it includes a children's carnival Thursday through Saturday nights and a Saturday morning parade.

BOONE AND SCENIC VALLEY RAILROAD (all ages)

225 10th Street, Boone 50036; (800) 626–0319 or (515) 432–4249, www.scenic-valleyrr.com, B&SVRR@tdsi.net. Train rides at 1:30 P.M. Monday through Friday and 1:30 and 4:00 P.M. Saturday and Sunday from Memorial Day weekend through October. $$ for adults, $ for ages 12 and under. There are also winter holiday, dessert, and dinner train rides.

A family favorite, this excursion train takes you on a two-hour 15-mile round-trip chug through the glorious Des Moines River Valley over two very high bridges. The train is pulled by an exotic-looking 116-ton Chinese steam engine. In the fall there's a special Thomas the Tank Engine train. To find the train depot, go north on Story Street through the business district to Tenth or Eleventh Street, then west six blocks.

MAMIE DOUD EISENHOWER BIRTHPLACE (ages 7 and up)

709 Carroll Street, Boone 50036; (515) 432–1896. Open 1:00 to 5:00 P.M. Tuesday through Sunday in April and May, 10:00 A.M. to 5:00 P.M. daily from June through October. $.

Tour this sweet little yellow frame house packed with Eisenhower family items. The former First Lady was born here in 1896.

SEVEN OAKS RECREATION AREA (all ages)

1086 222nd Drive, Boone 50035; (515) 432–9457, www.sevenoaksrec.com, sevenoaks@opencominc.com. Open winter and summer. Lifts open 4:00 to 9:00 P.M. Monday through Wednesday, 10:00 A.M. to 9:00 P.M. Friday and Saturday, and 11:00 A.M. to 9:00 P.M. Sunday from December through mid-March. $$–$$$, ages 5 and under with paying adult get a **Free** *ski package. Equipment rentals and lessons are available.*

Located on US 30 about 5 miles west of Boone, Seven Oaks has a snow tubing park with a T-bar lift and a separate area with eight runs for downhill skiing and snowboarding, with one triple chairlift and three tow-rope lifts. When the weather warms, there's golf, mountain biking, canoe rentals, and camping near the Des Moines River. Take US 30 to L Avenue South (Country Road R18).

KATE SHELLEY RAILROAD MUSEUM AND PARK (ages 4 and up)

1198 232nd Street, Boone 50036; (515) 432–1907. Park open dawn to dusk. Museum open 1:00 to 4:00 P.M. some weekends, or by appointment. Call ahead for reservations. Donation requested.

Kate Shelley's story reads like the plot of an American Girl novel. On July 6, 1881, fifteen-year-old Kate climbed across a railroad bridge during a fierce night storm to warn an oncoming passenger train of danger up the line. The museum, located about 5 miles southwest of Boone, is a restored railroad depot and features a video about Kate Shelley's life, some of her belongings, and a working telegraph. It's in a wooded corner of the sleepy hamlet of Moingona, with picnic tables and low-key hiking trails. Take US 30 west from Boone, then south on L Avenue (Country Road R18).

Talk like an Iowan To avoid being pegged as an out-of-stater, remember to pronounce the north central Iowa towns of Madrid and Nevada correctly. It's *MAD-rid* (not *mah-DRID*) and *ne-VAY-duh* (not *ne-VAH-da*).

LEDGES STATE PARK (all ages)

1519 250th Street, Boone 50156; (515) 432–1852, Ledges@dnr.state.ia.us. Open 4:00 A.M. to 10:30 P.M. daily. **Free.**

A family favorite, this popular 1,200-acre state park in the wooded Des Moines River Valley about 5 miles south of Boone is famous for its "canyon area" with up to 100-foot sandstone cliffs along Pea's Creek. Catch the scenic views by car or on foot. On the winding road informally known as Canyon Drive, you'll encounter several shallow water crossings. (The road is sometimes closed due to flooding.) Ledges also has two trails on either side of the canyon, most with steep portions winding through the woods to scenic overlooks. Kids love to play in the sandy area and slosh through the water in Pea's Creek. This is also a great place for fishing, picnicking, and canoeing (rentals available at Seven Oaks Recreational Area). With strollers and very young children, try an easy half-mile interpretive nature trail around Lost Lake, in the park's southwest area. There are also ninety-four campsites, with modern rest rooms, showers, and a playground. To get to Ledges take US 30 2 miles east of Boone to State Highway 17 south. Go 2 miles and turn west on 250th Street.

IOWA ARBORETUM (all ages)

1875 Peach Avenue, Madrid 50156; (515) 795–3216, www.iowaarboretum. com, arbiowa@pionet.net. Grounds open sunrise to sunset daily. $, ages 11 and under **Free.**

Located on 378 acres about 5 miles south of Boone, this "living museum" is a great place to learn about trees, shrubs, and flowers. You can walk on trails through woods and through pretty gardens with herbs, perennials, roses, dwarf conifers, and hostas. Try the Library Trail, which has nineteen different plant collections. There's also a children's garden and butterfly garden. Popular with school groups, the arboretum has a modern education center that offers occasional activities, from bird-watching to a family wildlife walk and a pancake breakfast. Call for the schedule. To get to the arboretum, take State Highway 17 to Luther, then go 2½ miles west on County Road E-57. Turn south onto a gravel road and follow the arboretum signs.

Where to Eat

Colorado Grill. *1514 South Marshall Street, Boone; (515) 433–7020.* Corn dogs and fish nuggets are among the children's menu items at this restaurant near US 30. Colorado Grill serves steak, ribs, chicken, and sandwiches for lunch and dinner in a room decorated with Rocky Mountain photos and ski gear. $–$$

Van Hemert's Dutch Oven Bakery. *605 Story Street, Boone; (515) 432–9567.* Yummy fresh doughnuts, apple fritters, cookies, and Dutch letters are served at this old-fashioned downtown bakery, which also offers deli sandwiches and soups. $

Where to Stay

AmeriHost Inn and Suites. *1745 SE Marshall Street, Boone; (515) 432–8168.* Two miles south of downtown, this chain motel has an indoor pool and sixty rooms, some with wood-beamed ceilings. $$–$$$$

Hook's Point Bed & Breakfast. *3495 Hook's Point Drive, Stratford; (515) 838–2781; www.hookspoint.com.* For a splurge with school-age children and up, visit this 1904 farmhouse about 15 miles north of Boone, with two rooms and a suite well suited to families. A full breakfast is included, plus the option for a six-course, all-homemade dinner for an additional fee (the food has been featured in several national magazines). $$–$$$

For More Information

Boone Chamber of Commerce, *806 Seventh Street, Boone 50036; (515) 432–3342, www.booneiowa.com.*

Jefferson

Jefferson is about 30 miles west of Boone on US 30.

MAHANAY BELL TOWER (all ages)

100 East Lincoln Way, Jefferson 50129; (515) 386–2155. Open 11:00 A.M. to 4:00 P.M. daily from Memorial Day through Labor Day, weekends in May and September or by appointment. $.

For a great view of Jefferson and surrounding farmland in seven counties, take a glass elevator to the 120-foot-high observation deck of this fourteen-story carillon.

DEAL'S ORCHARD (all ages)

1102 244th Street, Jefferson 50129; (515) 386–8279. Open during prime apple-picking season, 8:00 A.M. to 6:00 P.M. daily from mid-September through October; 9:00 A.M. to 5:30 P.M. Monday through Saturday from November through February and July to mid-September; generally closed March through June.

Pick your own apples at this third-generation orchard that has fifty-five acres of trees with thirty-five varieties. Other fresh produce available in season includes raspberries, cherries, tomatoes, sweet corn, and pumpkins. Each

Amazing Iowa Facts About 20 percent of the nation's corn is grown in Iowa, which has about 33.2 million acres of farmland.

year about 25,000 to 30,000 gallons of fresh apple cider are processed. Celebrate the harvest on the second weekend in October at the Annual

Fall Festival, featuring hayrides and games. To get to the orchard, go 3 miles west of Jefferson on Old Highway 30, then a half mile south on K Avenue to 244th Street.

A Rubiner Family Adventure

When our dear family friend Marion visited all the way from London, we wanted to make sure she had the quintessential Iowa experience. So on a crisp fall day, during the height of the corn and soybean harvest, we dropped a little surprise on her. Driving past burnt-umber fields of ripe soybeans dotted with huge green combines harvesting away, we stopped our van on a gravel road and flagged down a farmer, an acquaintance of my husband's whom we'd alerted in advance. We'll never forget Marion's stunned expression when we told her she was going on a combine ride with the farmer and our son Noah. A good time was had by all—and Marion even got to drive the combine.

Where to Stay

Limburg House. *305 West Lincolnway Street, Jefferson; (515) 386–4699.* Featuring a Mission-style staircase and antiques, this B&B in a 1905 house welcomes children and includes three suites, each with a sitting room and private bath. $$–$$$

For More Information

Jefferson Area Chamber of Commerce. *220 North Chestnut Street, Jefferson 50129; (515) 386–2155,* *www.jeffersoniowa.com, chamber@jefferson iowa.com.*

Fort Dodge

About 49 miles north of Jefferson off US 169 and US 20, Fort Dodge is the site of a former garrison built to protect residents from Native Americans in the mid-1860s. On the first full weekend in June, the city's Fort Museum is the site of Frontier Days, which includes a parade, live music, and a Buckskinner's Rendezvous. Special children's activities range from a puppet show to a spelling bee, petting zoo, and cowboy camp.

Rodeo Alert One of Iowa's best-known rodeos has been held for more than sixty years in the small town of Dayton, about 15 miles southeast of Fort Dodge on State Highway 175. It's held on Labor Day weekend and includes four shows, a carnival, and a parade. Call (515) 547-6336.

BLANDEN MEMORIAL ART MUSEUM (ages 5 and up)
920 Third Avenue South, Fort Dodge 50501; (515) 573–2316, www.blanden. org, info@blanden.org. Open 10:00 A.M. to 5:00 P.M. Tuesday, Wednesday, and Friday, 10:00 A.M. to 8:30 P.M. Thursday, and 1:00 to 5:00 P.M. Saturday and Sunday. **Free.**

Blanden, Iowa's first art museum, occasionally offers family programs and hands-on art activities for children. The museum is in a park setting and has an impressive collection of early twentieth-century American art, plus Asian, African, and European art. There are also traveling exhibits. Check the Web site for the special events.

FORT MUSEUM AND FRONTIER VILLAGE (ages 6 and up)
Junction of Museum Road and US 20 near US 169, Fort Dodge 50501; (515) 573–4231, www.fortmuseum.com, thefort@frontiernet.net. Open 9:00 A.M. to 5:00 P.M. Monday through Saturday, and 11:00 A.M. to 5:00 P.M. Sunday from May through mid-October. $$ for adults, $ for children, ages 5 and under **Free.**

Fort Dodge's original 1862 military fort was downtown. This museum, in the northwest part of town, is a re-created Civil War militia fort and village with twenty original and replica buildings, plus displays about pioneers, American Indians, and the military. There are also chuck wagon dinners during the summer months.

DOLLIVER MEMORIAL STATE PARK (all ages)

2757 Dolliver Park Avenue, Lehigh 50557; (515) 359–2539, www.state.ia.us/ dnr/organiza/ppd/dolliver.htm, dolliver@dnr.state.ia.us. Open 4:00 A.M. to 10:30 P.M. daily. **Free.**

Located 10 miles south of Fort Dodge, this 457-acre park on the Des Moines River and Prairie Creek is known for its bluffs, canyons, and Indian mounds. A trail leads past the Copperas Beds, unusual sandstone formations towering 100 feet above Prairie Creek. The high bluff includes mineral deposits, petrified logs, and sticks from a Mesozoic era riverbed. Popular for fishing and canoeing, Dolliver also has picnic areas, a playground, a recently renovated family cabin that sleeps four, and a forty-one-site campground with modern showers and rest rooms.

Where to Eat

Community Orchard. *2233 160th Street, Fort Dodge; (515) 573–8212.* Located at the northwest edge of the Fort Dodge airport, this family-friendly apple orchard has fall children's activities and a snack bar that serves lunch and desserts, including apple pie and dumplings. $

Picnic Possibilities In town, visit **Olson Park** on South 17th Street, which has a wading pool, playground, band shell, and small live animal area. North of town is **Kennedy Park** on a man-made lake with a beach, boating docks, and a playground. To get there take 15th Street north out of town about 5 miles (15th Street turns into Nelson Avenue).

Where to Stay

Best Western Starlite Village. *1518 Third Avenue Northwest, Fort Dodge; (800) 903–0009 or (515) 573–7177.* An Olympic-size indoor pool is a main attraction at this hotel. About 8 miles from the Fort Museum, the Best Western has 107 rooms, a restaurant, and a coffee shop. $$–$$$$

Country Inn. *3259 Fifth Avenue South, Fort Dodge; (515) 955–2259.* One of the newest motels in town, this fifty-two-room chain motel has an indoor pool. $$

Holiday Inn. *2001 Highway 169 South, (515) 955–3643.* Located six blocks from the Fort Museum and a mile from downtown, the Holiday Inn has ninety-four rooms, an indoor pool, and a playground. $$

For More Information

Fort Dodge Area Chamber of Commerce. *1406 Central Avenue, Fort Dodge 50501; (515) 955–5500,* *www.dodgenet.com/~chamber/index.html, info@fortdodgechamber.com.*

West Bend

If you're going to West Bend, you gotta go to the Grotto, one of Iowa's strangest attractions. West Bend is on State Highway 15 about 50 miles northwest of Fort Dodge. Take US 169 north and then County Road B63 west.

GROTTO OF THE REDEMPTION (all ages)

300 North Broadway, West Bend 50597; (800) 868–3641 or (515) 887–2371, www.nw-cybermall.com/grotto.htm, grotto@ncn.net. Open for tours 10:00 A.M. to 5:00 P.M. daily from May through mid-October, or by appointment. During tour season the grotto is lighted until 11:00 P.M. **Free** *but a donation is requested.*

This place must be seen to be believed. Take a tour to find out how and why this elaborate grotto (actually nine separate grottoes that show scenes from Christ's life) was constructed with stones and gems from around the world. Father Paul Dobberstein started building the Grotto in 1912. By his death in 1954, it covered a city block, and today bills itself as the world's largest grotto, with the world's largest concentration of minerals and "petrification" (estimated worth: $4.3 million).

Amazing Iowa Facts In 1994 seventy-three-year-old Alvin Straight drove an old lawn mower more than 300 miles from his north central Iowa hometown of Laurens to Mt. Zion, Wisconsin. Determined to visit his ailing brother in Wisconsin but unable to drive a car because of cataracts, Straight drove his 1966 John Deere mower 5 miles an hour for six weeks. His trip inspired the 1999 film *The Straight Story*, which earned actor Richard Farnsworth (who played Alvin) an Academy Award nomination. The G-rated movie was filmed along the route Alvin drove, and is filled with beautiful shots of Iowa.

Where to Eat

Grotto Park Restaurant. *301 North Broadway, West Bend; (515) 887–3591.* This small restaurant across from the Grotto is open primarily during the peak tour season from 8:00 A.M. to 8:00 P.M. daily. It features cafeteria-style and sit-down service, with meat-potato-vegetable meals and baked desserts, plus a Sunday lunch buffet. $

Picnic Possibilities
There are picnic areas just west and north of the Grotto, with tables and playground equipment beside a small pond.

Where to Stay

Grotto Campground. *300 North Broadway, West Bend; (800) 868–3641 or (515) 887–2371.* Owned by the Grotto and right next door, this campground has eighty electrical hookups available and tent camping, plus modern rest rooms with showers. $

Park View Inn and Suites. *14 Fourth Street NE, West Bend; (515) 887–3611.* One block north of the Grotto, this new thirty-six-unit motel has an indoor pool. $$–$$$

For More Information

West Bend Chamber of Commerce. *P.O. Box 366, West Bend 50597; (800) 868–3641 or (515) 887–2371.*

Bancroft

About 34 miles northeast of West Bend is Bancroft, located on US 169.

UNION SLOUGH NATIONAL WILDLIFE REFUGE (all ages)
1710 360th Street, Titonka 50480; (515) 928–2523, www.midwest.fws.gov/ UnionSlough/. Refuge open sunrise to sunset daily, but call ahead because some portions may be closed. Office open 7:30 A.M. to 4:00 P.M. daily. **Free.**

Located halfway between Bancroft and the smaller town of Titonka, this 3,400-acre national refuge is a wonderful place to see wildlife—from birds to turtles and frogs—on foot or by car. There's a mowed 1¼-mile nature trail through woodland and prairie trails overlooking a creek (easy enough for a sturdy stroller), and a 4-mile auto tour through the refuge (call ahead to check road conditions). There's also a picnic area at the refuge's southern end. The refuge was created at the confluence of two rivers in 1938 to protect waterfowl. Spring and fall are the best times to visit, when you'll see migrating ducks, geese, whistling swans, and shorebirds. In the summer, you'll see young animals, from deer fawns to baby wood ducks. Remember to bring bug spray, sunscreen, a hat, and binoculars. To get to the refuge from Bancroft, take US 169 south about a mile to County Road A42, where you'll see a sign to the refuge office.

Amazing Iowa Facts On May 10, 1879, a 437-pound meteor crashed to earth in a farm field near the town of Estherville, by the Minnesota border about 37 miles west of Bancroft. It's one of the largest meteorites known to have fallen in North America. You can see pieces of it at the Estherville public library.

Where to Eat

The Kettle Cafe. *109 West Ramsey Street, Bancroft; (515) 885–2752.* This diner-style spot on the main drag downtown serves daily breakfast and lunch, with meat loaf and roast beef specials, homemade soup, burgers, and homemade pies. Sunday brunch is served the first Sunday of the month. $

Where to Stay

AmericInn. *600 Highway 18 West, Algona; (515) 295–3333.* About 15 miles south of Bancroft, this chain motel in Algona has forty-one rooms, a pleasant lobby with a fireplace, and an indoor pool. $$–$$$$.

For More Information

Bancroft City Office. *105 East Ramsey Street, Bancroft 50517; (515) 885–2382.*

Britt

The small town of Britt, 35 miles southeast of Bancroft on US 18, has a strange reputation as an annual gathering place for hoboes. On the second weekend in August, the annual National Hobo Convention or "Hobo Days," held since 1900, features a carnival, flea market, and car show on Britt's three-block main street. Word has it that up to one hundred modern-day hoboes show up each year from around the country. But word of warning: Security was tightened after some 1998 arrests for drinking and fighting.

HOBO MUSEUM (ages 6 and up)

51 Main Avenue South, Britt 50423; (641) 843–9104, www.hobo.com. Open 10:00 A.M. to 5:00 P.M. Monday through Friday from the Tuesday after Memorial Day through Labor Day, or by appointment. $.

To Iowans, Britt is synonymous with hoboes, thanks to three locals who volunteered to take over a national hobo convention previously held in Chicago. Located in an old downtown movie theater, this museum—believed to be the only hobo museum anywhere—uses pictures and artifacts to depict 102 years of hobo history, and the gift shop sells hobo crafts. The museum defines hoboes as wandering itinerant workers. Fun fact: Hoboes got their name because they used to carry hoes while searching for work.

Where to Eat

Mary Jo's Hobo House. *72 Main Avenue South, (641) 843–3840.* Breakfast and lunch—including specials ranging from sandwiches to meat loaf, mashed potatoes, and gravy—are served at this downtown hangout near the Hobo Museum. $

Clear Lake

Clear Lake is famous for its old ballroom where rock 'n' rollers Buddy Holly, Ritchie Valens, and J. P. "The Big Bopper" Richardson performed their last concert before dying in a plane crash. It's also a popular outdoor playground, thanks to its 3,684-acre spring-fed lake, the state's third largest lake. Clear Lake is located off of Interstate 35 and US 18 about 20 miles east of Britt. In early December, the annual Christmas by the Lake celebration features a lighted evening Christmas parade, fireworks, free horse-drawn carriage rides, and a big bash at the Surf Ballroom.

CLEAR LAKE FIRE MUSEUM (ages 6 and up)

112 North Sixth Street, Clear Lake 50428; (641) 357–2613. Open 1:00 to 5:00 P.M. Saturday and Sunday from Memorial Day through Labor Day. **Free.**

Created by Clear Lake's Volunteer Fire Department, this small museum looks like an old fire station with a two-story arched engine door and a shiny brass pole. Inside, there's turn-of-the-twentieth-century firefighting equipment and a 1924 pumper truck.

LADY OF THE LAKE EXCURSION BOAT (all ages)

1500 South Shore Drive, Clear Lake 50428; (641) 357–2243; Cruises depart at 7:00 P.M. Monday through Thursday, 7:00 and 9:30 P.M. Friday, and several times on Saturday and Sunday from Memorial Day weekend through mid-September. $$ for adults, $ for ages 11 and under, babes in arms **Free.**

Enjoy the spring-fed lake by taking a ninety-minute cruise on this stern-wheeler ferry boat that once plied the Missouri River. It leaves from the dock behind Clear Lake City Park, located on Main Street and South Shore Drive. Reservations aren't necessary, but try to arrive fifteen minutes before departure time. You can sit outside on the top deck or inside on the lower deck.

SURF BALLROOM (ages 6 and up)

460 North Shore Drive, Clear Lake 50428; (641) 357–6151, www.surfball room.com. Open 9:00 A.M. to 4:00 P.M. Monday through Friday. Pre-arranged guided tours, $; **Free** *self-guided tours. Check schedule for family performances.*

Remember Don McLean's 1970s hit song "American Pie" about the day the music died? That day was February 3, 1959, when Buddy Holly, Ritchie Valens, and J. P. "The Big Bopper" Richardson died in a plane crash after performing at the Surf Ballroom.

Today the Surf still offers concerts—from swing to country to oldies—so check the calendar. (McLean sang "American Pie" here in 1994.) The best-known family events are the annual children's Halloween party and a Branson-style musical at Christmas. The funky old ballroom is also a rock 'n roll shrine and museum of sorts. Your best bet is a self-guided tour but guided tours can be arranged in advance.

Built in 1948 after the original 1933 ballroom burned down, the Surf has a "crash memorial" out front dedicated to Holly, Valens, and the Bopper. Inside is music memorabilia, including photos of famous performers and performances. You can also wander around the old-fashioned ballroom, site of countless concerts—big band, swing, rock, pop, country, even Garrison Keillor's crew. The Surf was designed to look like an ocean beach club on a South Seas island, with murals of the pounding surf, palm trees on stage, and clouds painted on the ceiling. In real life, it's across from Clear Lake.

o Jump in the Lake

For swimming, try the **Clear Lake City Beach,** a block south of the city park, or the two state parks with beaches. **Clear Lake State Park,** 2730 South Lakeview Drive (641-357-4212), is a fifty-five-acre park on the southeast shore about 2 miles south of town. It's fun for swimming, boating, sailing, and fishing. You can also boat over to a three-acre island in the middle of the lake for a picnic. **McIntosh Woods State Park,** 1200 East Lake Street in Ventura (641-829-3847), is a sixty-two-acre park on the northwest shore that's popular for boating and swimming.

FORT CUSTER MAZE

East Main Avenue, Clear Lake 50428; (641) 357–6102. Open 9:00 A.M. to 7:00 P.M. Monday through Friday and 10:00 A.M. to 6:00 P.M. Saturday and Sunday from Memorial Day through Labor Day weekend, weekends only in May and September. $, ages 3 and under Free.

One of the newest attractions in town, this two-acre maze made of stacked wooden pallets looks like a western fort with three bridges and towers at four corners and in the center. (The towers are a good lookout spot for anxious parents.) The maze, designed by a father and son from Clear Lake with the help of a British maze expert, has almost 2 miles of trails, including eight stations where you get a stamp recording your progress. In the summer there are weekly prizes for visitors who navigate the maze the fastest. (One speedy child made it through in seventeen minutes.) The maze design is changed weekly. There's also a small museum with Civil War and Native American artifacts. From Interstate 35 exit 193, drive one block west on County Highway B35 to 24th Street, then four blocks north to Main Avenue and one block east.

Where to Eat

Backyard Deli and Ice Cream. *300 Main Avenue, Clear Lake; (641) 357–2234.* After you've played at Clear Lake's City Park, go across the street to this deli for ice cream, sandwiches, barbecue, soups, and salads. $

Boathouse Bar and Grill. *468 North Shore Drive, Clear Lake; (641) 357–8688.* Right next to the Surf Ballroom, this

dinner-only steak house with nautical decorations has a children's menu, burgers, seafood, pasta, pizza, and sandwiches. $–$$$

Dock's. *475 North Shore Drive, Clear Lake; (641) 357–6338.* Across the street from the Surf Ballroom, this casual seafood restaurant decorated with oars, buoys, and mounted fish, overlooks the lake (with its own dock). Dock's offers a children's menu, and serves steaks, pastas, and sandwiches outside on a deck or inside rooms with panorama windows. Lunch only on weekends. $–$$$

Martha's. *305 Main Avenue, Clear Lake; (641) 357–8720.* This local hangout serves a hearty breakfast, plus hot dishes like roast beef and meat loaf spe-cials for lunch and dinner. Martha's is closed on Sunday. $

PM Park. *15297 Raney Drive, Clear Lake; (641) 357–2574.* A seasonal spot, open from May through mid-September on the lake's south shore, PM Park serves a down-home breakfast (try the hash browns) and lunch items ranging from short-order stuff to daily specials like creamed chicken on biscuits. $

*P*icnic Possibilities Try Clear Lake City Park, located downtown across the street from the lake, with a playground, band shell, and gazebo. Or visit Tourist Park on South Shore Drive, which has grills, volleyball courts, and a playground.

Where to Stay

AmericInn. *1406 North 25th Street, Clear Lake; (641) 357–8954.* This forty-eight-room chain motel located off Interstate 35 at exit 194 near the airport has an indoor pool. $–$$$$

Best Western Holiday Lodge. *2023 Seventh Avenue North, Clear Lake; (641) 357–5253.* One of the largest hotels in town, this 141-room hotel near downtown and the lake has an indoor swimming pool and a restaurant. $$–$$$

Budget Inn. *1306 North 25th Street, Clear Lake; (641) 357–8700.* Located near the lake at the junction of Interstate 35 and US 18, this sixty-room chain motel has an outdoor pool and a playground. $–$$

Heartland Inn, *1603 South Shore Drive, Clear Lake; (800) 334–3277 or (641) 357–5123.* The thirty guest rooms face the lake at this small, homey hotel, which also has an indoor pool and its own dock for fishing, boat launching, or sitting on benches to watch the sunset. $$$–$$$$

For More Information

Clear Lake Chamber of Commerce. *205 Main Avenue, Clear Lake 50428; (800) 285–5338 or (641) 357–2159,* *www.clearlakeiowa.com, chamber@netins.net.*

Mason City

Think Mason City. Think *The Music Man*. This is the hometown of the 1957 Tony-award winning musical's composer, Meredith Willson, as you'll soon find out when you arrive. Mason City is also known for its Prairie School architecture. It's 8 miles east of Clear Lake off State Highway 122 and US 65.

KINNEY PIONEER MUSEUM (all ages)

9184-G 265th Street, Mason City 50401; (641) 423–1259 or 357–2980. Open noon to 5:00 P.M. Wednesday through Sunday from May through September. $.

This is a re-created pioneer village with a one-room schoolhouse, log cabin, blacksmith shop, and living prairie. Pioneer crafts and trades are demonstrated on the weekends. You can also see fossils, dolls, and antique cars. It's located 7 miles west of town on State Highway 122 at the entrance to the Municipal Airport.

MEREDITH WILLSON BOYHOOD HOME (ages 6 and up)

314 South Pennsylvania Avenue, Mason City 50401; (641) 423–3534, www.themusicmansquare.org, musicman@mach3ww.com. Open 1:00 to 4:00 P.M. Monday through Sunday from May through October; 1:00 to 4:00 P.M. Saturday and Sunday from November through April, or by appointment. $, ages 5 and under Free.

This is the pretty Queen Anne–style 1895 home Meredith Willson grew up in. Once referred to as "a walking commercial for Iowa," Willson was born in 1902 in Mason City and later based *The Music Man,* set in River City circa 1912, on his childhood memories of Mason City. You can take a self-guided tour of the home, which is filled with family and musical memorabilia. Some guided tours are available. Willson left Mason City at age seventeen, lured by the bright lights of New York City. He died in California in 1984.

MUSIC MAN SQUARE (all ages)

308 South Pennsylvania Avenue, Mason City 50401; (641) 424–2852, www. themusicmansquare.org, musicman@mach3ww.com. Open 1:00 to 5:00 P.M. Monday through Sunday. Museum, $. It's Free *to enter the streetscape.*

The big new attraction in town, this $10 million limestone complex formally opened in 2002. From the outside it looks like a new convention center, except it's decorated with musical notes and the words from the *Music Man* song "76 Trombones." Step inside and you're in a re-created 1912 River City streetscape with set designs from the movie, an ice-cream parlor with a working soda fountain, and a candy shop. There's also a museum devoted to the musical with Willson memorabilia, wax statues of music greats, and a recording studio. Look for special children's programs inside the square at the Exploratorium, located in the Madison Park area.

CHARLES H. MACNIDER MUSEUM (ages 3 and up)

303 Second Street SE, Mason City 50401; (641) 421–3666, macnider@ macniderart.org. Open 9:00 A.M. to 9:00 P.M. Tuesday and Thursday, 9:00 A.M. to 5:00 P.M. Wednesday, Friday, and Saturday, and 1:00 to 5:00 P.M. Sunday. **Free.**

Don't miss the huge collection of puppets, marionettes, and related props in this graceful Tudor-style mansion overlooking Willow Creek. Some of the puppets were featured in the movie *The Sound of Music*. The museum also has a collection of nineteenth- and twentieth-century American art. A fun time to visit is during the annual arts festival held the third weekend in August, when there are many craft and art activities for children.

FRANK LLOYD WRIGHT STOCKMAN HOUSE (ages 7 and up)

530 First Street NE, Mason City 50401; (641) 421–3666. Open 10:00 A.M. to 5:00 P.M. Thursday through Saturday and 1:00 to 5:00 P.M. Sunday from June through August, 10:00 A.M. to 5:00 P.M. Saturday and 1:00 to 5:00 P.M. Sunday from September through October. $.

The Stockman House is the only Prairie School house Frank Lloyd Wright designed in Iowa. It's also the only middle-class home from Wright's Prairie School period that's open to the public. Lovingly restored, the Stockman House is full of Arts and Crafts furniture and period reproductions of Wright furniture.

BIRDSALL ICE CREAM COMPANY (all ages)

518 North Federal Avenue, Mason City 50401; (641) 423–5365. Open 10:30 A.M. to 10:00 P.M. daily except Christmas and Thanksgiving.

Little has changed at this old-fashioned ice-cream parlor that Addison Birdsall opened just north of downtown in 1931 (although there are now more flavors to choose from). You can still sit at the counter inside or along the wall outside and have a shake, sundae, cone, or malt. Vanilla, chocolate, and chocolate chip remain best-sellers, but a favorite, made only in August, is fresh peach. There are also Birdsalls at Music Man Square and the Southbridge Mall downtown.

Architectural Walking Tour

Mason City has the largest group of Prairie-style homes on one site in the nation, and the best way to see them is on foot. Pick up a helpful walking tour guide at the Mac-Nider Museum or the Stockman House and explore the Rock Glen–Rock Crest National Historic District. During the fourteen-block walk, you'll pass by eight private homes (you can't go inside) designed by Wright's Chicago colleagues and built between 1912 and 1917. You'll also cross pretty Willow Creek on the Music Man footbridge. The tour ends at the Stockman House.

LIME CREEK NATURE CENTER (all ages)

3501 Lime Creek Road, Mason City 50401; (641) 423–5309. Open 8:00 A.M. to 4:00 P.M. Monday through Friday, 9:00 A.M. to 5:00 P.M. Saturday, and 1:00 to 5:00 P.M. Sunday; closes at 4:00 P.M. Saturday and Sunday during the winter. **Free.**

This 406-acre nature center includes 4 miles of trails through restored prairie for walking, cross-country skiing, biking, and horseback riding. It also has a conservation education facility, a restored prairie, a nature center with animal displays, and special programs for children. It's on US 65 about 6 miles north of downtown.

A Rubiner Family Adventure

Hunger struck on a glorious summer day as my family was cruising across northern Iowa on a two-lane rural highway. We needed a place to unpack our picnic—fast. Suddenly, looming ahead of us like a mirage was a sign for a park. Following the sign, we turned onto a gravel road that led past cornfields and into the woods, right to a lovely secluded park along a grassy riverbank. We had it all to ourselves. We soon found out why. As we left the car, we were overpowered by a foul smell, the odor of many hogs somewhere nearby. For the first time, we truly understood why neighbors of the large hog-rearing operations that dot Iowa are complaining. And why the tourism folks are complaining. And why lawmakers are trying to mediate. We ate quickly, swung on some nearby swings quickly, and drove away. Quickly.

Where to Eat

Chandler's Eatery and Pub. *1617 Monroe Avenue, Mason City; (641) 421–1525.* A lunch and dinner spot, Chandler's has a varied menu with items including London broil, a Mediterranean salad, and grilled portobello mushrooms and salmon, plus pasta and cheesecake. $–$$

Northwestern Steakhouse. *304 16th Street NW, Mason City; (641) 423–5075.* Known for steaks and Greek food (from roasted chicken to stuffed grape leaves), this dinner spot in a small old brick building north of town is popular so make a reservation. $$$

Papa's American Cafe. *2960 Fourth Street SW, Mason City; (641) 424–1593.* Minnesota Vikings memorabilia decorates the walls of this casual restaurant best known for its barbecued ribs. Papa's also offers a ten-item children's menu and pizza, salads, dinners, and sandwiches. $

Where to Stay

Hanford Inn. *3041 Fourth Street SW, Mason City; (800) 424–9491 or (641) 424–9494.* Located in a commercial strip off Interstate 35 on State Highway 122 West, this seventy-two-room full-service hotel has an indoor pool, recreation room, and restaurant. $$

Holiday Inn. *2101 Fourth Street SW, Mason City; (641) 423–1640.* A full-service hotel near the junction of Interstate 35 and US 18, this 135-room hotel has a restaurant and "holidome" indoor recreation area with a pool and game room. $$–$$$

Super 8. *3010 Fourth Street SW, Mason City; (641) 423–8855.* This fifty-seven-room chain motel located at exit 193 of Interstate 35 near the airport has an indoor pool. $$–$$$

For More Information

Mason City Convention and Visitors Bureau. *15 West State Street, Mason City 50401; (800) 423–5724 or (641) 422–1663, www.masoncity tourism.com, cvb@masoncityia.com.*

Other Things to See and Do in North-Central Iowa

- **Grimes Conservation Farm.** Marshalltown, (641) 754–6303
- **Edel's Blacksmith Shop.** Haverhill, (641) 475–3299
- **Octagon Center for the Arts.** Ames, (515) 232–5331
- **Hoggatt School.** Ames, (515) 232–2148
- **Boone Speedway.** Boone, (515) 987–1220
- **Telephone Company Museum.** Jefferson, (515) 386–4141
- **Historic Sod House.** West Bend, (515) 887– 4721
- **Fort Defiance State Park.** Estherville, (712) 337–3211.
- **Winnebago Visitor Center.** Forest City, (641) 585–6936
- **I–35 Speedway.** Mason City, (641) 424–6515

Western Iowa

Y ou're following in famous footsteps when you explore western Iowa. Explorers Meriwether Lewis and William Clark were here in 1804. Today the region offers several Lewis and Clark attractions, with more to come during the bicentennial celebration of the expedition starting in 2003. Western Iowa also has the state's last patch of wilderness—the rare geological formation known as the Loess Hills—and other popular outdoor spots, including the Iowa Great Lakes, Storm Lake, and the Desoto National Wildlife Area.

For more cultivated fun, visit the museums of Sioux City and the Council Bluffs/Omaha area. You'll also find cultural reminders of Iowa's immigrant past (Danes in Elk Horn, Dutch in Orange City, and Swedes in Stanton) and rural roots (the Clay County Fair, the Sidney Rodeo, and the Henry Wallace Country Life Center).

For a counterclockwise tour, start in the region's northeast corner, in the Iowa Great Lakes, then go south on US 71 to Spencer and southwest to Le Mars and then Sioux City. Keep moving south along Interstate 29 (or smaller back roads) through the Loess Hills and Council Bluffs to Sidney in the state's southwest corner. Next travel east on State Highway 2 to Shenandoah, and then up north on State Highway 48 and east on State Highway 92 through Greenfield. Take Interstate 80 west to Elk Horn and then northeast to Coon Rapids, located on State Highway 141. Last stop, via US 71 North, is Storm Lake.

For More Information

Western Iowa Tourism Region.
103 North Third Street, Red Oak 51566;
(888) 623–4232 or (712) 623–4232,

www.traveliowa.org, witroffice@redoak.
heartland.net.

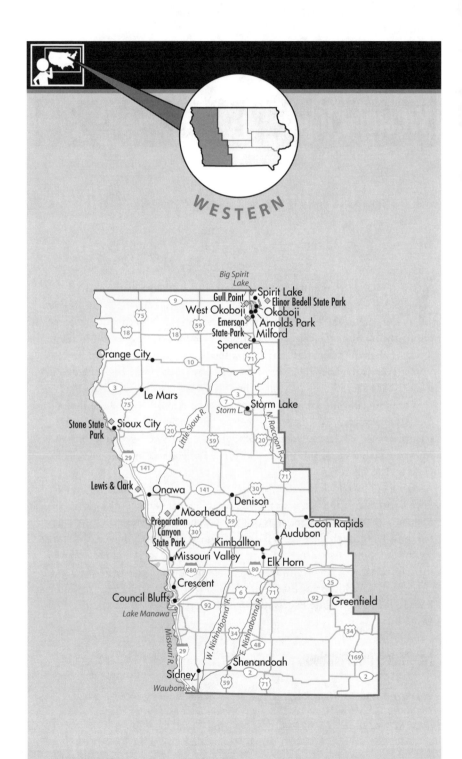

WESTERN

Big Spirit Lake
Gull Point
Spirit Lake
Elinor Bedell State Park
West Okoboji
Okoboji
Emerson
State Park
Arnolds Park
Milford
Spencer

Orange City

Le Mars

Storm Lake
Storm L.

Stone State
Park
Sioux City

Lewis & Clark
Onawa

Denison

Preparation
Canyon
State Park
Moorhead

Coon Rapids

Audubon

Kimballton

Missouri Valley
Elk Horn

Crescent

Council Bluffs
Lake Manawa

Greenfield

Little Sioux R.

N. Raccoon R.

Missouri R.

W. Nishnabotna R.

E. Nishnabotna R.

Sidney
Waubonsie

Shenandoah

Betsy's Top Ten
Picks for Fun in Western Iowa

1. Iowa Great Lakes

2. Clay County Fair, Spencer

3. Omaha's Henry Doorly Zoo, near Council Bluffs

4. Loess Hills Prairie Seminar

5. Ice Cream Capital Tour, Le Mars

6. Orange City Tulip Festival

7. Garst Farm Resorts, Coon Rapids

8. Danish Windmill Museum, Elk Horn

9. Preparation Canyon State Park, Moorhead

10. Miller's Country Zoo, Greenfield

Iowa Great Lakes

The Iowa Great Lakes, off State Highway 9 and US 71, include the resort towns of Okoboji, Spirit Lake, Arnolds Park, and Milford. This is one of the state's most popular recreational areas for summer and winter fun. West Lake Okoboji and Big Spirit Lake are the largest of seven lakes.

SPIRIT LAKE FISH HATCHERY (all ages)

122 252nd Avenue, Orleans 51360; (712) 336–1840. Guided tours 8:00 A.M. to 4:00 P.M. Monday through Friday. **Free.**

Located in a small town northeast of Spirit Lake, this hatchery collects, spawns, incubates, and raises walleye used throughout Iowa. Try to visit in early to mid-April when walleye spawning is in full swing.

ELINOR BEDELL STATE PARK (all ages)

Off County Road M56 on the east shore of East Lake Okoboji, Spirit Lake; (712) 337–3211, www.state.ia.us/government/dnr/organiza/ppd/bedell.htm, elinor_bedell@dnr.state.ia.us. Open 4:00 A.M. to 10:30 P.M. daily. **Free.**

One of the last open spaces in the Great Lakes, this eighty-acre park is Iowa's newest state park, opened in 1998. Perfect for picnicking, camping, and swimming, it also has a large playground and a lakeshore trail with a wildlife viewing blind. There's a small tent camping area, eight RV campsites with full hookups, and a modern rest room and shower. The park is just north of the YMCA Camp Foster area.

THE RANCH AMUSEMENT PARK (ages 3 and up)

1800 South Highway 71, Okoboji 51355; (712) 332–2159. Open 11:00 A.M. to 11:00 P.M. daily from Memorial Day through Labor Day weekend; call for May and September hours. $; discounts on Wednesday.

This outdoor entertainment park has children's rides, bumper boats, an arcade, and a miniature golf course with a Wild West theme. Kids age ten and up (at least 56 inches tall) can ride the Tiger Cat Go-Cart Racer on a speedway with hairpin turns. For ages five through ten, there's a kids-only mini go-cart track.

ulture for Kids

- **Boji Bantam Theatre,** 2001 Highway 71 North, Okoboji (712–332–7773, www.stephens.edu/www/PR/News/Okoboji.html), offers special summer productions for children. The theater is part of the Okoboji Summer Theatre, a summer-stock troupe.

- **Lakes Art Center,** 2001 Highway 71 North, Okoboji (712–332–7013, www.lakesart.org), located next to the Okoboji Summer Theatre, offers hands-on activities and art classes for children.

OKOBOJI QUEEN II EXCURSIONS (all ages)

243 West Broadway, Arnolds Park 51331; (800) 599–6995 or (712) 332–2183. Open noon to 8:00 P.M. daily from Memorial Day through Labor Day weekend, weekends in May and early September. $$, children less than 36 inches tall ride **Free.**

Ride on the open-air upper deck or in the enclosed lower deck of this 200-passenger excursion boat during an 18-mile narrated tour of West Okoboji Lake. There's food onboard.

ARNOLDS PARK AMUSEMENT PARK (all ages)

Highway 71 and Lake Street, Arnolds Park 51331; (800) 599–6995 or (712) 332–2183, www.arnoldspark.com. Open 11:00 A.M. to 10:00 P.M. (sometimes 7:00 P.M.) daily from Memorial Day through Labor Day weekend, weekends in May and early September. $$$, children less than 36 inches tall **Free.**

More than one hundred years old, Arnolds Park has thirty rides and attractions, including one of the nation's top ten wooden roller coasters, a giant Ferris wheel, and a new log ride, the Boji Falls Log Flume. There are also games, shows, go-carts, miniature golf, and souvenir shopping at the nearby Emporium and Queens Court shops.

Zany Winter Games The annual University of Okoboji Winter Games, one of Iowa's kookiest events, are held in late January, usually on Super Bowl weekend. This is your chance to see broom ball, a cross between soccer and hockey that's played on ice with a volleyball-size ball (but players don't wear ice skates). Teams from around the nation compete. Other events during the games include human bowling, the Freeze Your Fanny bike ride, kids' kite flying, and snowmobile races. There are also dogsled rides, snowball softball, an ice-fishing contest for kids, and a Friday night chili contest and feed. Several summer resorts and restaurants reopen for the Winter Games, which are held on Smith's Bay in West Lake Okoboji.

 IOWA GREAT LAKES MARITIME MUSEUM (ages 5 and up)
243 West Broadway Avenue, Arnolds Park 51331; (800) 270–2574 or (712) 332–2107. Open 9:00 A.M. to 9:00 P.M. daily from Memorial Day through Labor Day weekend, shorter hours the rest of the year. $.

Located on West Lake Okoboji, this maritime museum traces the region's nautical history. It features a raised wooden boat that once sank, and a theater that shows movies about lake history.

Outdoor Fun

- Good beaches on West Lake Okoboji include **Pike's Point,** off State Highway 9 to the northeast, **Gull Point State Park,** off State Highway 86 to the west, and **Terrace Park** to the south.

- Boat rentals, including kayaks, boats, canoes, and Jet Skis, are available at **Funtime Rentals** (712–332–2540), **Mau Marine** (712–332–5626), and **Oak Hill Marina** (800–266–6858 or 712–332–2701).

- Hiking, biking, and in-line skating can be enjoyed on the **Spine Trail,** a 14-mile stretch of old railroad bed between Milford and Spirit Lake.

University of Okoboji You'll see University of Okoboji bumper stickers and T-shirts worn across Iowa, but guess what? It doesn't exist. The phantom college was invented by the Three Sons, an outdoor clothing store in Milford that sells the "U of O" gear.

TREASURE VILLAGE (all ages)

2023 Highway 86, Milford 51351; (712) 337–3730. Open 9:00 A.M. to 10:00 P.M. Monday through Saturday and 10:00 A.M. to 10:00 P.M. Sunday from Memorial Day through Labor Day weekend. $.

This amusement park three miles northwest of Milford offers live children's theater performances of classics like *Snow White*, plus a twenty-seven-hole miniature golf course, antique flea markets, and other special events.

BOJI BAY WATER PARK (all ages)

2207 Okoboji Avenue (US 71), Milford 51351; (712) 338–2473. Open 11:30 A.M. to 6:00 P.M. daily from Memorial Day through Labor Day weekend. $$$ for adults, $$ for children, ages 3 and under Free.

This family water park at the corner of US 71 and State Highway 86 has four water slides, a wave pool, tube rides, a lazy river ride, sand volleyball, a wading pool for young children, a children's pool and beach, an indoor game area, and concessions.

Where to Eat

Bavarian Gardens Bar and Grill. *144 Lakeshore Drive, Arnolds Park; (712) 332–2990.* After playing at the Arnolds Park amusement park or shopping at the Central Emporium, pick up a burger here—you can even drive your boat up. $

Crescent Beach Restaurant. *1620 Lakeshore Drive, Wahpeton; (800) 417–1117 or (712) 337–3351.* Located off State Highway 86 at the Crescent Beach Resort, this lakefront restaurant serves filet mignon, Iowa chops, and fresh fish, and has a children's menu. Kids who finish early can play at the nearby island playground. $$–$$$

The Dry Dock. *Highway 71, Arnolds Park; (712) 332–9449.* This restaurant is best known for its great lake views and sandwiches (try the French dip or sirloin steak). There's also a Friday night fish fry and a children's menu. $

Smokin' Jakes. *117 West Broadway Street, Arnolds Park; (712) 332–5152.* Open April through November, this is the place for smoked meat dinners and sandwiches (ribs, pork chops, beef, chicken), plus steaks and ice cream. $–$$$

The Tacos House. *1614 Terrace Park Boulevard, Milford; (712) 262–2192.*

Open March through October, this popular local hangout on the edge of US 71 about a mile south of Arnolds Park serves Mexican fast food and ice cream at indoor and outdoor tables. $

The Wharf. *Highway 71, Okoboji; (712) 332–2744.* This waterside spot is known for its burgers, steaks, seafood,

and pasta. There's also a children's menu. $–$$

Yesterdays. *131 West Broadway, Arnolds Park; (712) 332–2353.* Open April through December, this fine-dining spot specializing in fresh seafood has a children's menu. $$

Great Lakes Menus Online To browse more than thirty restaurant menus in the Okoboji area, visit www.iowagreatlakes.com/ _din/_menus/.

Where to Stay

Arnolds Park Classic Cottages. *35 Zephyr Drive, Arnolds Park; (712) 332–5320.* Near many local attractions, these ten old-fashioned cottages include air-conditioning and heat, kitchenettes, a covered picnic area with a patio and grill, and public dock access. $$$$

Crescent Beach Lodge. *1620 Lakeshore Drive, Wahpeton 51351; (800) 417–1117 or (712) 337–3351, www.crescentbeachlodge.com.* This old-fashioned resort on West Lake Okoboji's Emerson Bay just outside Milford on US 86, offers lodging May through September (with a three-night minimum) in forty-four hotel-style rooms including suites, four condos, and a cottage. A children's recreational program, boats, and a playground with rocket slide and miniature golf are available. $$$–$$$$

Emerson Bay State Park. *3100 Emerson Street, West Okoboji; (712) 337–*

3211. First-come first-served lakeshore camping is available (with nearby swimming, boating, fishing, and some cable TV sites) at this state park 2½ miles northwest of Milford on US 86. $

Fillenwarth Beach. *87 Lakeshore Drive, Arnolds Park; (712) 332–5646, www.fillenwarthbeach.com.* A children's recreation program and a baby-sitting service are provided at this old-fashioned resort on West Lake Okoboji. It has ninety-three rooms (including cabins) with kitchens and air-conditioning, plus a beach, tennis courts, boating, cruises, and indoor and outdoor pools. $$–$$$

Gull Point State Park. *1500 Harpen Drive, Wahpeton; (712) 337–3211, www.state.ia.us/dnr/organiza/ppd/gullpt.htm.* Located 3½ miles north of Milford on US 86, this beautiful 193-acre preserve on West Okoboji Lake offers first-come first-served lakeshore camping. There are 112 sites with modern facilities, a historic 1930s lodge, a 1½-mile hiking trail, and nearby swimming, boating, and fishing. $

The Inn at Okoboji. *3301 Lakeshore Drive, Okoboji; (877) 265–4386 or (712) 332–2113.* More than 100 years old, the Inn at Okoboji has a recreation program for children ages three to twelve. There are 152 rooms (including several suites and a cottage), plus a playground, indoor and outdoor pools, a

nine-hole golf course, sand volleyball, and boat rental. The inn is open from April to October. $$$$

Village East Resort. *1405 Highway 71, Okoboji; (800) 727–4561 or (712) 332–2161, www.villageeastresort.com.* This resort has one hundred rooms and suites, a children's playground, an outdoor pool, and an indoor heated Olympic-size pool. $$$–$$$$

For More Information

Okoboji Tourism Committee. *P.O. Box 215, Okoboji 51355; (800) 270–* *2574 or (712) 332–2209, www.vacation okoboji.com, info@vacationokoboji.com.*

Spencer

Located 15 miles south of the Iowa Great Lakes at the junction of US 71 and US 18, Spencer has one of the Midwest's largest and most diverse collections of 1930s architecture (the downtown was rebuilt after a devastating 1931 fire) and one of the world's best county fairs, a nine-day extravaganza in September.

INKPADUTA CANOE TRAIL (all ages)
Runs from Spencer south to the Woodbury County town of Smithland; (712) 225–5959; for a map call (712) 262–2187.

This slow-moving 130-mile portion of the Little Sioux River is perfect for fishing, canoeing, and spotting otters, white-tailed deer, and great blue herons. It starts in Spencer and has many other access points.

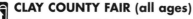

CLAY COUNTY FAIR (all ages)
Fairgrounds at 1404 Fourth Avenue West, Spencer 50130; (712) 262–4740, www.claycountyfair.com, clayfair@ncn.net. Open nine days in mid-September. $, ages 7 and under **Free.**

This is Iowa's largest and best-known county fair, dating back to the early 1900s. It usually begins the second week in September and includes carnival rides and games, live music by nationally known performers, tractor pulls, livestock shows, rodeos, a classic car show, car races, and "Blaze," the balloon-blowing goat. Camping is available at the fairgrounds.

Where to Eat

Carroll's Bakery and Deli. *416 Grand Avenue, Spencer; (712) 262–4575.* Sandwiches, baked chicken, barbecued pork, salads, and yummy creme horns are served at this downtown lunch spot. $

Hava Java. *12 West Fourth Street, Spencer; (712) 262–3207.* Hava Java is a coffeehouse that also serves sandwiches and soup. $

Picnic Possibilities Try **River View Park**, at 612 47th Street Southeast, a sixty-acre park with landscaped lawns, nature trails, aquatic center, and tennis courts.

Where to Stay

AmericInn. *1005 Thirteenth Street Southwest, Spencer; (712) 262–7525.* This chain motel off US 71 south of downtown has a large indoor pool and forty-six rooms, including two-room suites. $$–$$$$

Hannah Marie Country Inn. *4070 Highway 71 South, Spencer; (712) 262–1286, www.nwiowabb.com/hannah.htm.* A real treat, this award-winning inn is located in two country Victorian houses on a 200-acre farm 4 miles south of Spencer. It has six individually themed guest rooms, and its dining rooms are painted to resemble an English village and an Italian courtyard. A hearty breakfast is served. $$$–$$$$

For More Information

Spencer Chamber of Commerce. *122 West Fifth Street, Spencer 51301; (712) 262–5680, www.spenceriowachamber.org, spencerchamber@smunet.net.*

Orange City

Settled by Dutch immigrants in 1870 and named after the Dutch leader William of Orange, this city revels in its Dutch-ness during an annual three-day Tulip Festival held the third weekend in May. Orange City is about 52 miles southwest of Spencer on State Highway 10.

VOGEL WINDMILL (ages 5 and up)

1020 Albany Place, Orange City 51041; (712) 737–8880. Open by appointment. Guided tours by request. **Free.**

Touring this replica of a windmill, you'll learn how wind power turns heavy gears to grind paint pigment. The windmill was built in 1967 by Andrew Vogel, an Orange City entrepreneur who founded the national paint brand Diamond Vogel, now one of Orange City's top employers (with headquarters behind the windmill). The windmill also has a replica of an old Dutch bedroom; vegetables are stored under the bed for freshness. To visit the windmill, pick up the key at the customer service office of the Diamond Vogel headquarters.

Tulip Festival Held since 1935, Orange City's three-day Tulip Festival begins with street cleaning. During this Dutch tradition, men and boys douse the streets with water, followed by women and girls in long aprons and lace caps pushing heavy brooms. The festival also features Dutch delicacies like tulip lollipops and spicy saucijzebroodjes (pigs in blankets), plus Dutch dancing, music, and fashions amid thousands of blooming tulips. The festival runs from Thursday through Saturday; daily activities include parades at 2:15 and 6:30 P.M., tours of the Vogel Windmill, and wooden clog-making demonstrations at the Old Factory, a shop at 110 Fourth Street Southwest.

Where to Eat

Dutch Bakery. *221 Central Avenue Northeast, Orange City; (712) 737–4360.* Watch doughnuts and Dutch letters (S-shaped almond-filled pastries) being made in the back of this bakery that also serves soup and salad and offers daily lunch specials. $

Hatchery. *121 Third Street Northwest, Orange City; (712) 737–2889.* Reservations are recommended at this lunch and dinner spot serving steaks, burgers, and Mexican food in what used to be an old egg hatchery. $$

Picnic Possibilities Visit **Windmill Park** downtown, which has a playground, windmill, band shell, shelter, and tulip gardens.

Where to Stay

Dutch Colony Inn. *706 Eighth Street Southeast, Orange City; (712) 737–3490.* Located on a commercial strip of State Highway 10 East on the south side of town, this hotel has thirty-eight rooms and a free continental breakfast. $$

Super 8. *810 Lincoln Place, Orange City; (712) 737–2600.* This chain motel near State Highway 10 East has thirty-four rooms, including two family suites. $$

For More Information

Orange City Chamber of Commerce and Visitors Center. *509 Eighth Street Southeast, Orange City 51401;*

(712) 707–4510, www.orangecityiowa.com, octulip@frontiernet.net.

Le Mars

Le Mars bills itself as the ice-cream capital of the world. (Read on to find out why.) It's 17 miles southwest of Orange City at the junction of State Highways 60 and 3 and US 75.

ICE CREAM CAPITAL OF THE WORLD VISITOR CENTER (ages 4 and up)

16 Fifth Avenue Northwest, Le Mars 51031; (712) 546–4090, www.bluebunny. com. Open 11:00 A.M. to 5:00 P.M. Monday through Friday, 9:00 A.M. to 5:00 P.M. Saturday, and 1:00 to 5:00 P.M. Sunday from September through April 1; 9:00 A.M. to 5:00 P.M. Monday through Saturday and 1:00 to 5:00 P.M. Sunday from early April through August. $, ages 3 and under Free.

Learn the history of ice cream and how it is made at the home of Wells' Dairy and Blue Bunny Ice Cream, located at the junction of US 75 and State Highway 3. The visitor center includes a simulated production line with equipment and videos of real ice-cream production, a theater with ice-cream history films, and an interactive computer area with ice-cream-related computer games. End your visit by stopping at the 1920s-style sweet shop and ice-cream parlor for a phosphate, malt, shake, specialty sundae (try the *Avalanche*), or hard-dip cone. The Wells family opened this dairy in 1913, and family members still live in Le Mars, which claims to produce more ice cream by a single company than any other city in the world. An annual Ice Cream Days celebration with a children's learning fair, band concerts, an art fair, and cook-off contest is often held around July 4.

Where to Eat

Archie's Waeside. *224 Fourth Avenue Northeast, Le Mars; (712) 546–7011.* Don't miss the Benny Weiker filet mignon, bone-in rib eye, and huge pork chops for dinner at this western Iowa institution that's been owned by the same family since 1949. There's a children's menu. $$–$$$

Bob's Drive Inn. *Highway 75 South, Le Mars; (712) 546–5445.* Pick up a "Bob-dog" (a hot dog) and "Rootbeer Whip" (a root beer with whipped ice milk) at this popular local drive-in. $

Where to Stay

Amber Inn. *635 Eighth Avenue Southwest, Le Mars; (800) 338–0298.* About 1½ miles from the Ice Cream Visitor Center on US 75 South, this locally owned, cheap, and clean motel has seventy rooms. $–$$.

For More Information

Le Mars Chamber of Commerce. *50 Central Avenue Southeast, Le Mars 51031; (712) 546–8821, www.LeMarsiowa.com.*

Sioux City

Iowa's fourth largest city sits on the state's western border overlooking the Missouri River at the junction of Interstate 29, US 75, and US 20, about 26 miles southwest of Le Mars. A major nineteenth-century port and twentieth-century meatpacking center, Sioux City offers museums, lively historic districts (including the two-block "Historic Fourth Street" and the Rose Hill District), and attractions that pay homage to its famous visitors, Lewis and Clark. (The local baseball team is the Explorers.) Thanks to a major 1990s redevelopment effort, especially along the riverfront at Chris Larsen Park, Sioux City boasts several attractions and trails on the Missouri, plus restored buildings such as the Orpheum Theatre, an old movie palace that offers some family-friendly live entertainment.

K.D. STATION (ages 2 and up)

2001 Leech Avenue, Sioux City 51101; (712) 277–8787. Open 9:00 A.M. to 11:00 P.M. Sunday through Thursday, 9:00 A.M. to 1:00 A.M. Friday and Saturday. **Free.**

Sort of a combo museum and mall, this family fun center—with miniature golf, bowling, restaurants, and shops, including a very good specialty meat and fish store—is located in what was once an enormous meatpacking plant (the bowling alley is in an old freezer). The dark brown factory, beside now empty stockyards, was built in 1918 and is a national historic site. Located off US 75, K.D. Station also has a new railroad museum.

Amazing Iowa Facts The Missouri River is the nation's longest river, flowing 2,250 miles through seven states from the Rocky Mountains to the Mississippi River. Today environmentalists, farmers, and boaters are battling over the future of "The Big Muddy." Man-made dams, dikes, and channels have tamed the once unruly river. This has prevented flooding, spurred barge traffic, and created fun places to boat and fish, but it has also harmed native fish and birds. Environmentalists want the river returned to a more natural state to save endangered animals, but farmers fear their fields will flood.

SIOUX CITY ART CENTER (ages 4 and up)

225 Nebraska Street, Sioux City 51101; (712) 279–6272. Open 10:00 A.M. to 5:00 P.M. Tuesday, Wednesday, Friday, and Saturday, noon to 9:00 P.M. Thursday, and 1:00 to 5:00 P.M. Sunday. **Free** *except for special exhibits.*

There's a terrific hands-on gallery for children in this art center. Built in 1996, it also has a dramatic three-story glass atrium silo and a 900-piece collection of contemporary and traditional art. Special exhibits are being planned for the Lewis and Clark Bicentennial. An annual Labor Day weekend arts festival is held in downtown Sioux City on the riverfront at the state-of-the-art Anderson Dance Pavilion. It features artists from around the country, a children's activity center, free entertainment, and concession stands. The pavilion also hosts the annual July 4th parade, a Mardi Gras–style parade, plus Kidsville, a special area with children's activities, including a petting zoo and carnival games.

What Do Western Iowa and Northern China Have in Common?

They're the only two places in the world with a rare land formation: hills made from unusually deep layers of loose river silt (*loess* in German, pronounced "luss"). Iowa's Loess Hills are a 200-mile-long narrow band of bluffs stretching from near Sioux City south to the Missouri border. The bluffs are made of loess that's up to 200 feet deep. Erosion by wind and water has sculpted some of the area's strange formations, from bumpy ridge crests that resemble an animal's back to "cat steps"—zigzagged terraces that look like long narrow staircases. These are best found to the north in the Iowa counties of Harrison, Monona, Woodbury, and Plymouth, near the towns of Castana, Hornick, Mondamin, Moorhead, Onawa, Pisgah, and Turin.

SERGEANT FLOYD RIVERBOAT MUSEUM (ages 7 and up)

1000 Larsen Park Road, Sioux City 51103; (712) 279–0198. Open 8:00 A.M. to 6:00 P.M. daily from May through September, 9:00 A.M. to 5:00 P.M. daily from October through April. **Free.**

This Missouri River history museum is located on a diesel inspection ship that worked the river for fifty years. There's a large display of scale Missouri River steamboat and keelboat models, plus a special focus on the Lewis and Clark expedition. Located at exit 149 of Interstate 29, the museum also has an Iowa Welcome Center with tourism information.

Sioux City Sports

- **Sioux City Explorers,** a minor-league baseball team, plays at the new Lewis and Clark Park, 340 Line Drive, Sioux City (exit 143 off Interstate 29); (712) 277–9467, www.xsbaseball.com.

- **Sioux City Musketeers,** a championship-winning junior A League hockey team, plays at the Municipal Auditorium, 401 Gordon Drive, Sioux City; (712) 252–2116, www.musketeershockey.com. They'll play at a new arena, the Tyson/IBP Events Center, scheduled to open in late 2003.

- **Sioux City Bandits,** an indoor arena football team, also plays at the Municipal Auditorium and will also play at the new arena. The team's Web site is www.scbandits.com.

Lewis and Clark History Lesson

In 1803 President Thomas Jefferson commissioned Captains Meriwether Lewis and William Clark to lead an expedition into the vast Louisiana Purchase to find a Northwest Passage connecting the Atlantic and Pacific Oceans. During their epic adventure, they mapped a way west, but they never found that passage. In May 1804 the thirty-one-member Corps of Discovery began its 8,000-mile journey in a 55-foot-long keelboat with two smaller boats, traveling up the Missouri River from St. Louis. That year, they spent several months exploring Iowa and Nebraska. In August 1804 near Sioux City, Sergeant Charles Floyd became the expedition's first and only casualty (cause of death: a ruptured appendix). Today, he's honored in Sioux City by a 1,000-foot-high stone obelisk, near K.D. Station. For more information visit www.lewisandclarkne-ia.com/pages/mapframe.html.

 LEWIS AND CLARK INTERPRETIVE CENTER (ages 5 and up)
900 Larsen Park Road, Sioux City 51103; (712) 224–5254. Open 8:00 A.M. to 6:00 P.M. daily from Memorial Day through Labor Day weekend, 9:00 A.M. to 5:00 P.M. Tuesday through Sunday the rest of the year. **Free.**

Try out to be a member of the Lewis and Clark Expedition at this new museum, which opened in 2002 to mark the bicentennial of the journey. Children receive a journal to write in and choose a role they'd like to play on the expedition. Then they tour exhibits pegged to expedition events that occurred in the Sioux City area. Displays highlight the everyday members of the expedition, the nature they encountered, plus eighteenth-century medicine and military life. There's also a short video about Sergeant Floyd, the expedition member who died near Sioux City. The center is located next to the Sergeant Floyd Riverboat Museum.

 **DOROTHY PECAUT NATURE CENTER IN STONE STATE PARK (all ages)**
4500 Sioux River Road, Sioux City 51109; (712) 258–0838, www.woodbury parks.com. Center open 9:00 A.M. to 5:00 P.M. Tuesday through Saturday and 1:00 to 4:00 P.M. Sunday year-round, until 8:00 P.M. Tuesday and Thursday from May through October. Park open 4:00 A.M. to 10:30 P.M. daily. **Free.**

A "walk-under" prairie, natural history dioramas, and a 400-gallon aquarium filled with native fish are highlights of this $1.4 million nature center that explains the Loess Hills' unusual ecosystem. It's located in 1,029-acre Stone Park, which is in northwest Sioux City along State Highway 12, 4 miles north of Interstate 29. At the nature center, kids can handle furs, fossils, antlers, and other artifacts in the children's discovery area and hike on 2 miles of trails around the center. The park also is a great place to picnic, hike, cross-country ski, mountain bike, and camp. There are wonderful views of the Loess Hills' wooded valleys and dry prairie ridges, plus views of neighboring South Dakota and Nebraska. Late April and early May are the best times to see woodland wildflowers. The park has thirty-two campsites, twelve with electric hookups, flush toilets, and showers. Reservations are required. For more information call (712) 255–4698. To get to the nature center from Interstate 29, take exit 151 to State Road 12 North. Continue 3 miles, passing a Dairy Queen, four-way intersection, and railroad tracks, to a T intersection. Go left on Sioux River Road (State Highway 12) and drive 1 mile to a sign for the nature center.

*E*xploring the Loess Hills The best way to experience the Loess Hills' subtle beauty is on foot or on a bike. (One of the best hikes is up Murray Hill, near Pisgah. Onabike is a one-day organized bike ride through the hills in August.) Other options include cycling, birdwatching, fishing, hunting, cross-country skiing, mushroom hunting, camping, and autumn leaf-gazing. You can also drive on the Loess Hills Scenic Byway, which runs parallel to Interstate 29, traveling through seven western Iowa counties, each with its own scenic loop, some gravel, some paved. Try the Spring Valley Loop near Sidney, the Preparation Loop near Turin, or the Ridge Road Loop near Westfield. For a brochure call (888) 623–4232 or (712) 886–5441. Or call the Loess Hills Hospitality Association in Moorhead at (800) 886–5441.

Where to Eat

Aggie's. *107 Sergeant Square Drive, Sergeant Bluff; (712) 943–8888.* Smoked (not soaked) baby back ribs and brisket, plus yummy sides and homemade cobbler are worth the drive to Aggie's, a barbecue smokehouse 7 miles south of Sioux City. $$

Daily Grind. *511 Fourth Street, Sioux City; (712) 277–2020.* In the Historic Fourth Street area dotted with nineteenth-century buildings that house restaurants, retail stores, and condos, this fancy coffee bar also has some quick-lunch options, including design-your-own chef salads, sandwiches (try the chicken salad or albacore tuna), and homemade soup. Save room for a huge white-frosted cinnamon bun and rich turtle cheesecake. $

Green Gables. *1800 Pierce Street, Sioux City; (712) 258–4246.* Try the walleye pike, matzoh ball soup, chicken salad, and hot fudge sundaes (the fudge comes in a pour-your-own pitcher) at this longtime family favorite and third-generation-owned restaurant. $-$$

Sweet Fanny's. *1024 Fourth Street, Sioux City; (712) 258–3434.* Located in the historic warehouse district with old brick buildings featuring huge windows, this WWII-themed restaurant serves burgers, seafood, and prime rib for lunch and dinner. $-$$$

Tastee Inn and Out. *2610 Gordon Drive, Sioux City; (712) 255–0857.* Pick up a Tastee Sandwich (loose ground beef on a bun) and onion chips at this longtime drive-thru with a walk-up window (and no seats). $

Amazing Iowa Facts Iowa is a top popcorn producer. In 1914 Cloid Smith (yes, Cloid) and his son Howard shelled, cleaned, and packaged the first official brand of popcorn in the basement of their Sioux City home. Jolly Time Popcorn is still sold today.

Where to Stay

Hilton Inn. *707 Fourth Street, Sioux City; (800) 593–0555 or (712) 277–4101.* You'll find an indoor pool, 193 rooms, and Missouri River views at this high-rise hotel downtown. $$$

Holiday Inn. *701 Gordon Drive, Sioux City; (800) 238–6147 or (712) 277–9400.* The Holiday Inn has a convenient downtown location (exit 147B off Interstate 29), an indoor pool, and living-room suites among its 114 rooms. $$-$$$

Sioux City Sisters The original advice columnists Ann Landers and Abigail "Dear Abby" Van Buren were born in Sioux City in 1918 and lived there until after high school. At birth, the identical twins were named Pauline "Po-po" and Esther "Eppie" Friedman.

For More Information

Sioux City Convention and Visitors Bureau. *801 Fourth Street, Sioux City* *51102; (800) 593–2228 or (712) 279–4800, www.siouxcitytourism.com.*

Onawa

About 36 miles south of Sioux City along the Missouri River near Interstate 29, Onawa claims to have the nation's widest Main Street. It's a Loess Hills gateway and another Lewis and Clark stop.

LEWIS AND CLARK KEELBOAT DISPLAY/LEWIS AND CLARK STATE PARK (all ages)

Highway 175 West five miles west of Onawa, 51040; (712) 423–2829. Open 8:00 A.M. to 6:00 P.M. daily from May through October. **Free.**

The Lewis and Clark Expedition arrived here on August 10, 1804, and stayed a while to observe the geography, plants, and animals. Today the thirty-acre park on 250-acre Blue Lake includes a full-size replica of the explorers' keelboat *Discovery.* It's the site of an annual June celebration of the Lewis and Clark Expedition, which features living history demonstrations. The park also offers hiking trails, boating, fishing, swimming, and camping; all eighty-one campsites along the lakeshore have electrical hookups.

The annual Lewis and Clark Festival is held in Onawa's Lewis and Clark Park. This three-day event held the second weekend in June is your big chance to ride the replica of the explorers' keelboat. Rides are offered in Blue Lake. The festival also includes demonstrations by buckskinners in frontier dress, bluegrass music, an adventure walk, and hawk throw. There's an arts and crafts fair and a Friday afternoon Buffalo Burger Feed at Gaukel Park, on 12th Street north of downtown near the Monona County Historical Museum.

THE SYLVAN RUNKEL STATE PRESERVE (all ages)

178th Street and Oak Avenue intersection, near Onawa; (712) 423–2426, www.state.ia.us/parks/sylvan.htm. Open 24 hours a day. **Free.**

Located near the site of the annual Loess Hills Prairie Seminar, this is a 330-acre preserve with classic Loess Hills scenery: steep, crested hills with long narrow summits, branching spurs, and footpaths on the main ridgetops. Getting to the preserve is tricky. From State Highway 175 and County Road L12 just east of Onawa, go north on L12 for about 7 miles to Nutmeg Avenue. Turn east, cross a bridge over the Little Sioux River, and turn south onto 178th Street, then go 2 miles to Oak Avenue. Just northeast of this intersection is an entrance to the footpath by a preserve sign.

A Rubiner Family Adventure

The camping is rugged at the annual Loess Hills Prairie Seminar, which is held each June in a wilderness area near Onawa. But when my family went to the weekend seminar, the toughest part was deciding which workshops to go to. Started more than twenty-six years ago, this once small "back to nature" seminar now draws more than 300 people for dozens of free workshops led by volunteers on the area's flora, fauna, nature, geology, and history. While my daughter Lily trooped off to a plant-sketching class, my son Noah went to "Reptiles and Amphibians," led by an enthusiastic mother-daughter team who pulled frogs, turtles, and snakes out of their van like magicians pulling rabbits out of a hat. Noah later went to a skulls, bones, and fur workshop, while Lily made nachos in a solar oven during a campfire cooking class and joined an archaeological dig during which someone found a 3-inch piece of petrified bone (from a giant ground sloth, the guide guessed).

But the weekend's highlight was a hike along a classic Loess Hills ridge, surrounded by open land and sky. Walking single-file on a bumpy, narrow dirt trail, we felt like we were walking along an animal's spine. On either side of us, the land dropped. In the distance, slopes blanketed with green native grasses and gullies filled with trees rose and fell like a warm, bumpy bed. To the west, past the vast floodplain, snaked the Missouri River. And, to my children's embarrassment, I couldn't resist: I flung my arms in the air, whirled like a dervish, and belted out, "The hills are alive with the sound of music."

For a seminar brochure call the Western Hills Area Education Agency at (712) 274–6000.

E.G.'S PUMPKIN FARM (all ages)

27126 Hazel Avenue, Onawa 51040; (800) 810–3276, www.egsfarm.com. Open noon to 10:00 P.M. from mid-September through October. $.

Each fall, this farm south of Onawa comes up with an enormous new maze design for kids to navigate. (A portrait of trumpeter Louis Armstrong one year, a giant electric guitar another year.) It also offers pumpkin picking, hayrides, pedal cart racing, straw bale bowling, farm animals, build-your-own scarecrows, pumpkin painting, and a Pumpkin Cafe and Boo-tique. On the weekends there's live music. From Onawa, go south on County Highway K45 to 260th Street, then west to Hazel Avenue and south to the farm.

Amazing Iowa Facts Onawa is the home of the Eskimo Pie. The chocolate-coated ice-cream treat was created here in 1919 and is proudly served at Oehler Brothers, a local cafe just off Interstate 29.

Where to Stay

Cabins at Little Sioux Park. *1746 Obrien Avenue, Correctionville; (712) 258–0838.* Built in 2001, these four cabins in a park about 20 miles northeast of Onawa near State Highway 31 and US 20 include twin bunk beds, running water, heating, air-conditioning, and electricity. They're available May through October by reservation only, with a minimum two-night stay required on weekends. Tent and RV camping is also available at the 375-acre park, which has a lakefront beach with lifeguards. $

Country Homestead Bed and Breakfast. *22133 Larpenteur Memorial Road, Turin; (712) 353–6772.* Nestled in a tiny Loess Hills town 7 miles east of Onawa, this pretty 1855 white farm-house decorated with family antiques is on a small working farm and has two guest rooms, each with private bath. A full farm breakfast is served. $$-$$$

The Inn at Battle Creek. *201 Maple Street, Battle Creek; (877) 365–4949.* Located in a small town on the edge of the Loess Hills about 30 miles north-east of Onawa off State Highway 175, this 1899 Victorian home has five antique-furnished guest rooms with private bath, including two that are adjoining and one with a double bed and pull-out day bed. Breakfast is included. A gourmet dinner is available at extra cost. $$$-$$$$

For More Information

Onawa Chamber of Commerce. *1009 Iowa Avenue, Onawa 51040; (712)* *423–1801, www.onawa.com, chamber@onawa.com.*

Moorhead

About 23 miles southeast of Onawa on State Highway 183, Moorhead is another Loess Hills outpost.

PREPARATION CANYON STATE PARK (all ages)
32257 Pecan Avenue, near Moorhead; (712) 423–2829, www.state.ia.us/ government/dnr/organiza/ppd/prepcan.htm. Open 4:00 A.M. to 10:30 P.M. daily. Free.

This remote 344-acre Loess Hills park has glorious views and is a great place to hike and picnic, with several trails that wind through the rugged hills past streams and springs. It's located off State Highway 183, 5 miles southwest of Moorhead. Camping is allowed only at nine hike-in sites, each with a table and fireplace, in the park's eastern half.

LOESS HILLS STATE FOREST OVERLOOK (all ages)

On 314th Street, between Moorhead and Pisgah; (712) 423–2829, www.state.ia.us/government/dnr/organiza/ppd/prepcan.htm. **Free.**

One of the best places to soak in the beauty of the Loess Hills and feel on top of the world, this is a large wooden deck and ramp with stunning views in a secluded spot near Preparation Canyon State Park. Take State Highway 183 about 3 miles south of Moorhead to 314th Street and turn west. Follow the road until the pavement ends and turn right onto gravel. Continue a few miles to the overlook.

Amazing Iowa Facts In 1955 a young girl discovered 5,500-year-old human bones in a gravel pit in the tiny Loess Hills town of Turin (population 103). The bones—actually the remains of four skeletons—were soon dubbed "Turin Man." Old-timers still talk about the crowds that flocked to Turin to see this major archaeological discovery.

Where to Eat

Blue Bonnet Cafe. *113 Oak Street, Moorhead; (712) 886–5465.* Home-cooked lunch specials from fried chicken to meat loaf and roast beef are served at this small-town cafe. Dinner is served on Friday night. $

Small's Fruit Farm. *2074 Highway 183, Mondamin; (712) 646–2193.* About 15 miles south of Moorhead, this pick-your-own orchard, which has a mill where you can watch apple cider being made, serves fresh apple, cherry, and strawberry pie. $

Loess Hills Orchards

- **Heartland Orchard.** 24164 Cottonwood Road, Council Bluffs; (712) 328-6875.

- **Stephen's Garden.** 29280 185th Street, Honey Creek; (712) 545-3680.

Where to Stay

Loess Hills Hideaway Cabins and Campground. *337th and Plum Streets, Moorhead; (402) 551–0690, www.loess hillshideaway.com/location.html.* This thirty-two-acre private campground on a wooded site has four rustic one-room housekeeping cabins built in 1997. Each sleeps up to seven people and has air-conditioning and kitchen facilities. There are also six campsites with modern facilities and hiking trails. $–$$

For More Information

Loess Hills Hospitality Center.
119 Oak Street, Moorhead 51558;
(800) 886–5441 or (712) 886–5441.

Missouri Valley

Missouri Valley is another Loess Hills gathering spot, south of Moorhead near the junction of Interstates 29 and 680.

DESOTO NATIONAL WILDLIFE REFUGE (all ages)

1434 315th Lane, Missouri Valley 51555; (712) 642–4121, midwest.fws.gov/ desoto/dsotobro.html. Refuge open during daylight hours; visitor center open 9:00 A.M. to 4:30 P.M. daily except holidays. **Free.**

Bald eagles, geese, and ducks flock to this 8,000-acre refuge with wetlands, grasslands, woodlands, and croplands along the Missouri River near US 30. The visitor center has weekend wildlife films, nature exhibits, and bird-viewing areas, plus artifacts from a supply boat that was heading to the Montana goldfields when it sank in 1865. Located 6 miles west of Missouri Valley, the refuge also has several hiking trails and a 12-mile auto tour with numbered stops. Pick up a brochure with information about the stops. Camping is available nearby at Wilson Island Recreation Area.

Where to Stay

Wilson Island Recreation Area.
32801 Campground Lane, Missouri Valley;
(712) 642–2069. Eleven miles south- west of Missouri Valley, just south of the DeSoto Refuge off State Highway 362, this secluded 577-acre area along

the Missouri River has 140 shady campsites with modern facilities, one cabin,
hiking trails, and picnic spots. $

For More Information

**Missouri Valley Chamber of Com-
merce.** *400 East Erie Street, Missouri
Valley 51555; (712) 642–2553, www.* *missourivalley.com, chamberofcommerce@
juno.com.*

Crescent

Crescent is located about 16 miles south of Missouri Valley on State Highway
183.

 ### MT. CRESCENT SKI AREA (ages 4 and up)
*17034 Snow Hill Lane; Crescent 51526; (712) 545–3850, www.skicrescent.
com, crescent@skicrescent.com. Season runs from December into March. Open
9:00 A.M. to 5:00 P.M. Monday through Thursday and 9:00 A.M. to 9:00 P.M. Fri-
day through Sunday. $$–$$$$.*

This ski area has a double chairlift, quad chairlift, ski classes, week-
end snow tubing, equipment rental, a snowmaking machine, and a
lodge with restaurants. To get here, take Interstate 29 to the Crescent
exit. Go 2 miles east to the town of Crescent and turn left onto State
Highway 183, and continue north 2 miles.

Council Bluffs

Council Bluffs is across the Missouri River from Omaha, Nebraska, at the
junction of Interstates 80 and 29 (about 5 miles south of Crescent). A stop on
both the Lewis and Clark Expedition and the Mormon Trail, Council Bluffs is
today best known by tourists for its two riverboat casinos.

COUNCIL BLUFFS DRIVE-IN THEATER (all ages)
*1130 West South Omaha Bridge Road, Council Bluffs 51501; (712) 366–
0422. $$, ages 11 and under* **Free.**

This is one of Iowa's few remaining drive-in movie theaters. First-run
movies are shown from April through October, starting at dusk.

Omaha Zoo

Omaha Zoo Lizards, poisonous snakes, a bat-eared fox, pumas, and other desert dwellers are all under the thirteen-story-tall, one-acre Desert Dome made of see-through acrylic panels at the Henry Doorly Zoo in Omaha, Nebraska. Billed as the world's largest indoor desert (with a 30-foot-tall sand dune), the dome re-creates the diverse animal and plant life of Australia's Red Center, southwestern Africa's Namib Desert, and the Sonoran Desert of the southwestern United States. Other zoo highlights include a tropical rain forest, an IMAX Theatre, and an aquarium where you walk through a glass-enclosed tunnel, surrounded by fish. The zoo is located at 3701 South 10th Street. It's open 9:30 A.M. to 5:00 P.M. daily. Call (402) 733–8401 or visit www.omahazoo.com.

SQUIRREL CAGE JAIL (ages 5 and up)

226 Pearl Street, Council Bluffs 51503; (712) 323–2509. Open noon to 4:00 P.M. Saturday and Sunday in May and September, 10:00 A.M. to 4:00 P.M. Wednesday through Saturday and noon to 4:00 P.M. Sunday from June through August. $.

This is one of the nation's three remaining "Lazy Susan" jails, which means it has a three-story rotating cell block with stone walls instead of bars. Built in the 1880s, it's on the National Register of Historic Places.

RAGBRAI

RAGBRAI Each July, more than 8,500 bicyclists spend a week pedaling across Iowa during the Register's Annual Great Bicycle Ride Across Iowa (RAGBRAI). Many more tag along for a day or two. More than thirty years old, RAGBRAI is the world's oldest, largest, and longest bicycle touring event. Riders start by dipping their back tires in the Missouri River and end by dipping their front tires in the Mississippi River. A different route is chosen each year. For more information visit www.ragbrai.org.

Where to Eat

Jonesy's Taco House. *1117 16th Avenue, Council Bluffs; (712) 322–8747.* Tacos and other Mexican fare are favorites at this south side restaurant. $.

Pizza King. *1101 North Broadway, Council Bluffs; (712) 323–4911.* Pizza King, on the east side, serves thin-crust pizza and steak. $-$$

Tony and Verla's. *418 Main Street, Malvern; (712) 624–8007.* Try the lemon meringue pie or sausage-and-pancakes breakfast at this cafe in a small town about 30 miles south of Council Bluffs. $

Picnic Possibilities Try the south side of **Lake Manawa State Park,** near the Dream Playground, which was designed by children. The 1,500-acre park, located at 1100 South Shore Drive, is on an oxbow lake just south of Council Bluffs.

Where to Stay

Ameristar Casino Hotel. *2200 River Road, Council Bluffs; (712) 328–8888.* Linked with the riverboat casino of the same name, this Queen Anne–style hotel on the Missouri River has 160 rooms, an indoor and outdoor pool, a children's activity center, and several restaurants. $$$–$$$$

Fairfield Inn by Marriott. *520 30th Avenue, Council Bluffs; (712) 366–1330.* Located near the intersection of Interstates 80 and 29, this sixty-two-room chain hotel has an indoor pool. $$

For More Information

Council Bluffs Convention and Visitors Bureau. *7 North Sixth Street, Council Bluffs 51502; (800) 228–6878 or* *(712) 325–1000, www.councilbluffsiowa.com, cvb@councilbluffsiowa.com.*

Sidney

Sidney is about 40 miles south of Council Bluffs on US 275 and State Highway 2 in Iowa's southwest corner.

 SIDNEY CHAMPIONSHIP RODEO (ages 4 and up)
Rodeo grounds off Maple Street, Sidney 51652; (800) 845–2250 or (712) 374–2695, www.sidneyrodeo.com. $$–$$$.

Sidney hosts one of Iowa's most famous rodeos, a four-day event held in late July and early August. Almost eighty years old, the rodeo includes bucking broncos, charging bulls, carnival games, and mutton-busting (an event featuring kids riding sheep). Camping is available on the rodeo grounds.

Where to Eat

Penn Drug. *714 Illinois Street, Sidney; (712) 374–2513.* This famous soda fountain, more than a century old, has been in the same family for four generations and serves sandwiches as well as ice-cream treats. $

Whip's Steak House. *812 Illinois Street, Sidney; (712) 374–2728.* Open for lunch and dinner, this steak house also serves huge pork tenderloins. $$

Where to Stay

Waubonsie State Park. *2559 Highway 239, Hamburg; (712) 382–2786.* Six miles south of Sidney, this park has fifty-five campsites with modern

shower and rest room facilities, plus hiking and equestrian trails that lead along windswept ridges into gorges and valleys. $

For More Information

Sidney City Hall. *604 Clay Street, Sidney 51652; (712) 374–2223.*

Shenandoah

Shenandoah is 16 miles east of Sidney near the junction of State Highway 2 and US 59.

WABASH TRACE NATURE TRAIL (all ages)
Trailheads at Sportsman's Park on Ferguson Avenue, Argus Road near the cemetery, and State Highway 2 five miles south of Shenandoah; (712) 246–4444, wabashtrace.heartland.net. Day pass for ages 12 and up, $.

Shenandoah is one of the best places to get on this 64-mile crushed limestone trail that runs along a converted railroad bed from the Missouri Border north to Council Bluffs through the Loess Hills. Use it to hike, bike, cross-country ski, and horseback ride.

Glenn Miller Festival in Clarinda
Famed 1940s bandleader Glenn Miller grew up in Clarinda (19 miles east of Shenandoah), which honors him each June with a festival featuring big bands from around the world, plus dancing, picnics, and tours of Miller's birthplace. Call (712) 542-2461 or visit www.glennmiller.org/festival.

Where to Eat

Mondo's. *309 South Fremont Street, Shenandoah; (712) 246–1325.* Burgers, chicken, and steak plus homemade pies, cinnamon rolls, and shakes dominate the American fare at this family-style restaurant with a children's menu. $-$$

Amazing Iowa Facts
The southwest Iowa town of Stanton boasts the world's largest coffee pot and coffee cup. Both are water towers shaped and painted like Swedish china. They honor Stanton's Swedish heritage and a hometown girl gone Hollywood, actress Virginia Christine who portrayed Mrs. Olsen in 1960s television coffee commercials. (Fun fact: The coffee cup water tower could hold 2.4 million cups of coffee.) While in downtown Stanton, try some Swedish pancakes and fruit-of-the-forest pie at Susie's Kitchen (*Susie's Kok* in Swedish).

Where to Stay

Country Inn. *1503 Sheridan Avenue, Shenandoah; (712) 246–1550.* This sixty-five room chain motel has an indoor pool. $-$$

For More Information

Shenandoah Chamber. *301 Maple Street, Shenandoah 52601; (712) 246–1669.*

Greenfield

Greenfield is at the junction of State Highways 92 and 25 (13 miles south of the Menlo exit 86 of Interstate 80), 88 miles northeast of Shenandoah.

MILLER'S COUNTRY ZOO (all ages)

2964 Highway 92, Greenfield 50849; (641) 743–6345, milrzoo@mddc.com. Open 1:00 to 6:00 P.M. Wednesday through Sunday from Memorial Day through September, or by appointment. $.

Located 7 miles east of Greenfield on State Highway 92, this private zoo has a large display of animals and birds, including cougars, bears, camels, zebras, deer, buffalo, goats, sheep, lemurs, monkeys . . . (oh my). Also included are a petting area and homestead area with a chicken coop.

HENRY A. WALLACE COUNTRY LIFE CENTER (ages 7 and up)

2773 290th Street, Orient 50858; (641) 337–5019, www.henryawallacecenter. com, haw@mddc.com. Open 10:00 A.M. to 5:00 P.M. Monday through Friday and 1:00 to 5:00 P.M. Saturday and Sunday from April through October. **Free.**

Learn about a major chapter of the nation's agriculture history at the birthplace farmstead of one of Iowa's most famous sons, Henry A. Wallace. A former vice president (under Franklin D. Roosevelt), Wallace founded Pioneer Hi-Bred, a major Iowa-born company that popularized hybrid seed corn, which spurred meat-eating by Americans because it increased the quantity and quality of livestock feed. This forty-acre outdoor interpretive center is a tribute to Wallace, highlighting his ideas, philosophies, and achievements via artwork, gardens, crops, and a walking trail. Guided tours are available in the summer. To get here, take State Highway 92 east from Greenfield.

Amazing Iowa Facts Television talk show host Johnny Carson was born in the southwestern Iowa town of Corning in 1925 and lived in nearby Red Oak and Avoca before moving at age eight to Nebraska. He has helped fund community projects in several southwest Iowa towns.

For More Information

Greenfield Chamber of Commerce,
201 South First Street, Greenfield 50849;

(641) 743–8444, www.greenfieldiowa.com, greenfld@mddc.com.

Elk Horn/Kimballton

Velkommen to the site of the nation's largest rural Danish settlement. Founded in the late 1800s, Elk Horn and its smaller sister city, Kimballton, offer proud tribute to their Scandinavian heritage with Danish architecture, food, crafts, and festivals. The towns are on State Highway 173, 7 miles north of Interstate 80 exit 54 and 52 miles northwest of Greenfield.

Danish Fests A parade, Danish folk dancers, and Danish foods are among the offerings at Tivoli Fest, an annual Memorial Day weekend celebration in Elk Horn. Jule Fest, held Thanksgiving weekend in Elk Horn and Kimballton, is a Christmas festival with a large gift boutique. Kimballton is also home to the annual Iowa State and National Hand Cornhusking Contest. Held on the second full weekend in October, it features old-fashioned cornhusking contests for all ages, pioneer craft demonstrations, and a Danish ethnic breakfast with *aebleskiver* (pancakes) and sausage.

🏛 BEDSTEMOR'S HUS (GRANDMA'S HOUSE) (ages 7 and up)

2015 College Street, Elk Horn 51531; (800) 759–9192 or (712) 764–6082, www.dkmuseum.org, dkmus@netins.net. Open for tours 1:00 to 4:00 P.M. daily from May through September. $.

This gingerbread house with a white picket fence is listed on the National Register of Historic Places and furnished to show how Danish-American families lived during the early twentieth century.

DANISH IMMIGRANT MUSEUM (ages 7 and up)

2212 Washington Street, Elk Horn 51531; (800) 759–9192 or (712) 764–7001, www.dkmuseum.org. Open 9:00 A.M. to 6:00 P.M. Monday through Saturday and noon to 5:00 P.M. Sunday from Memorial Day through Labor Day, 9:00 A.M. to 5:00 P.M. Monday through Saturday and noon to 5:00 P.M. Sunday from September through May. $.

Take a self-guided tour of exhibits tracing the immigration of Danes to the United States through arts, culture, and a genealogy center. There are also Legos (a Danish invention) to play with.

DANISH WINDMILL MUSEUM (ages 4 and up)

4038 Main Street, Elk Horn 51531; (800) 451–7960 or (712) 764–7472, www.danishwindmill.com, info@danishwindmill.com. Open 8:00 A.M. to 7:00 P.M. Monday through Saturday and 10:00 A.M. to 7:00 P.M. Sunday from Memorial Day through Labor Day, 9:00 A.M. to 5:00 P.M. Monday through Saturday and noon to 5:00 P.M. Sunday from September through May. $.

This is America's only authentic working Danish windmill. Built in Denmark in 1848 and imported to Elk Horn, it was rebuilt by community volunteers in 1976. During a brief tour you can climb to the top of the 60-foot-high windmill and watch a fifteen-minute video about its history.

Walnut: Antique City

Walnut: Antique City Even if your kids—like mine—don't like antiquing, the pretty little turn-of-the-century town of Walnut, known as Iowa's Antique City, is worth a stop. Stretch your legs by window-shopping on the redbrick main street, which is lined with small shops and antiques malls. Each year on the three-day weekend after Thanksgiving, the Annual Antique Christmas Walk features horse-drawn carriage rides, strolling carolers, a community bazaar, and antiques dealers from across Iowa and Nebraska. Call (712) 784–2100 or visit www.walnutia.com.

Where to Eat

Danish Bakery. *4234 Main Street, Elk Horn; (712) 764–2151.* Stop here to get your Kringle, a thin, delicate Danish pastry. $

Danish Inn. *4116 South Main Street, Elk Horn; (712) 764–4251.* A daily buffet packed with American and Danish food is served in this restaurant near the town's windmill. $–$$

Simply Sweet. *2104 Elm Street, Elk Horn; (712) 764–4030.* Homemade bread, soups, pie, ice cream, and bread are served at this perfect-for-lunch spot just north of the town's windmill. $

Picnic Possibilities

Picnic Possibilities Try **Little Mermaid Park** in Kimballton, which has a replica of Copenhagen's famous little mermaid statue, a farmer's cottage, a mini Danish windmill, and a children's playground.

Where to Stay

Hansen's Kro. *2113 Park Street, Elk Horn; (800) 606–2052.* This modern two-story house downtown is stuffed with Danish items and has a large family-friendly suite with queen-size bed, private bath, living room, and two couches and a daybed in an adjoining room. A complete Danish breakfast with *aebleskiver* (pancakes), cheeses, and meats is served. $$

For More Information

The Danish Windmill Corporation. *4038 Main Street, Elk Horn 51531; (712) 764–7472, www.danishwindmill.com, info@danishwindmill.com.*

Audubon

Visitors to Audubon are greeted by Albert the Bull, the world's largest anatomically correct bull, a 30-foot-tall, 45-ton steel-and-concrete tribute to the beef industry. Audubon is on US 71 about 17 miles north of Elk Horn.

NATHANIEL HAMLIN PARK AND MUSEUM (all ages)
1745 160th Street, Audubon 50025; (712) 563–2516. Museum open 2:00 to 4:00 P.M. Saturday and Sunday from June through September, or by appointment. **Free.**

Two elk greet visitors to this park, along with eighteen antique windmills donated by local farmers. Also included are a preserved prairie, a bluebird house trail, and a museum with the world's largest nail collection (yes, nail collection). It's located about a mile south of Audubon on US 71.

For More Information

City of Audubon. *410 North Park Place, Audubon 50025; (712) 563–3269, www.audubon.biz.*

Coon Rapids

Soviet Premier Nikita Khrushchev helped put Coon Rapids on the map (see below). It's on State Highway 141, about 27 miles northeast of Audubon.

GARST FARM RESORTS (ages 4 and up)

1390 Highway 141, Coon Rapids 50058; (712) 684–2964, www.farmresort. com, gresort@pionet.net. Open year-round; call for hours, tour schedule, and rates.

At the height of the Cold War in 1959, Soviet Premier Nikita Khrushchev visited this classic farm to learn more about the hybrid corn being championed by the farm's gregarious owner, Roswell Garst. Today, Garst Farm is still a working farm, but it also offers recreational activities and overnight accommodations in a classic Iowa homestead that's been converted into a bed-and-breakfast. There are also other lodgings on the 4,500-acre property that sits in a river valley. Especially good for families are Hollyhock Cottage, Woodland Carriage House, and Oak Ridge Farm House. Outdoor activities at the resort include rid-

A Rubiner Family Adventure Before we stayed at Garst Farm Resorts, we thought we were old hands at "agritainment." We'd been to pumpkin patches, hayrides, and farm-animal petting zoos. But we'd never slept near a pungent feedlot, peered into a manure lagoon, or learned how to make silage until our Garst farm visit. We lived for several days in Hollyhock Cottage, a former chicken coop with a large yard, a white picket fence, pink hollyhocks, and a huge cottonwood tree. Beyond that were a gravel road, weathered barns, cattle in the feedlot, and buffalo in the pasture. A truck carrying silage rumbled by day and night. To learn about the farm, we took a self-guided tour. On what turned out to be an uncomfortably hot, humid day, we trudged around the cattle operation, dutifully reading a helpful pamphlet. Tiny biting flies defied our insecticide, but we all perked up when we walked through Feed Alley and met the cattle eye to eye. We also glimpsed no-nonsense agribusiness at a nearby seed-corn processing plant, watching ears of corn tumble from a huge truck hoisted almost vertical by a hydraulic lift. But the kid's favorite part of the trip was a scenic trail ride through the resort property, led by a plucky guide. We were not experienced riders, but the guide had us trotting, navigating a wooded trail, and forging a river where, to everyone's amusement, my horse started kicking, leaving me half soaked.

ing, fishing, hiking, draft horse wagon rides, and canoeing. Don't miss the self-guided farm tour or the Dark Sky tour, offered by a local and very enthusiastic amateur astronomer who installed a high-powered scope on a lonely hilltop after determining that Coon Rapids is one of Iowa's darkest places.

Denison

At the junction of US 30 and US 59, Denison is about 43 miles northwest of Coon Rapids. It makes the map thanks to a hometown girl who made it big in Hollywood, actress Donna Reed.

 ## THE DONNA REED PERFORMING ARTS FESTIVAL
(ages 7 and up)

The Donna Reed Center for the Performing Arts, 1305 North Broadway, Denison 51442; (712) 263–3334, www.donnareed.org, info@donnareed.org. Center open for drop-in tours 8:00 A.M. to 4:00 P.M. Monday through Friday, or by appointment. June festival tuition, $$$$.

Remember Donna Reed? She starred with Jimmy Stewart in the 1946 film classic *It's a Wonderful Life* and played the quintessential good mom in the 1960s television sitcom *The Donna Reed Show*. Folks in Denison certainly remember Donna Reed. She grew up here. Today, aspiring actors, dancers, and singers attend an annual festival named after Reed, held the third full weekend in June. For more than seventeen years, the festival has imported Hollywood and Broadway types to teach acting, music, modeling, and dance classes—many for adults, some for children. Community events (some free) during the festival include a Saturday parade and a musical theater showcase performed by festival students. The Donna Reed Center is in a restored 1914 opera house with a theater for live performances and first-run movies, an old-fashioned soda fountain, and a miniature model of Bedford Falls, the mythical town from *It's a Wonderful Life*. A Donna Reed Museum will open in the center, possibly by summer 2003.

 ## DENISON AQUATIC FUN CENTER (all ages)

710 North 16th Street, Denison 51442; (712) 263–8130. Open 1:00 to 8:00 P.M. Sunday through Friday and 1:00 to 6:00 P.M. Saturday from June through August, 3:30 to 8:00 P.M. Monday through Friday and 2:00 to 6:00 P.M. Saturday and Sunday from September through May. $.

This aquatic center has an indoor pool with spa and an outdoor pool with two water slides, a young children's pool, geysers, and a fountain. Mini golf and concessions are available.

Where to Eat

Cronk's Cafe. *812 Fourth Avenue South, Denison; (712) 263–4191.* This lively evening spot, opened in 1929, serves stick-to-your-ribs pork tenderloin sandwiches and chicken-fried steak, plus has a salad bar and Sunday brunch. $–$$

Where to Stay

Park Motel. *803 Fourth Avenue South, Denison; (712) 263–4144, www.thepark motel.com/location.htm.* This funky old motel in a 1940 Spanish Colonial Revival building is near the junction of US 30, US 59, and State Highway 141. It has thirty-two rooms, including seven themed suites (a Donna Reed Suite *and* a Moose Suite), and is listed on the National Register of Historic Places. $–$$$

For More Information

Denison Chamber of Commerce. *18 South Main Street, Denison 51442; (712) 263–5621, www.denisonia.com, dsnchmbr@frontiernet.net.*

Storm Lake

About 56 miles north of Denison, Storm Lake is another popular summer resort area located off US 71 and State Highway 7.

STORM LAKE (all ages)
1001 Sunrise Park Road, Storm Lake 50588; (712) 732–8000, www.storm lake.org/city/pages/laketrail.htm. Free.

    With 3,200 acres, Storm Lake is Iowa's fourth largest natural lake and one of the most visitor-friendly because public city parks, not private homes, border much of it. You'll find several sandy beaches for swimming along Lake Trail, a 5-mile recreation trail that connects Sunrise Park in the east with Frank Starr Park in the west. The paved trail wraps around about 75 percent of the lake and is good for walking, jogging, and biking. Sunrise Park has a campground, playground, swimming beach, and pool, plus a nearby boat rental (Lakeside Marina). Storm Lake is also a good place to sail and fish for walleye, catfish, and sunfish.

SANTA'S CASTLE (all ages)

200 East Fifth Street, Storm Lake 50588; (712) 732–3780 or 299–4565, www.stormlakeonline.com/santascastle.html. Open 6:00 to 8:00 P.M. Monday through Friday and 1:00 to 4:00 P.M. Saturday and Sunday between Thanksgiving and Christmas Eve; additional weekday hours from 2:00 to 4:00 P.M. starting in early December; open year-round by appointment. $.

This is billed as the Midwest's largest operating collection of mechanical Christmas figures, including classics from old department store holiday windows of the 1920s and 1930s. Located in a former Carnegie Library, the admission price includes a half-hour guided tour.

Where to Eat

Baker's Court. *Highway 7 West, Storm Lake; (712) 732–6298.* Featuring Storm Lake's only soup/salad/ice-cream bar, this restaurant serves a daily special, from Alaskan walleye to prime rib, and Sunday brunch. There's also a children's menu. $–$$

BozWellz Pub and Eatery. *507 Erie Street, Storm Lake; (712) 732–3616.* Homemade pastas, hand-cut steaks, prime rib, burgers, salads, and homemade desserts are among the offerings at BozWellz. $–$$

Picnic Possibilities Try Sunset Park's **Living Heritage Tree Museum,** a paved walkway past thirty-four trees with markers explaining their historic significance. (Ask for a guide at the Storm Lake Visitor's Bureau.) There's also a playground near the picnic area.

Where to Stay

Lighthouse Inn Motel. *1601 East Lakeshore Drive, Storm Lake; (712) 732–5753, www.lighthouseinniowa.net.* There are twenty-five rooms, including ten with individual design themes, at this recently refurbished 1950s drive-up motel off Business Highway 71 on the lake. $$–$$$

Sunrise Campgrounds. *1001 Sunrise Road, Storm Lake; (712) 732–8023, www.stormlake.org/city/pages/campgrounds. htm.* Located in Sunrise Park on the lake and open from April through October (weather permitting), this campground with modern facilities doesn't take reservations. $

For More Information

Storm Lake Area Convention and Visitors Bureau. *119 West Sixth Street,* *Storm Lake 50588; (888) 752–4692 or (712) 732–3780, www.stormlake.org.*

Other Things to See and Do in Western Iowa

- **Cayler Prairie.** Near Big Spirit Lake, (712) 332–2209
- **Sioux City Public Museum.** Sioux City, (712) 279–6174
- **Iowa Aviation Museum.** Greenfield, (641) 343–7184
- **General Store Museum.** Kimballton, (712) 773–2430
- **Prairie Rose State Park.** Walnut, (712) 773–2701
- **Harrison County Historical Village.** Missouri Valley, (712) 642–2114
- **RailsWest Railroad Museum/HO Model Railroad.** Council Bluffs, (712) 323–5182
- **Western Historic Trails Center.** Council Bluffs, (712) 366–4900
- **Lake Icaria.** Corning, (641) 322–4793
- **Buena Vista County Historical Society.** Storm Lake, (712) 732–4955

Appendix: Events and Celebrations

H ere is a month-by-month list of some of Iowa's most interesting or quirky annual celebrations for families (the ones I haven't already mentioned). For a more complete listing of Iowa events, call (800) 345-IOWA.

JANUARY

Bald Eagle Weekend. Guttenberg, (877) 252-2323. Live animal presentations, ice sculptures.

Winterfest. Strawberry Point, (563) 933-4958. Sleigh rides, magic show, bonfire, fireworks.

Winterfest's Winter Wonderland of Lights. Council Bluffs, (712) 545-3850. Animated displays, 18-foot fountain of lights, 250-plus holiday decorations.

FEBRUARY

Children's Cross-Country Ski Event. Decorah, (563) 382-9681. Noncompetitive cross-country skiing.

Saylorville Eagle Watch. Johnston, (515) 556-0620. Bald-eagle spotting, education programs.

Boys' State Wrestling Tournament. Des Moines, (515) 323-5400. Wildly popular high school tournament.

MARCH

Maple Syrup Festival. Cedar Rapids, (319) 362-0664. Demonstrations, music, pancakes.

Boys' State Basketball Tournament. Des Moines, (515) 323-5400. Popular high school tournament.

Children's Easter Egg Hunt. Clarinda, (712) 542-2166. Mad dash for eggs.

APRIL

Waverly Midwest Horse Sale. Waverly, (319) 352-1804. Huge draft and riding horse sale.

Earth Fair. Cedar Falls, (319) 277-2187. Earth Day celebration with canoeing, fishing, hiking, bird-watching, tree planting.

Annual Doll, Toy, and Bear Show and Sale. Des Moines, (515) 223-4468. Rare dolls on display.

MAY

Syttende Mai: Norwegian Constitution Day Celebration. Decorah, (563) 382-9681. Children's parade, activities, music.

My Waterloo Days. Waterloo, (319) 233-8431. Hot-air balloon rally, parade, dragon boat race, fireworks.

Maifest. Amana Colonies, (800) 579-2294. Maypole dancers, German music, food, parade.

Taste Louisiana Cajun Fest. Amana Colonies, (888) 594-3903. Bayou feast, zydeco music, costume parade.

Riverfest. Iowa City, (319) 335-3273. Outdoor music, food, art fair, and kidfest craft activities, rides, and games.

Beaux Arts Festival. Davenport, (563) 323-9042. Art, food, kids' activities, entertainment.

JUNE

Laura Ingalls Wilder Day. Burr Oak, (800) 463-4692. "Little Miss Laura" crowning, parade, children's activities.

Lawn Chair Nights. Waverly, (800) 251-0360. Free family concert series on courthouse lawn.

Iowa Arts Festival. Iowa City, (319) 337-7944. World music, culinary arts, fine art.

Kalona Days Celebration. Kalona, (319) 656–2660. Races, games, parades, entertainment.

Bentonsport Riverside Rendezvous. Bentonsport, (319) 592–3579. Early 1800s celebration with skill contests, black powder shoot, craft demonstrations.

Johnston Green Days. Johnston, (515) 251–3707. Kids' carnival, parade, music.

Raspberry Festival. Webster City, (515) 832–9193. Raspberry pancake breakfast, pie-eating contest, children's games, fireworks, stage shows.

DeSoto Refuge Fest. Missouri Valley, (712) 642–2772. Free fishing, fly-tying demonstration, boating, children's games.

The Big Parade. Sioux City, (712) 279–4800. Mardi Gras-style parade, Cajun music, fireworks.

Renaissance Faire of the Midlands. Council Bluffs, (402) 345–5401. Costumed performers, period music, jousting, swordplay, "wee folks glen" with children's activities.

Kinderfest. Manning, (800) 292–0252. German children's festival with games, rides, parade.

JULY

Stacyville Bratwurst Daze. Stacyville, (641) 737–2428. Five-mile "brat trot," tractor pull, water ball fight, parade.

Ridiculous Days. Strawberry Point, (563) 933–2120. Garage sales, kids' games, tractor pull.

Balloons and Toons on the Square. Indianola, (515) 961–6269. Hot-air balloons, music, games.

Croatian Fest. Centerville, (641) 856–3391. Ethnic food and entertainment, accordion band.

Independence Day at Living History Farms. Urbandale, (515) 278–5286. Old-fashioned games, spelling bee, brass band, parade.

Riverbend Rally. Iowa Falls, (641) 648–5549. July 4th parade, talent show, carnival rides, fireworks, kids' games, and fishing contest.

Star-Spangled Spectacular. Storm Lake, (712) 732–3780. Parade, kids' train and pony rides, water show, fireworks.

LakeFest/Iowa Storytelling Festival. Clear Lake, (641) 357-2159. Midwest storytellers, art, Dixieland bands.

Krewe de Charlie Sioux Mardi Gras Gala. Sioux City, (712) 279-4800. Costumes, bands, Cajun cookout.

Derby Down Davis. Corning, (641) 322-5229. Children's soapbox derby races down Davis Avenue, food and entertainment.

AUGUST

Iowa Renaissance Festival and Harvest Faire. Amana Colonies, (800) 579-2294. Sixteenth-century festival with horseback jousting, strolling minstrels, merchants bazaar, hands-on activities.

Taste of Cedar Rapids. Cedar Rapids, (319) 398-0449. Music, fireworks, kids' activities.

Albia Restoration Days. Albia, (641) 932-5108. Historic town square celebration.

Old Settler Celebration. Corydon, (641) 872-2600. Carnival, free concerts, street dances, and food.

Adel Sweet Corn Festival. Adel, (515) 993-5472. Free sweet corn, parade, entertainment.

Prairie Festival. Huxley, (515) 597-3879. Parade, carnival, farmers' market, dog show, music.

Lincoln Highway Days. Nevada, (515) 382-6538. Rodeos, parade, carnival, street dance, games.

Sweet Corn Days. Estherville, (712) 362-3541. Family festival with free corn, parade, rubber duck derby on river.

Old-Time Country Music Contest. Avoca, (712) 762-4363. Performers, arts, crafts, food.

Great Iowa Balloon Race. Storm Lake, (712) 732-3780. Bathtub races, parade, ice-cream social, water fights.

SEPTEMBER

Scandinavian Food Fest. Decorah, (800) 463-4692. Traditional Norwegian food sampling.

Ag Appreciation Day. Grinnell, (641) 236-6555. Petting zoo, antique tractor parade, entertainment.

Beaverdale Fall Festival. Des Moines, (515) 255-6105. Huge neighborhood celebration with popular parade, fireworks, food, and music.

Pelican Festival. Granger, (515) 323-5300. Pelican viewing by telescope, educational presentations.

International Horse Archery Festival. Fort Dodge, (515) 573-5996. Archery-from-horseback competitions, storytelling, costumes.

Oktemberfest. Marshalltown, (800) 697-3155. Carnival, go-cart races, marching band competition, parade.

Nodaway Corn Carnival. Nodaway, (712) 785-3501. Parade, draft horse pull, "kiddie pedal pull," pet show, petting zoo.

Popcorn Day Festival. Hamburg, (712) 382-1313. Children's activities, pet parade, free popcorn.

Balloon Days. Creston, (641) 782-7021. Hot-air balloon and bathtub races, pet show, parade.

OCTOBER

Pick-a-Pumpkin Days. Guttenberg, (563) 252-3820. Wagon rides, petting zoo, arts and crafts, pumpkin picking.

Oktoberfest. Amana Colonies, (800) 579-2294. German music, food, dancing, parade, family activities.

Fall Harvest Days at Living History Farms. Urbandale, (515) 278-5286. Traditional harvest activities, food.

Dogtoberfest. West Des Moines, (515) 222-3642. "Howl'a-ween" fun for dogs and owners with dog costume contest, dog/owner look-alike contest.

Great Iowa Pet Expo. Des Moines, (515) 242-3669. Trade show with pet-related workshops and entertainment, including pet costumes, stupid pet tricks, ferret follies obstacle course.

Oktoberfest. Manning, (800) 292-0252. German-American dancing and choirs, horse rides and horse-drawn wagon rides, pumpkin painting.

NOVEMBER

Hometown Christmas. Mount Vernon, (319) 895-8214. Carolers, Santa, live Nativity performances.

A Christmas Past. West Branch, (319) 643-2541. Free admission to Hoover library-museum, horse-drawn rides, free activities.

Quad City Arts Festival of Trees. Davenport, (563) 324-3378. Decorated trees, gingerbread village, holiday parade, pops concert.

Lighted Christmas Parade. Perry, (515) 465-4601. Lighted floats, Santa, food.

Home for the Holidays. Mason City, (641) 423-6688. Downtown Christmas lights, strolling carolers, live Nativity and window displays, horse-drawn sleigh rides.

Weihnachtsfest. Manning, (800) 292-0252. German Christmas festival with fireworks, lighted parade, Father Christmas.

DECEMBER

Dickens of a Christmas. Indianola, (515) 951-6269. Victorian celebration with living windows, carolers, horse-drawn wagon rides, costumed Dickens characters.

Prelude to Christmas. Amana Colonies, (800) 579-2294. Craft demonstrations, candle-lit streets, holiday foods, cookie walk.

Norwegian Christmas at Vesterheim Museum. Decorah, (563) 382-9681. Traditional Norwegian foods, customs, Christmas elf visit, hands-on crafts.

Las Posadas. Perry, (888) 424-4268. Traditional Hispanic religious procession, music, piñatas, food at Hotel Pattee.

Santa Lucia Fest. Swedesburg, (319) 254-2317. Reading of Lucia story, music, Swedish meal.

General Index

A

Adventureland, 115
Airpower Museum, 78
Altoona, 114–15
Amana Colonies, 40–43
Amana Colonies Nature Trail, 42
Amazing Maize Maze at Carter Farm, The, 55
Amboy Trail Ranch, 111
American Gothic House, 77
Ames, 143–46
Amish, 73
Amish meals, 93
Anamosa, 61–63
Appleberry Farm, 140
Aquarium, The, 14
Arnolds Park Amusement Park, 172–73
Arsenal Island, 53–54
Audubon, 199

B

Backbone State Park, 11
Bald Eagle Watch, Keokuk, 100
Bald Eagle Watching, Red Rock, 85
Bancroft, 157–58
Battle of Pea Ridge, 100
Bedstemor's Hus, 197
Belinda Church Toy and Antique Museum, 92
Bellevue, 58–59
Bellevue Butterfly Gardens, 58–59
Bentonsport National Historic District, 98
Big Creek State Park and Lake, 133
Big Treehouse, 139–40

Bily Clocks Museum/Antonin Dvořák Museum, 25
Birdsall Ice Cream Company, 164–65
Blackhawk Children's Theatre, 27
Blanden Memorial Art Museum, 154
Blank Park Zoo, 121
Bluedorn Science Imaginarium, 28
Bock's Berry Farm, 49
Boji Bantam Theatre, 172
Boji Bay Water Park, 174
Bonaparte National Historic District, 98
Boone, 149–52
Boone and Scenic Valley Railroad, 149
Bridges of Madison County, 90
Britt, 158–59
Brucemore, 65
Brunnier Art Museum, 143
Buffalo Bill Museum/The SS *Lone Star Steamer,* 55
Burlington, 104–6
Burlington Bees Baseball, 104

C

Canoeing, 13, 21, 22
Carroll's Pumpkin Farm, 39
Casino Gambling, 5
Cedar Falls, 31–34
Cedar Falls Municipal Band, The, 31
Cedar Rapids, 63–70
Cedar Rapids City Parks, 66
Cedar Rapids History Center, 65
Cedar Rapids Kernels, 66
Cedar Rapids Museum of Art, 66
Cedar Rapids Rough Riders Hockey Team, 66

Cedar Rapids Symphony, 65
Cedar Valley Arboretum and Botanic
   Gardens, 29
Cedar Valley Nature Trail, 64
Centerville, 96–97
Central Iowa Trails, 129
Channel Cat Water Taxi, 52–53
Chariton, 92–95
Charles H. MacNider Museum, 164
Cherry Sisters, 64
Chief Black Hawk, 30
Cinder Path Trail, 93
Clay County Fair, 176
Clear Lake, 159–62
Clear Lake Fire Museum, 159–60
Clinton, 56–58
Clinton Lumberkings, 57
Colfax, 113
Community Orchard, Fort Dodge, 155
Coon Rapids, 200–201
Cordova Observation Tower, 84
Corn Mazes, 9
Corydon, 95
Council Bluffs, 191–93
Council Bluffs Drive-In Theater, 191
Country Heritage Community Maize
   Maze, 9
Country Relics Village, 148
Crescent, 191
Crystal Lake Cave, 6
Cumming, 89–90
Cumming Orchard, 89
Cyclones Maze, 145
Czech Village, 67
Czipar's Apple Orchard, 6

Davenport/The Quad Cities, 52–56
Davenport River Bandits, 53
Deal's Orchard, 152–53
Decorah, 20–24
Decorah Hatchery, 21
Decorah Trout Hatchery, 21
Denison, 201–2
Denison Aquatic Fun Center, 201–2
Des Moines, 116–33
Des Moines Art Center, 123–24
Des Moines Arts Festival, 122
Des Moines Botanical Center, 120
Des Moines Buccaneers Hockey, 128
Des Moines Civic Center, The, 126
Des Moines Downtown Farmers'
   Market, 121
Des Moines Menace Soccer, 125
Des Moines Metro Opera, 87, 126
Des Moines Parks, 127
Des Moines Symphony, The, 126
Desoto National Wildlife Refuge, 190
Devonian Fossil Gorge and Coralville
   Lake, 45–46
Dolliver Memorial State Park, 154–55
Donna Reed Performing Arts Festival,
   The, 201
Dorothy Pecaut Nature Center in Stone
   State Park, 183–84
Downtown School, The, 122
Drake Relays, The, 125
Drake University Bulldogs Basketball
   and Football, 124–25
Dubuque, 3–8
Duffy's Collectible Cars, 67
Dyersville, 8–10

D

Dan-D Farms Corn Maze, 85
Danish Immigrant Museum, 197–98
Danish Windmill Museum, 198

E

E.G.'s Pumpkin Farm, 187
Eagle Point Park, 7
Effigy Mounds National Monument, 18

Eldon, 77–78
Elinor Bedell State Park, 171–72
Elk Horn/Kimballton, 197–99
Elkader, 12–14
Eskimo Pie, 188
Eulenspiegel Puppet Theatre
    Company, 44

F

Fairfield, 77
Family Museum of Arts and Science,
    54–55
Farm House Museum, 143
Farmers' Market, Iowa City, 47
Felix Adler Museum, 57
Fenelon Place/Fourth Street, 3
Field of Dreams, 9–10
Five Flags Theater, 4
Fort Atkinson State Preserve, 25
Fort Custer Maze, 163–66
Fort Dodge, 153–55
Fort Madison, 102–4
Fort Museum and Frontier Village, 154
Frank Lloyd Wright Stockman
    House, 164
Fredericksburg, 26
Fun Valley Ski Area, 40

G

Gable, Dan, 112
Garst Farm Resorts, 200–201
Geode State Park, 105
George M. Verity Riverboat
    Museum, 100
Glenn Miller Festival, 195
Grand Opera House, 4
Grant Wood Art Gallery, 61
Gray's Lake Park, 127
Great River Road, The, 6
Green's Sugar Bush, 25

Greenfield, 196–97
Grinnell, 38–40
Grotto of the Redemption, 156
Grout Museum of History and
    Science, 27
Guttenberg, 14–16

H

Hartman Reserve Nature Center, 31
Hawkeye Buffalo Ranch, 26
Henry A. Wallace Country Life
    Center, 196
Herbert Hoover National Historic Site
    and Presidential Museum, 48
Heritage Carousel in Union Park, 118
Hickory Park Restaurant, 146
Historic Valley Junction, 127–28
Hobo Museum, 159
Holly, Buddy, 159–60
Hotel Pattee, 133–34
Howell Tree Farm/Howell Floral and
    Greenhouse, 89–90

I

Ice Cream Capital of the World Visitor
    Center, 179–80
Ice Cream Shops, Des Moines, 131
Ice House Museum, 31
Indianola, 87–88
Ingersoll Dinner Theater, 126
Inkpaduta Canoe Trail, 176
International Wrestling Institute and
    Museum, 112
Iowa Arboretum, 151
Iowa Caucuses, 119
Iowa Children's Museum, 43
Iowa City, 43–47
Iowa Cubs Baseball, 120
Iowa Falls, 148

Iowa Great Lakes Maritime Museum, 173
Iowa Great Lakes, 171–76
Iowa Historical Building, 119
Iowa International Raceway, 139
Iowa State Capitol, 118–19
Iowa State Center, 144
Iowa State Fair, 117
Iowa State University Cyclones, 144
Iowa Youth Chorus, 126

J

Jefferson, 152–53
Jester Park, 130
John Deere Collectors Center, 52
John Ringling, 16
John Wayne Birthplace, 91
Jordan House, 128

K

K.D. Station, 181
Kalona, 73–75
Kalona Historical Village and Museums, 74
Karkosh Korners Display Gardens at Pearl City Perennial Plantation, 50
Kate Goldman Children's Theater at the Des Moines Playhouse, 127
Kate Shelley Railroad Museum and Park, 150
Keokuk, 100–101
Kinney Pioneer Museum, 163
Knoxville, 83–86

L

Lacey-Keosauqua State Park, 98
Lady of the Lake Excursion Boat, 160
Lake Red Rock, 84

Lakes Art Center, The, 172
Laura Ingalls Wilder Park & Museum, 23
Le Mars, 179–80
Ledges State Park, 150–51
Lewis and Clark, 169, 182–83, 186
Lewis and Clark Interpretive Center, 183
Lewis and Clark Keelboat Display/Lewis and Clark State Park, 186
Lime Creek Nature Center, 165
Living History Farms, 129
Lockmaster's House Heritage Museum, 14–15
Loess Hills, 182–84, 186, 188–90
Loess Hills Prairie Seminar, 187
Loess Hills State Forest Overlook, 189
Lone Tree, 49
Lost Island Water Park, 29

M

Mahanay Bell Tower, 152
Maid-Rite Sandwich, 50
Mamie Doud Eisenhower Birthplace, 149
Maquoketa, 59–61
Maquoketa Caves State Park, 60
Maharishi U, 77
Marshalltown, 139–41
Maxwell Museum, 142
Maytag Dairy farms, 112
McCaughey septuplets, 86
McFarland Park, 145
McGregor/Marquette, 16–20
Meredith Willson Boyhood Home, 163
Meskwaki Powwow, 37
Midwest Old Threshers Heritage Museums, 76
Miller's Country Zoo, 196
Mines of Spain Recreation Area, 5
Mini-Americana Barn Museum, 41
Mississippi River Museum, 4–5

Mississippi River Visitor Center, 53
Missouri River, 181
Missouri Valley, 190–91
Moline, 52
Montezuma, 40
Moorhead, 188–90
Mount Crescent Ski Area, 191
Mount Pleasant, 75–77
Muscatine, 49–51
Museum of Amana History, 41
Museum of Natural History, 45
Music Man Square, 163–64

N

Nathaniel Hamlin Park and
    Museum, 199
National Balloon Museum, 87
National Czech and Slovak Museum, 67
National Farm Toy Museum, 10
National Motorcycle Museum, 62
National Sprint Car Hall of Fame and
    Museum, 84
Nauvoo, 102
Neal Smith National Wildlife Refuge
    and Prairie Learning center, 113–14
Nelson Pioneer Farm Museum, 79
New Pioneer Co-op, 47
Newton, 111–13
Nightfall on the River, 122
Northeast Iowa trails, 12

O

Okoboji, 171
Okoboji Queen II Excursions, 172
Old Capitol Museum, 44
Old Fort Madison, 102–3
Omaha Zoo, 192
Onawa, 186–88
Orange City, 177–79

Osborne Nature Center, 13
Oskaloosa, 79–80
Ottumwa, 78–79

P

Paint Creek Riding Stables and
    Campground, 18–19
Paper Moon, 17
Pearl Button Museum, 49
Pella, 81–83
Pella Historical Village, 81–82
Pella Opera House, 8
Penitentiary Museum, 61–62
Perry, 133–34
Pierce's Pumpkin Patch, 93
Pikes Peak State Park, 16
Pinky The Elephant, 18
Piper's Grocery Store, 93–94
Pleasantville, 85
Polk City, 133
Prairie City, 113–14
Prairie Lights, 46
Prairie Trails Museum of Wayne
    County, 95
Prairie-style homes, Mason City, 165
Preparation Canyon State Park, 188–89
Princess Sweet Shop/Cafe, 148
Putnam Museum of History and
    Natural Science/IMAX Theatre, 54

R

RAGBRAI, 192
Ranch Amusement Park, The, 172
Rathbun Fish Hatchery, 96
Rathbun Lake, 96
Reagan, Ronald, 124
Reiman Gardens, 145
Renaissance Festival, Water Works
    Park, 123

River Junction Trade Company, 17
Rock Island Arsenal Museum, 54
Rodeo, Dayton, 154
Rustic Hills Carriage Tours, 4

S

Salisbury House, 123
Sanderson, Cael, 112, 144
Santa's Castle, 203
Saylorville Lake Visitor Center, 130
Science Center of Iowa, 124
Science Station and McLeod/Busse
    IMAX Dome Theatre, 64–65
Seed Savers Exchange/Heritage Farms,
    22–23
Seminole Valley Farm and Park, 68
Sergeant Floyd Riverboat Museum, 182
Seven Oaks Recreation Areas, 149–50
Shenandoah, 194–95
Sidney, 193–94
Sidney Championship Rodeo, 193–94
Sioux City, 180–85
Sioux City Art Center, 181
Sioux City Sports, 182
61 Drive-In, 60
Sleepy Hollow Sports Park, 118
Snake Alley, 104
Spencer, 176–77
Spillville, 24–26
Spirit Lake Fish Hatchery, 171
Spirit of Dubuque Sightseeing
    Cruises, 5
Spook Cave and Campground, 17–18
Squirrel Cage Jail, 192
St. Donatus, 6
Stanhope, 148
Starr's Cave Nature Center and
    Preserve, 104–5
State Center, 142
Stone City, 62

Stone's Restaurant, 140
Storm Lake, 202–4
Story City, 147
Story City Antique Carousel, 147
Storybook Hill Children's Zoo, 7
Straight, Alvin, 156
Strawberry Point, 11–12
Sullivan Brothers, 28
Sundown Mountain Ski Resort, 7
Surf Ballroom, 160
Sylvan Runkel State Preserve, The, 186

T

Tama/Toledo, 37–38
Tama County Historical Museum, 37
Temple for the Performing Arts, 126
Terrace Hill, 122
The Beach Ottumwa, 78
The Play Station, 64
Theatre Cedar Rapids, 65
Toolesboro Indian Mounds, 106
Trainland U.S.A., 113
Treasure Village, 174
Tri-State Rodeo, 103
Trolleys of Dubuque, 4
Tulip Festival, Orange City, 178
Tulip Time, Pella, 81
Turkey River, 13

U

U.S. Cellular Center, 65
Union Slough National Wildlife Refuge,
    157–58
University of Iowa Hawkeyes, 44
University of Iowa Museum of Art, 44
University of Iowa's Hancher
    Auditorium, 44
University of Northern Iowa
    Museum, 32

University of Northern Iowa
    Panthers, 32
University of Okoboji, 174
University of Okoboji Winter
    Games, 173
Upper Iowa River, 21–22

V

Valle Drive-In, 112
Veishea, 144
Vesterheim Norwegian-American
    Museum, 21–22
Veterans Memorial Auditorium, 126
Villages of Van Buren County, 97–100
Vogel Windmill, 178
Volga River, 13

W

Wabash Trace Nature Trail, 194
Walnut, 198
Wapello, 106
Waterloo, 27–30

Waterloo Black Hawks Hockey, 28
Waterloo Bucks Baseball, 28
Waterloo Center for the Arts, 27
Waterloo/Cedar Falls Symphony
    Orchestra, 31
Watson's Grocery Store, 142
Weather Beacon, The, 118
West Bend, 156–57
West Branch, 48
West Liberty, 44
Whitewater University Fun Park, 116
Willowglen Nursery, 23
Willson, Meredith, 163
Wilson's Orchard, 46
Wilton Candy Kitchen, 51–52
Wilton, 51–52
Winterset, 90–92
Wood, Grant, 61–62, 77

Y

Yellow River State Forest, 19
Youngville Cafe, The, 68

Activities Index

AGRITAINMENT

Amazing Maize Maze at Carter Farm, The, 55

Amish meals, 93

Appleberry Farm, 140

Bock's Berry Farm, 49

Carroll's Pumpkin Farm, 39

Clay County Fair, 176

Community Orchard, Fort Dodge, 155

Corn Mazes, 9

Country Heritage Community Maize Maze, 9

Cumming Orchard, 89

Cyclones Maze, 145

Czipar's Apple Orchard, 6

Dan-D Farms Corn Maze, 85

Deal's Orchard, 152–53

Des Moines Downtown Farmers' Market, 121

E.G.'s Pumpkin Farm, 187

Farmers' Market, Iowa City, 47

Garst Farm Resorts, 200–201

Green's Sugar Bush, 25

Hawkeye Buffalo Ranch, 26

Howell Tree Farm/Howell Floral and Greenhouse, 89–90

Iowa Arboretum, 151

Iowa State Fair, 117

John Deere Collectors Center, 52

Karkosh Korners Display Gardens at Pearl City Perennial Plantation, 50

Loess Hills Prairie Seminar, 187

Nelson Pioneer Farm Museum, 79

Pierce's Pumpkin Patch, 93

Reiman Gardens, 145

Seed Savers Exchange/Heritage Farms, 22–23

Willowglen Nursery, 23

Wilson's Orchard, 46

FUN PARKS/AMUSEMENTS

Adventureland, 115

Arnolds Park Amusement Park, 172–73

Big Treehouse, 139–40

Boji Bay Water Park, 174

Country Relics Village, 148

Field of Dreams, 9–10

Fort Custer Maze, 163–66

Heritage Carousel in Union Park, 118

K.D. Station, 181

Lost Island Water Park, 29

Ranch Amusement Park, The, 172

Santa's Castle, 203

Story City Antique Carousel, 147

The Beach Ottumwa, 78

The Play Station, 64

Treasure Village, 174

Whitewater University Fun Park, 116

HISTORIC SITES AND HOMES

American Gothic House, 77

Arsenal Island, 53–54

Battle of Pea Ridge, 100

Bedstemor's Hus, 197

Bentonsport National Historic District, 98

Bonaparte National Historic District, 98

Boone and Scenic Valley Railroad, 149

Bridges of Madison County, 90

Brucemore, 65

Czech Village, 67

Fenelon Place/Fourth Street, 3

Frank Lloyd Wright Stockman
    House, 164
Historic Valley Junction, 127–28
Iowa State Capitol, 118–19
Jordan House, 128
Mamie Doud Eisenhower
    Birthplace, 149
Meredith Willson Boyhood Home, 163
Nauvoo, 102
Pella Historical Village, 81–82
Prairie-style Homes, Mason City, 165
River Junction Trade Company, 17
Rustic Hills Carriage Tour, 4
Salisbury House, 123
Squirrel Cage Jail, 192
Surf Ballroom, 160
Terrace Hill, 122
Toolesboro Indian Mounds, 106
Villages of Van Buren County, 97–100
Vogel Windmill, 178
Watson's Grocery Store, 142
Wilton Candy Kitchen, 51–52
Youngville Cafe, The, 68

MUSEUMS

Airpower Museum, 78
Belinda Church Toy and Antique
    Museum, 92
Bily Clocks Museum/Antonin Dvořák
    Museum, 25
Blanden Memorial Art Museum, 154
Bluedorn Science Imaginarium, 28
Brunnier Art Museum, 143
Buffalo Bill Museum/The SS *Lone Star
    Steamer,* 55
Cedar Rapids History Center, 65
Cedar Rapids Museum of Art, 66
Charles H. MacNider Museum, 164
Clear Lake Fire Museum, 159–60
Danish Immigrant Museum, 197–98
Danish Windmill Museum, 198

Des Moines Art Center, 123–24
Des Moines Arts Festival, 122
Des Moines Botanical Center, 120
Duffy's Collectible Cars, 67
Family Museum of Arts and Science,
    54–55
Farm House Museum, 143
Felix Adler Museum, 57
Fort Museum and Frontier Village, 154
George M. Verity Riverboat
    Museum, 100
Grant Wood Art Gallery, 61
Grout Museum of History and
    Science, 27
Henry A. Wallace Country Life
    Center, 196
Herbert Hoover National Historic Site
    and Presidential Museum, 48
Hobo Museum, 159
Ice Cream Capital of the World Visitor
    Center, 179–80
Ice House Museum, 31
International Wrestling Institute and
    Museum, 112
Iowa Children's Museum, 43
Iowa Great Lakes Maritime
    Museum, 173
Iowa Historical Building, 119
John Wayne Birthplace, 91
Kalona Historical Village and
    Museums, 74
Kate Shelley Railroad Museum and
    Park, 150
Kinney Pioneer Museum, 163
Lakes Art Center, The, 172
Laura Ingalls Wilder Park &
    Museum, 23
Lewis and Clark Interpretive Center, 183
Living History Farms, 129
Lockmaster's House Heritage Museum,
    14–15
Maxwell Museum, 142

Maytag Dairy Farms, 112
Midwest Old Threshers Heritage
  Museums, 76
Mini-Americana Barn Museum, 41
Mississippi River Museum, 4–5
Museum of Amana History, 41
Museum of Natural History, 45
Music Man Square, 163–64
Nathaniel Hamlin Park and
  Museum, 199
National Balloon Museum, 87
National Czech and Slovak Museum, 67
National Farm Toy Museum, 10
National Motorcycle Museum, 62
National Sprint Car Hall of Fame and
  Museum, 84
Neal Smith National Wildlife Refuge
  and Prairie Learning Center, 113–14
Old Capitol Museum, 44
Old Fort Madison, 102–3
Pearl Button Museum, 49
Penitentiary Museum, 61–62
Prairie Trails Museum of Wayne
  County, 95
Putnam Museum of History and
  Natural Science/IMAX Theatre, 54
Rock Island Arsenal Museum, 54
Science Center of Iowa, 124
Science Station and McLeod/Busse
  IMAX Dome Theatre, 64–65
Sergeant Floyd Riverboat Museum, 182
Sioux City Art Center, 181
Tama County Historical Museum, 37
Trainland U.S.A., 113
University of Iowa Museum of Art, 44
University of Northern Iowa
  Museum, 32
Vesterheim Norwegian-American
  Museum, 21–22
Waterloo Center for the Arts, 27

OUTDOOR RECREATION

Backbone State Park, 11
Big Creek State Park and Lake, 133
Canoeing, 13, 21, 22
Cedar Rapids City Parks, 66
Cedar Valley Arboretum and Botanic
  Gardens, 29
Crystal Lake Cave, 6
Des Moines Parks, 127
Desoto National Wildlife Refuge, 190
Devonian Fossil Gorge and Coralville
  Lake, 45–46
Dolliver Memorial State Park, 154–55
Dorothy Pecaut Nature Center in Stone
  State Park, 183–84
Eagle Point Park, 7
Effigy Mounds National Monument, 18
Elinor Bedell State Park, 171–72
Fort Atkinson State Preserve, 25
Geode State Park, 105
Gray's Lake Park, 127
Hartman Reserve Nature Center, 31
Iowa Great Lakes, 171–76
Jester Park, 130
Lacey-Keosauqua State Park, 98
Lady of the Lake Excursion Boat, 160
Lake Red Rock, 84
Ledges State Park, 150–51
Lewis and Clark Keelboat Display/Lewis
  and Clark State Park, 186
Lime Creek Nature Center, 165
Loess Hills State Forest Overlook, 189
Loess Hills, 182–84, 186, 188–90
Maquoketa Caves State Park, 60
McFarland Park, 145
Mines of Spain Recreation Area, 5
Okoboji, 171
Osborne Nature Center, 13
Pikes Peak State Park, 16
Preparation Canyon State Park, 188–89
Rathbun Lake, 96

Saylorville Lake Visitor Center, 130

Seminole Valley Farm and Park, 68

Spook Cave and Campground, 17–18

Starr's Cave Nature Center and
Preserve, 104–5

Storm Lake, 202–4

Sylvan Runkel State Preserve, The, 186

Turkey River, 13

Union Slough National Wildlife Refuge,
157–58

Upper Iowa River, 21–22

Volga River, 13

Yellow River State Forest, 19

PERFORMING ARTS/THEATERS

Blackhawk Children's Theatre, 27

Boji Bantam Theatre, 172

Cedar Falls Municipal Band, The, 31

Cedar Rapids Symphony, 65

Council Bluffs Drive-In Theater, 191

Des Moines Civic Center, The, 126

Des Moines Metro Opera, 87, 126

Des Moines Symphony, The, 126

Donna Reed Performing Arts Festival,
The, 201

Eulenspiegel Puppet Theatre
Company, 44

Five Flags Theater, 4

Glenn Miller Festival, 195

Grand Opera House, 4

Ingersoll Dinner Theater, 126

Iowa State Center, 144

Iowa Youth Chorus, 126

Kate Goldman Children's Theater at
The Des Moines Playhouse, 127

Meskwaki Powwow, 37

Nightfall on the River, 122

Pella Opera House, 8

Renaissance Festival, Water Works
Park, 123

61 Drive-In, 60

Temple for the Performing Arts, 126

Theatre Cedar Rapids, 65

U.S. Cellular Center, 65

University of Iowa's Hancher
Auditorium, 44

Valle Drive-In, 112

Veterans Memorial Auditorium, 126

Waterloo/Cedar Falls Symphony
Orchestra, 31

SPORTS

Amboy Trail Ranch, 111

Burlington Bees Baseball, 104

Cedar Rapids Kernels, 66

Cedar Rapids Rough Riders Hockey
Team, 66

Clinton Lumberkings, 57

Davenport River Bandits, 53

Denison Aquatic Fun Center, 201–2

Des Moines Buccaneers Hockey, 128

Des Moines Menace Soccer, 125

Drake Relays, The, 125

Drake University Bulldogs Basketball
and Football, 124–25

Fun Valley Ski Area, 40

Iowa Cubs Baseball, 120

Iowa International Raceway, 139

Iowa State Center, 144

Iowa State University Cyclones, 144

Mount Crescent Ski Area, 191

Okoboji Queen II Excursions, 172

Paint Creek Riding Stables and
Campground, 18–19

RAGBRAI, 192

Seven Oaks Recreation Areas, 149–50

Sioux City Sports, 182

Sleepy Hollow Sports Park, 118

Sundown Mountain Ski Resort, 7

University of Iowa Hawkeyes, 44

University of Northern Iowa
  Panthers, 32
University of Okoboji Winter
  Games, 173
Waterloo Black Hawks Hockey, 28
Waterloo Bucks Baseball, 28

TRAILS

Amana Colonies Nature Trail, 42
Cedar Valley Nature Trail, 64
Central Iowa Trails, 129
Cinder Path Trail, 93
Inkpaduta Canoe Trail, 176
Northeast Iowa trails, 12
Wabash Trace Nature Trail, 194

ZOOS AND ANIMALS

Aquarium, The, 14
Bald Eagle Watch, Keokuk, 100
Bald Eagle Watching, Red Rock, 85
Bellevue Butterfly Gardens, 58–59
Blank Park Zoo, 121
Decorah Hatchery, 21
Decorah Trout Hatchery, 21
Miller's Country Zoo, 196
Omaha Zoo, 192
Rathbun Fish Hatchery, 96
Rodeo, Dayton, 154
Sidney Championship Rodeo, 193–94
Spirit Lake Fish Hatchery, 171
Storybook Hill Children's Zoo, 7
Tri-State Rodeo, 103

About the Author

etsy Rubiner, a Michigan native, has lived in Des Moines since 1990 and is a freelance writer specializing in children, families, and travel. During her twenty-year journalism career, she has worked as a feature writer at several newspapers, most recently the *Des Moines Register*. Her work has appeared in *FamilyFun, Parenting, Time,* the *New York Times,* the *Washington Post,* and *Better Homes and Gardens,* among other publications.